THE STATE OF THE HISTORY OF ECONOMICS

This collection explores emerging areas in the history of economics and provides a valuable insight into contemporary research in the field. The papers focus on four areas:

- *Science and Economics* Authors investigate how science is perceived and how its history has been retold, detail a history of the concept of "probability" and examine "cyberpunk" – a science fiction genre that draws heavily on modern economic ideas
- *David Ricardo's contribution to international trade theory* Texts by David Ricardo are re-examined to provide a framework for a more consistent and coherent interpretation of Ricardo and to demonstrate how history of economic thought approaches can be applied to the treatment of current theory and policy concerns
- *The contributions of individual economists* Economists considered include: Joseph A. Schumpeter, Werner Sombart and John Maynard Keynes. There is also a comparison of Hicks' and Lindahl's views on monetary stability
- *Economics and events before Adam Smith* An investigation into English policies toward Ireland at the time of Cromwell's occupation is followed by explorations of the ideas of Vincent de Gournay and debates in French economic journals in the period 1750–70

Professor James P. Henderson, Valparaiso University, holds degrees from Beloit College and Northern Illinois University. He was President of the History of Economics Society in 1995–6 and is Vice-President of the Association for Social Economics. He is the author of *Early Mathematical Economics: William Whewell and the British Case*.

THE STATE OF THE HISTORY OF ECONOMICS

Proceedings of the
History of Economics Society

Selected papers from the History of
Economics Society Conference 1995

Edited by James P. Henderson

Routledge
Taylor & Francis Group

LONDON AND NEW YORK

First published 1997
by Routledge
2 Park Square, Milton Park, Abingdon, Oxfordshire OX14 4RN

Simultaneously published in the USA and Canada
by Routledge
711 Third Avenue, New York, NY 10017

First issued in paperback 2015

Routledge is an imprint of the Taylor and Francis Group, an informa business

Typeset in Garamond by
RefineCatch Limited, Bungay, Suffolk

British Library Cataloguing in Publication Data
A catalogue record for this book is available from the British Library

Library of Congress Cataloging in Publication Data
The state of the history of economics : proceedings of the History of
Economics Society / edited by James P. Henderson.
p.   cm.
Includes bibliographical references and index.
1. Economics–History–Congresses.   I. Henderson, James P.
II. History of Economics Society.
HB75.S695   1997
330′.09–dc21   97-4159
CIP

ISBN 13: 978-1-138-88090-0 (pbk)
ISBN 13: 978-0-415-13354-8 (hbk)

Publisher's Note

The publisher has gone to great lengths to ensure the
quality of this reprint but points out that some
imperfections in the original may be apparent

For Judy

CONTENTS

Contributors   ix

INTRODUCTION   1
James P. Henderson

1 THE HISTORY OF ECONOMICS AND THE HISTORY OF
  AGENCY   6
  Andrew Pickering

2 THE HISTORY OF CLASSICAL AND FREQUENTIST
  THEORIES OF PROBABILITY   19
  Philip Mirowski

3 CYBERPUNK AND CHICAGO   39
  Craufurd D. Goodwin and Alex Rogers

4 HETEROGENEOUS LABOR IN A SIMPLE RICARDIAN
  MODEL   56
  John B. Davis and Amitava Krishna Dutt

5 INTERNATIONAL TRADE, MACHINERY, AND THE
  REMUNERATION OF LABOR: A REEXAMINATION OF
  THE ARGUMENT IN THE THIRD EDITION OF
  RICARDO'S *PRINCIPLES OF POLITICAL ECONOMY
  AND TAXATION*   68
  Robert E. Prasch

6 REFLECTIONS ON SCHUMPETER'S *HISTORY OF
  ECONOMIC ANALYSIS* IN LIGHT OF HIS UNIVERSAL
  SOCIAL SCIENCE   81
  Yuichi Shionoya

7 JOHN MAYNARD KEYNES ON SOCIO-ECONOMIC
  CLASSES IN TWENTIETH-CENTURY CAPITALISM   105
  John E. Elliott and Hans E. Jensen

CONTENTS

8 HICKS AND LINDAHL ON MONETARY INSTABILITY: ELASTICITY OF PRICE EXPECTATIONS VERSUS ELASTICITY OF INTEREST EXPECTATIONS   130
Domenica Tropeano

9 (DIS)TRUSTING THE TALE: WERNER SOMBART AND THE NARRATIVE OF ECONOMICS   143
Jonathon Mote

10 CROMWELL'S OCCUPATION OF IRELAND AS JUDGED FROM PETTY'S OBSERVATIONS AND MARX'S THEORY OF COLONIALISM   157
Patrick J. Welch

11 VINCENT DE GOURNAY, OR *"LAISSEZ-FAIRE WITHOUT LAISSEZ-PASSER"*   173
Pascale Pitavy-Simoni

12 STORM OVER ECONOMIC THOUGHT: DEBATES IN FRENCH ECONOMIC JOURNALS, 1750–70   194
Philippe Steiner

Index   215

CONTRIBUTORS

John B. Davis (Chapter 4) is in the Department of Economics, Marquette University, Milwaukee, Wisconsin

Amitava Krishna Dutt (Chapter 4) is in the Department of Economics, University of Notre Dame, Indiana

John E. Elliott (Chapter 7) is at the University of Southern California, Los Angeles

Craufurd D. Goodwin (Chapter 3) is in the Department of Economics, Duke University, Durham, North Carolina

James P. Henderson (editor) is Professor of Economics at Valparaiso University, Valparaiso, Indiana

Hans E. Jensen (Chapter 7) is at the University of Tennessee, Knoxville

Philip Mirowski (Chapter 2) is Koch Professor of Economics and the History of Science, University of Notre Dame, Indiana

Jonathon Mote (Chapter 9) is with the Pew Charitable Trusts, Philadelphia, Pennsylvania

Andrew Pickering (Chapter 1) is in the Department of Sociology, University of Illinois at Urbana-Champaign

Pascale Pitavy-Simoni (Chapter 11) is with GRESE, Université de Paris I (Panthéon-Sorbonne), France

Robert E. Prasch (Chapter 5) is Visiting Assistant Professor of Economics, Vassar College, Poughkeepsie, New York

Alex Rogers (Chapter 3) is in the Department of Economics, Duke University, Durham, North Carolina

Yuichi Shionoya (Chapter 6) is Professor Emeritus of Hitotsubashi University, Tokyo, Japan

CONTRIBUTORS

Philippe Steiner (Chapter 12) is at Université de Paris IX (Paris-Dauphine), ENS Fontenay St Cloud, Fontenay aux Roses, France

Domenica Tropeano (Chapter 8) is Professor at Dipartimento di Instituzioni Economiche e Finanziarie, Università di Macerata, Italy

Patrick J. Welch (Chapter 10) is in the Department of Economics, Saint Louis University, St Louis, Missouri

INTRODUCTION

James P. Henderson

The twenty-second annual meeting of the History of Economics Society was held at the University of Notre Dame on June 2–5, 1995. The theme, "The History of Economics: The State of the Art," is reflected in the title of this volume. That also was the title of the first meeting of the History of Economics Society. The Society's founders – William D. Grampp, Vincent J. Tarascio, Warren J. Samuels, William R. Allen, Craufurd D. Goodwin, and Robert V. Eagly – were honored at a special dinner: "Remembering our own Past."

There was a change in the format of the traditional President's Banquet. The President's Lecture was presented before the banquet. Professor Laurence S. Moss of Babson College, our President in 1994, spoke on: "Finding New Wine in Old Bottles: what to do when Leontief's coefficients are no longer the designated drivers of economic research." The Society's awards were presented at the President's Banquet.

The Society now presents two awards annually for outstanding scholarly contributions to the history of economics. The winner of the new "History of Economics Society Best Paper Award" was selected by a committee which included Allin Cottrill (Wake Forest University), Phil Mirowski (University of Notre Dame), and Gary Mongiovi (St. John's University). Articles appearing in the Society's two official publications: *Journal of the History of Economic Thought* and the selection of papers presented at the annual meeting which appear in the *Perspectives* volume are automatically eligible. Articles by members of the Society which appear in other publications may be nominated for consideration by the Committee. The recipient of the first "History of Economics Society Best Paper Award" was Maria Cristina Marcuzzo, for her article: "At the Origin of Imperfect Competition: different views?" published in Volume 10 (63–78) of the *Perspectives on the History of Economic Thought* edited by Karen I. Vaughn. The competition for this year's "Joseph Dorfman Prize for the Best Dissertation" was particularly strong. For the first time, the judges recommended that one of the dissertations be given Honorable Mention: *Economic Thought and Policy Advice in New Zealand: Economists and the Agricultural Sector circa 1918–1939* by Grant Fleming. The committee to select the "Dorfman Prize" winner included Jeff Biddle of Michigan State University (chair), Dan Hammond of Wake Forest University and Don Moggridge of the University of Toronto. Given the high quality of this year's submissions, it is remarkable that the judges were unanimous in their choice for the "Dorfman Prize." Esther-Mirjam Sent completed her dissertation, *Resisting Sargent*, at Stanford University under the supervision of Kenneth Arrow. Sent's use of analytical tools developed in the sociology of scientific knowledge to analyze the production of economic knowledge breaks important ground. Her willingness to reach beyond traditional economic methodology makes her dissertation deserving of special recognition.

The decision, by the Society's Executive Committee, to publish this volume of papers with Routledge led to several important innovations. For the first time there is an editorial board. The members chosen to serve on that board: Warren J. Samuels of Michigan State University, Phil Mirowski of the University of Notre Dame, and John B. Davis of Marquette University, played an important role in bringing forth this volume. In addition to the refereeing done by those on the editorial board, a number of members offered their time and expertise to referee papers submitted. These include: Donald A. Walker of Indiana University of Pennsylvania (editor of the Society's *Journal of the History of Economic Thought*), Professor James A. Gherity of Northern Illinois University, Professor Amitava Krishna Dutt of the University of Notre Dame, Professor Robert F. Hebert of Auburn University, Professor Todd Lowry of Washington and Lee University, Professor Richard Gonce of Grand Valley State University, Professor Esther-Mirjam Sent of the University of Notre Dame, and Professor Hans Jensen of the University of Tennessee, Knoxville. Of course, those referees who submitted papers for this volume had no voice in the selection or rejection of their own submissions.

The twelve papers in this volume represent some of the best scholarship on the history of economics. The first three papers reflect science themes. Professor Andy Pickering of the University of Illinois gave the "Distinguished Guest Lecture" which opened the meeting. We are pleased to include his lecture: "The History of Economics and the History of Agency," in this volume. Pickering is a leading figure in the relatively new field of the sociology of scientific knowledge. His paper focuses on the issues of "theory and historiography, about how we think about science and tell its history." Philip Mirowski's paper: "The History of Classical and Frequentist Theories of Probability," breaks new ground by offering a "synoptic history" of one of the key concepts in our discipline. His paper is "a first attempt to sketch in some of the early history of that notoriously slippery notion of 'Probability.'" The third paper, on science fiction: "Cyberpunk and Chicago," is written by Professor Craufurd D. Goodwin of Duke University and an undergraduate student of his, Alex Rogers. One of the innovations of the History of Economics Society meeting at Notre Dame was to invite graduate students to present their work. This is the first time that the Society has published an article co-authored by an undergraduate student. The paper draws on the literary tradition of addressing the same issues as economists, by authors who use "different heuristic and rhetorical devices. Typically this literature consists of fiction, poetry, drama, editorializing in the media, and reflective essays of various kinds." Goodwin and Rogers examine a genre of science fiction literature "from the 1980s referred to as 'cyberpunk' that both draws heavily on modern economic ideas and deals with them in a way that is reminiscent of but distinctly different from the earlier humanistic commentary."

The next two papers treat the contributions of David Ricardo. John B. Davis of Marquette University and Amitava Krishna Dutt of the University of Notre Dame offer an analysis of "Heterogeneous Labor in a Simple Ricardian Model." Devising a simple model based on Ricardo's *Principles*, they seek to "increase our understanding of the dynamics of growth and distribution first developed informally by Ricardo," by means of a "modification of Ricardo's original framework." Their simple model "interchanges the roles of land and labor in the original Ricardian model," thereby providing "a potentially useful way of modeling an economy with labor heterogeneity." They examine the policy implications that follow from the analysis. The result informs the reader of how history of economic thought approaches can be applied to the treatment of current theory and policy concerns. The other paper, "International Trade, Machinery, and the Remuneration of Labor: a reexamination of the argument in the third edition of Ricardo's *Principles of Political Economy and Taxation*" is by Robert E. Prasch of Vassar College. The author shows that "a consistent reading of the chapters on trade and machinery in the third edition of Ricardo's *Principles* can be achieved by reflecting on the various effects that trade in luxuries, trade in wage-goods, changes in 'art and skill,' and the construction of machinery, can be thought to have on the size of the wage-fund." He concludes that "the existence of a wage-fund . . . provides a framework for a more consistent and coherent interpretation of Ricardo," because that doctrine "enabled Ricardo to consistently support a regime of free international trade as being in the best interests of the capitalists and, as a result of enhanced accumulation, the working class."

The third group of papers considers the contributions of individual economists. The paper by Yuichi Shionoya of the Social Development Research Institute in Tokyo: "Reflections on Schumpeter's *History of Economic Analysis* in Light of his Universal Social Science," leads off. The author seeks to "identify Schumpeter's theoretical framework in the *History of Economic Analysis* and to review a number of fundamental issues in the history of economics by using his framework." The next paper is co-authored by Professors John E. Elliott of the University of Southern

California and Hans E. Jensen of the University of Tennessee, Knoxville, both of whom have served as President of the Association for Social Economics. It is an important social economic issue that they address in their paper, "John Maynard Keynes on Socio-economic Classes in Twentieth Century Capitalism." Elliott and Jensen are particularly interested in Keynes's views on socio-economic classes with respect to "their relations to his theory of involuntary unemployment." In keeping with the traditions of social economics, they focus on his policy positions, which "substantially motivated" his theoretical conceptualizations. Thus Keynes's "underlying views on the changing institutional and class structure of modern economic society are more important and have greater implications for his economic theory than might well otherwise be the case." The paper, "Hicks and Lindahl on Monetary Instability: elasticity of price expectations versus elasticity of interest expectations" by Domenica Tropeano of the University of Macerata in Italy compares "Hicks's and Lindahl's views on stability in economies with inside money." This approach differs from the more familiar "Keynesian macromodels with money" where the "existence and stability of equilibrium was either simply assumed or demonstrated by relying on some real balance effect mechanism." The next paper, "(Dis)Trusting the Tale: Werner Sombart and the narrative of economics," by Jonathon Mote, of the Pew Charitable Trusts, was one of several papers presented on Sombart at the Notre Dame meeting. Here Mote addresses the question "What is the nature of the disciplinary historical narrative which serves to exclude the Institutional and German Historical Schools from the discipline?" in order to explain why "contemporary economic theory is bereft of historical and empirical forces." He finds that Sombart's "noö-sociology" was a rather successful "attempt to construct a more encompassing methodology for not only economics, but all of the social sciences" that ought to be better appreciated by modern economists.

The final group of papers deals with people or events before Adam Smith wrote his *Wealth of Nations*. The first paper, "Cromwell's Occupation of Ireland as Judged from Petty's Observations and Marx's Theory of Colonialism" is by Patrick J. Welch of Saint Louis University. He focuses on Sir William Petty's *The Political Anatomy of Ireland* and *The History of the Survey of Ireland Commonly Called the Down Survey* and Karl Marx's *Capital* (volume I) and *On Colonialism* to judge English policies toward Ireland at the time of Cromwell's occupation. After describing Cromwell's occupation and policies toward Ireland, Welch employs "elements of Marx's theory of colonization, along with a discussion of conditions in Ireland that relate to each element," and explains why "Marx paid only passing attention to this episode in Irish history." The next paper is by Pascale Pitavy-Simoni of GRESE, Université de Paris I Panthéon Sorbonne, on "Vincent de Gournay, or '*Laissez-faire* without *Laissez-passer*'." This article consists of two parts. In the first part, he "explains why Gournay wanted to free production from the impediments imposed by the mercantilist (or Colbertist) straightjacket," this is *laissez-faire*, an expression of the freedom of labor and manufacture. The topic of the second part is *laissez-passer*, where domestic trade is distinguished from international trade. It is in "its international application" that his economic liberalism "is seriously compromised by Gournay's defense of a Navigation Act." Pitavy-Simoni's work reveals "how protectionism is part and parcel of economic liberalism" in Gournay's thought. Finally, the "Debates in French Economic Journals, 1750–1770" are examined by Philippe Steiner, of the Université Paris IX-Dauphine, ENS Fontenay Saint Cloud. His paper sheds light on "French political economy, a field whose first vigor dates from this period." He maintains that by doing so one can understand how the very appearance of physiocracy was possible, how that school first entered into "economic thought." This leads him to "consider physiocracy as one component of French economic thought among others."

What you are about to read is indeed *The State of the History of Economics*, as reflected in work of this representative group of economists who are members of the History of Economics Society. It was a distinct honor to serve as the President of the History of Economics Society in 1995 and a pleasure to read and edit the papers in this volume.

1

THE HISTORY OF ECONOMICS AND THE HISTORY OF AGENCY

Andrew Pickering

I am honored to be asked to speak here, and I'm pleased because it gives me the chance to say that some of the recent writing that most interests me comes from historians of economics and adjacent fields.[1] But I have to enter the standard disclaimer, required of all aliens entering the US: "I am not now, nor have I ever been, a member of the History of Economics Society." So I don't have any special knowledge of the history of economics, and most of what I do know I learned from members of this audience. I take it, therefore, that my brief is to talk about theory and historiography, about how we think about science and tell its history. That being the case, I will start off by talking about a double displacement that I see happening in the history of science – or, more realistically, that I would like to see happening there. Then I'll talk about how the history of economics might look under these displacements.

To begin, we need a baseline, which, in the history of science, is the genre known as history of ideas. In its canonical form this tries to understand scientific ideas as evolving under their own inner logic, though much mileage has recently been got by sociologizing and contextualizing the picture. Thus the sociology of scientific knowledge approach has sought to display the social interests that sustain the particular bodies of knowledge that one finds associated with particular groups; and, less theoretically, the historiographic avant garde would probably agree that the best history of ideas is contextualist, relating specific ideas to their historical, cultural, social, etc., contexts. The point I want to stress, though, is that all these variants share the view that science is, above all else, a knowledge-producing enterprise; and that we should therefore put scientific knowledge at the centre of our historical accounts and arrange everything else around it.[2] The first displacement I want to recommend is, then, to do away with this obsession with knowledge. A strange suggestion, I know, but one that might seem less strange if I put forward an alternative.

Over the past decade or so, led by Bruno Latour (1987) and the theorists of the actor-network, science studies have become increasingly concerned with issues of agency (Pickering 1995a). And, to cut a long story short, out of that concern has grown an image of science as a zone of encounter between human and nonhuman agency – a place of struggle where human agency in its many guises (the scale and social relations of human actors, their interests and disciplined practices, and so on) is reciprocally reconfigured in relation to the contours and powers of nonhuman agents like machines, instruments, and experimental set-ups. Science, that is, and technology, which is not essentially different from science on this account, is in the business of dealing with nonhuman powers – warding them off, capturing them, seducing them – in a process that continually reconfigures science itself. And this theoretical development suggests to me a historiographic one: namely, that instead of writing the history of science as a history of ideas, we should write it as a *history of agency*: a history of the becoming of social agents in relation to the becoming of material agents – machines, drugs, and whatever. I should add that writing a history of agency does not entail the denial that scientists do produce ideas and knowledge; it suggests instead that we think of knowledge as part and parcel of struggles in fields of agency, as one of our ways of coping with otherness. A history of agency would thus be a rebalanced one, that went beyond the traditional obsession with knowledge to include a recognition of science's material and social engagements.[3]

So far so good, I hope. Now for my second displacement. There is a feeling in the world that over the past few decades we have done too many microstudies and written too many specialized monographs, and that for our own benefit, as well as that of our students and the literate public, it is time we started again producing the kind of synthetic overviews that historians used to produce (Secord 1993). I certainly feel this – perhaps because I have done too many microstudies myself, but also because I think that historical syntheses can be politically important in helping to take stock of just who we are, what the late twentieth century is like, and how it got to be that way. So the second historiographic displacement I want to recommend is the construction of historical big pictures, capable of making sense of the wealth of specialized information already at our disposal, and indicating directions for future research. But then, to go back to my first displacement, what would a big picture of the history of agency look like? My answer goes like this.

Just as scientific knowledge always occupies center stage in the history of ideas, so the central foci of concern in a macrohistory of agency would be the great and enduring sites of the intersection of human and nonhuman agency – the battlefield, for example (understood as iconic of military endeavor in general), and, since the Industrial Revolution, the factory (understood as iconic of industrial production). And that is my basic idea: we should collectively engage in writing synthetic narratives of the history of science as a history of agency centered on places like the factory and the battlefield, as the places from which sciences continually emerge and to which they continually return. Of course, I say, "we should" try writing that

7

way because a macrohistory of agency doesn't exist at the moment; it is a vision of the future, though Donna Haraway's "Manifesto for Cyborgs" (1985) might also serve as a manifesto for what I have in mind. So what I want to do for the rest of this talk is to think about how one might start to fill in the outlines, with particular reference to the history of economics. My idea is to try to exemplify what amounts to a shift in sensibilities that goes with my historiographic displacements; to show, in other words, that the overall history of economics might look somewhat different from the perspective of a history of agency than it does from that of the history of ideas. And my hope is to persuade you that the differences are interesting and important and worth pursuing. And worth correcting, too: I said at the start that I am not a historian of economics, and I am by no means confident that all that follows will stand up to expert scrutiny. I want to acknowledge now that in trying to get to grips with the field I have benefited enormously from numerous E-mail tutorials with Robert Leonard – thanks very much, Robert – but I have to enter another standard disclaimer here: Robert deserves the credit, but egregious errors that remain are definitely my own responsibility.

Now for the history of economics and the history of agency. The first point to make is that the history of agency might sound like bad news for the history of science in general, inasmuch as it denies the specialness of science asserted by the history of ideas. Instead of seeing science as an autonomous essence existing in its own Platonic realm, which only occasionally descends to the sublunary world of production and destruction – from the light to the darkness – the history of agency sees science as being typically there in the sublunary plane, as just one part of the bigger story of human production, consumption, and destruction. It might further seem that the history of agency is especially bad news for historians of economics, since economists have hardly ever engaged in the struggles with material agency that it thematizes.[4] But there is, fortunately, another way of looking at things. It could equally well be said that the history of agency should be great news for historians of economics. Why? Because industrialization is at the heart of the history of agency over the past couple of hundred years, and economics is, in some sense, the science of this process: with Adam Smith, at least, economics as a discipline has emerged directly from and has continually intertwined with the history of machines, factories, disciplined labor, capital, and so on. Of course, economics was not the only science to emerge from the Industrial Revolution; Michel Foucault (1979, for example) has a nice line on the emergence of the social sciences as techniques for managing an industrializing population, and, of course, many natural sciences were either born of industrialization or significantly inflected by it – John Desmond Bernal (1953a,b) compiled some useful lists: thermodynamics and the steam engine, electromagnetic theory and the telegraph, microbiology and brewing, and so on. But there is a difference amongst these industrial sciences that I find worth pondering upon, and which concerns their underlying ontologies.

The nineteenth-century social sciences that interested Foucault were purely about human beings, about counting people and classifying them; they were, one can say, *humanist*. At the opposite end of the spectrum, one finds natural sciences like thermodynamics or electromagnetism which are *antihumanist*, inasmuch as they theorize a world from which human beings might just as well be absent. Such social and natural sciences, then, instantiate the dichotomy of Nature and Society that one might think of as characteristic of modernity. But economics is different. It has, or had, a mixed ontology of people and things: machines, factories, labor, circuits of production and consumption. In this sense, economics was the first great posthumanist or *cyborg science* of modernity; the nineteenth-century equivalent of alchemy. I mention this because it gives economics a special place in the history of agency, as the symmetric science of the coupling of the human and the nonhuman. (I also mention it because it contradicts Bruno Latour's argument in *We Have Never Been Modern* (1993) that the dualist separation of Nature and Culture is the motor of modernity — far from slowing things down, cyborg sciences like economics are centrally concerned with speeding things up.)

So, economics as a field of thought is crucially connected into my speculative history of agency via its ontology of production and consumption. But there are some less obvious connections that I also want to mention. One can think of industrialization as, first of all, an *attack on the body* — a devaluation of human agency in relation to the agency of the new machines: steam engines, spinning jennies, and so on. But it is slowly dawning upon me that, running in parallel with this attack on the body, the nineteenth century was also the site of an *attack on the mind* — a proliferation of attempts to industrialize thought. I first began to see this when I read a paper by Simon Schaffer called "Babbage's intelligence: calculating engines and the factory system" (1994). As is well known, between 1822 and 1834 Charles Babbage was engaged in ultimately unsuccessful attempts to build his famous Difference and Analytical Engines, which we now think of as mechanical forerunners of the electronic computer. But what fascinates me about them is how closely engaged they were with contemporary developments in industry and economic theory.

Thus Babbage's inspiration in the construction of his engines was the late eighteenth-century program of the Frenchman Gaspard Riche de Prony, who extended the principle of the division of manual labor, characteristic of the factory system, to the mental labor of calculation. "By his own account inspired by Adam Smith's paean to the division of labour in the first chapters of *The Wealth of Nations*," as Lorraine Daston (1994, 188) puts it, "I [Prony] conceived all at once the idea to apply the same method to ... manufacture logarithms as one manufactures pins" (quoted ibid., 193). And Babbage simply took this characteristic strategy of the Industrial Revolution one step further, seeking to build *machines* that would emulate the operations of Prony's disciplined human calculators. The move from the attack on the body to the attack on the mind is beautifully played out here. Of course, it might seem that, with Babbage's machines, we drift away from the history of economics into that of mathematics and astronomy, but not entirely. Although Babbage is primarily remembered as a mathematician, he was also an economist (see also Romano 1982). And in just the period that he was working on his calculating engines, Babbage was intensely interested in understanding the political and domestic economy of the factory, publishing a highly regarded book entitled *On the Economy of Machinery and Manufactures* in 1832. These two projects, furthermore – the construction of calculating engines and economic enquiries into the factory system – were not, in fact, independent of one another: as Schaffer (1994, 209) notes, the project of economically regulating labor by atomizing and mechanizing the production process became known as the "Babbage principle" and was understood to apply "equally to the regulation of the factory and the calculating engines." Here, then, we can see how the history of economics and the history of the nonhuman computer have intertwined at the heart of the history of agency.

This is most of what I wanted to say about Babbage, but before leaving him behind I have one remark to add. I started by talking about a double displacement in the historiography of science, from the micro to the macro and from ideas to agency. But actually there is a third displacement that I would also like to encourage, and which I thought I would save until I had an example to discuss, namely a move from contextualist history to what one might call a *history of reciprocal alignments*. My idea is this. The standard way of thinking about the developments just mentioned would be a *contextualist* one. One could think about the factory and economic thought as providing an explanatory context for the history of the Difference and Analytical Engines. The division of physical labor might count as part of the explanation of why Babbage organized his attack on the mind in the way that he did. This would not be a totally mistaken way of thinking, but it would be, I think, importantly misleading, in the following sense. The tendency in contextualist history is to write as if context were a fixed and reliable explanatory resource, something that independently endures and hence more or less causes changes in something else. In contrast to this, I want to emphasize that in the developments at issue content and context were, as the physicists say, strongly coupled to one another, and were reciprocally transformed in relation to one another. To give an example of what I mean, the material work of building Babbage's engines stretched English machinists and machine tools to the limit. Great engineers of the period like Joseph Whitworth circulated through the engine projects, developing their skills and building their reputations there, before establishing themselves as independent producers. As Schaffer (1994, 210, emphasis added) puts it, "The calculating engines were themselves products of the system of automatic manufacture which Babbage sought to model. [And at the same time] They were some of that system's most famous and most visible *accomplishments*."

So the content/context split, central to contextualist historiography, breaks down in episodes like this. It is not the case that there was some unproblematic context that suffused Babbage's work on calculation from without. Rather, the industrialization of Britain was pushed in a specific direction in one and the same movement that included the shift from the attack on the body to the attack on the mind, the construction of Babbage's engines, and Babbage's economic enquiries. And this, I am inclined to say, is typical of what one would expect a history of agency to look like: it would be a history of the reciprocal alignment of a multiplicity of cultural elements, all emergently intertwining with one another and none having the necessary independence and stability required to count as an explanatory context for the others. Personally, I find this kind of historiographic image in which everything becomes in relation to everything else a fascinating one, though it is not easy to hold on to it. The problem is, I think, that the absence of a center vitiates our traditional quasi-mechanical explanatory schemas, but I won't go into that now. Instead, I just want to note that the history of Babbage's engines and economics seems to me that much more interesting and important when understood as part of the overall evolution – and I use the word "evolution" advisedly – of the wider cyborg assemblage that was industrializing Britain.

So that was the third historiographic displacement I wanted to recommend: the move from contextualism to a history of alignments. I will come back to it again later, but now back to history itself. I described economics earlier as the prototypical cyborg science of modernity, and to continue that line of thought, I can remark that it seems to me that, as a cyborg science, economics reached its zenith in the mid-nineteenth century in the work of Karl Marx – who else? – with his complex synthetic vision of the material, economic, social, legal, and political arrangements of industrial–capitalist societies. I have nothing special to say about Marx, but I mention him here in order to note that, after Marx, economics clearly changed its character. I am thinking, needless to say, of the neoclassical revolution of the 1870s, on which I can make some very tentative observations.

First, viewed from the traditional perspective of the history of ideas, the neoclassicist mathematicization of economics was probably a great lurch forwards (though in *More Heat than Light* Philip Mirowski (1989) has managed to tell the story with a negative sign in front of it). But seen from the perspective of a history of agency, the picture seems more complicated. Thus it is interesting to remark that the emergence of neoclassicism amounted to a kind of *purification* of economics. As Mark Blaug (1978, 4) puts it:

In the first half of the nineteenth century, economics itself was regarded as an investigation of "the nature and causes of the wealth of

11

nations," "the laws which regulate the distribution of the produce of the earth," and "the laws of motion of capitalism." After 1870, however, economics came to be regarded as a science that analyzed "human behaviour as a relationship between given ends and scarce means which have alternative uses."

In my terms, then, in the neoclassical revolution economics ceased to be a cyborg science, concerned with "the nature and causes of the wealth of nations," and became instead a distinctly humanist science (like sociology or psychology) centered on "human behaviour as a relationship between given ends and scarce means." Economics came, in other words, to center on the rational actions of distinctively human beings (rather than, for example, intertwinings of the productive capacities of machines with the social relations of labor).

I want to make two remarks concerning this reconfiguration of economics. The first is to hazard the opinion that the neoclassical revolution as a step forward in the realm of ideas might also be seen as a step backwards, inasmuch as the coherent social/material/conceptual overview of who we are which had been constructed by the classical political economists, preeminently Marx, was lost in the process of humanist purification. (I am reminded of Paul Feyerabend's comments on similar losses in going from the Aristotelian world-view to Galilean heliocentrism.) In some ways, of course, my putative history of agency is an attempt to put the pieces back together, and, consistently with this impulse, I am not, I have to admit, terribly interested in the substance of neoclassical economics and I won't therefore have anything else to say about it. Except to make my second point, which is this. I have the impression that the neoclassical revolution more or less coincided with the institutionalization of economics in the universities: it marked the point at which the discipline set off on a long loop from the darkness into the light – away from the factory and into the clean world of the academy (Maloney 1985). I wonder therefore whether one could establish a connection between the new humanism in economics and the traditionally dualist organization of learning. I have no idea whether this suggestion has any substance, but I would be interested in finding out.[5]

I return now to the attack on the mind, and, first, just briefly observe that I am struck by how large a part economists have played in this process. Besides Babbage and his computing engines, one can make quite a list. Stanley Jevons, for instance, one of the principals of the neoclassical revolution, also in 1869 designed a logic machine which solved complicated syllogisms mechanically (Gardner 1982, ch. 5). John von Neumann, himself partly an economist, was the key figure in the development of game theory as a formalization of intrinsically social aspects of human thought. (Wearing another of his hats, von Neumann was also instrumental in bringing to fruition Babbage's project in the construction of the ENIAC electronic computer in the Second World War.) And Herbert Simon, Nobel Laureate in economics, was one of the principals in the postwar emergence of artificial intelligence (Simon 1991, chs 12, 13). Perhaps I should not be so surprised by all this, since questions of how rational actors behave have become central to economics as a discipline, but still I want to say that this theme of the attack on the mind deserves further exploration by historians of economics – if only as a way of reclaiming a fascinating topic from the historians of computing and their hard-technology predilections.[6]

Second, I want to pick up one particular thread from the lines of work just mentioned, namely the history of game theory, which I know is a topic that looms quite large in the history of economics literature (and here I bow towards persons such as Robert Leonard, Philip Mirowski and Roy Weintraub). Von Neumann worked on game theory from the 1920s onwards, and my first comment is that I resent his prewar work enormously.[7] I think it stands as a particularly vicious, nasty, and indeed gratuitous extension of the attack on the mind. I can see the rationale behind industrializing scientific, industrial, and military thought, but I can see no point whatsoever in industrializing the playing of games. Games, it seems to me, are rather a nice hangover from our pre-industrial past, and I wish von Neumann had left them alone.[8] (I wish von Neumann had left a lot of things alone, to tell the truth.) But that isn't the point I wanted to dwell upon. Instead, I want to note that, as Robert Leonard (1992) has shown, game theory did not interest anyone in particular in the 1920s and 1930s. It was, in fact, only the publication of the intimidating *Theory of Games and Economic Behavior* in 1944 that created an interested readership, and what interest me most are the developments that followed. Von Neumann's coauthor, Oskar Morgenstern, was, of course, an economist, and, as the book's title made clear, it was addressed in part to economists. However, as we know, game theory was slow to make much impact in economics, and it was quickly taken up instead by mathematicians, especially mathematicians based at the RAND Corporation, who developed it in very specific ways, concentrating on minimax solutions to two-person zero-sum games.

One obvious question to ask here is why game theory developed in this direction in the postwar era, and Philip Mirowski has found a pretty convincing answer, namely the Cold War. In his essay "When Games Become Deadly Serious" (1991) he does a very nice sociology-of-scientific-knowledge-style job of showing that the specific trajectory of technical development of game theory at RAND was structured by a preoccupation with thermonuclear exchanges between the US and the Soviet Union. And here I need to make two comments. One is that this bit of the history of game theory clearly traverses the heart of a history of agency: material agency doesn't come more densely packed than in atom and hydrogen bombs, though now we are talking about destructive rather than productive

13

agency: we have moved from the factory to the other key site of the history of agency, the battlefield. The other is that a question of interpretation remains, which takes us back to my earlier remarks on contextualist historiography. If one operates in a contextualist mode, one is inclined to say that the Cold War caused or explains the postwar history of game theory. This is, I think, a reasonable gloss on Mirowski's essay – as it is on an enormous range of writing on the postwar history of the physical sciences and engineering – and, as I said earlier, I don't want to say that it is just wrong. But still, as with Babbage, I feel that this kind of historiography misses something important.

What's on my mind is this. Back around 1944, with the encouragement of the military, scientists began to engage, for the first time I think, in long-range planning, futurology. General Hap Arnold, for example, the man behind the establishment of the RAND Corporation, asked Theodor von Kármán, the aerodynamics wizard, to give him a report on what air warfare would be like "in five years, or ten, or sixty-five" into the future (Gorn 1988, 13). Von Kármán, described as a "gentle, warm-hearted man," obliged, and quickly came back with the famous *Toward New Horizons* report, which was, essentially, a detailed technological blueprint for fighting a future atomic war with the Soviet Union (Gorn 1988, ch. 1). Now, this was 1944–5 remember, so it seems pretty implausible to invoke an independently existing Cold War to explain the production and contents of *Toward New Horizons*. And, conversely, it seems much more plausible and interesting to see the scientists and mathematicians, from von Kármán on through the RAND game-theorists, as, in a sense, *constructing the Cold War* – as dreaming and specifying in detail its technoscientific contours.

Of course, I am not denying that there were tensions between the USA and the Soviet Union before the scientists began to engage in futurology; nor would I suggest that visions of hi-tech thermonuclear warfare exhaust the basic scenarios of the Cold War. But what I do suggest is that there is an important symmetry here that tends to disappear in contextualist histories of science: namely, that just as the Cold War context helped to specify the content of game theory, for example, so the development of game theory helped to specify the substance of the Cold War. Particular visions of the Cold War and particular mathematical structures were aligned with and *interactively stabilized* one another, as I would put it, without either having the enduring explanatory priority that contextualism assumes. And, just to register my suspicion of contextualism in one more way, let me emphasize that the history of the Cold War is, in my opinion, much more important than the history of game theory *per se*. To understand the half-century the world has just lived through, we have to understand the Cold War, and to do so we need to think of game theory as an integral part of the overall object, rather than just an index, as it were, of something outside itself. Again, this is a reason to prefer a history of the reciprocal alignment of multiple cultural elements to a contextualized history of ideas.

I can continue with the story of game theory at RAND because it reconnects with the history of economics and the history of agency. In his account of "War as a 'Simple Economic Problem'," Robert Leonard (1991) notes that while RAND was initially the exclusive preserve of physicists, engineers, and mathematicians, it soon acquired Social Science and Economics Divisions, and he regards this development as an upshot of the wartime collaboration of mathematicians and economists. But Fred Kaplan (1991) adds another angle in his book *Wizards of Armageddon*. He notes that the man behind the incorporation of economics at RAND was John Williams, the head of the maths division, and that Williams was "particularly entranced" with game theory. Further (ibid., 67):

> Williams realized that if game theory were to grow and have true relevance to economic problems or international conflict, and if RAND were to lead the way in this intellectual movement, then RAND would have to hire social scientists and economists who could study the "utility functions" of consumers and the actual behavior of various nations. The mathematicians, who certainly know nothing of such things, could then incorporate their findings into the matrixes of game theory.

I repeat this story really just because I love the irony of it. Having been offered game theory by von Neumann and Morgenstern, and spurned it, the economists then surfaced at the RAND Corporation as the hired help of the mathematicians who had taken it up.[9] Less ironically, it is interesting to note how game theory at RAND thus became once more what I would call a cyborg science, a science of mixed ontology, bringing together in the game-theory matrix the work of mathematicians, economists, and social scientists, and itself an integral part of the Cold War history of destructive agency.

To stay with this line of development for a little while longer, there is a further irony in that the hired help in the RAND Economics Department quickly took their revenge on the mathematicians in the elaboration of a new and not very mathematical approach to futurology that became known as *systems analysis*. Exemplified in the early 1950s in Albert Wohlstetter's forward-basing study (Smith 1966, ch. 6), it is worth emphasizing that, like game theory before it, systems analysis was not a mere product or symptom of the Cold War; it was, again, part of the construction and specification of the Cold War. Wohlstetter was, as far as I can make out, the first to imagine nuclear warfare in terms of "first strikes" and "second strikes," "hardened bases" and so on – the language we all now know and love. These terms had no real referent – a nuclear war never having been fought – Wohlstetter had to dream them up, whence they invaded and transformed the Cold War imaginary of generals and civilians alike. And, to wrap the story up, I can mention one last irony. In the 1960s, the systems analysts moved to Washington, recruited to the Department of Defense by operations researcher Robert Strange McNamara, where, needless to say, they sought to transplant their techniques from the dream-world of thermonuclear exchanges to the real war in Vietnam (Leonard 1991; Edwards 1996). The irony is, of course, that in Vietnam all of the cyborg forces of destruction growing out of the Second World War met the naked agency of people and jungles, and lost. There is something there that we historians of agency need to meditate upon.

That, I suspect, is enough for today on the history of economics as a history of agency. To sum up, I have been trying to exemplify in the history of economics a shift of sensibilities that comes with my trinity of historiographic displacements: from ideas to agency, from micro to macro, and from contextualism to a history of reciprocal alignments. There are, actually, many interesting topics that I've looked into in preparing this talk which I have not had time to mention, especially relating to the Second World War as a discontinuity in world history.[10] The histories of operations research and linear programming are fascinating, for example, as is the transference of ideas about servomechanisms and cybernetics from gun controls, maths, and engineering into postwar economics (as well as the other social sciences). I even once wanted to include in this talk some discussion of chaos theory and economics – but other people will have to follow Philip Mirowski's lead there. However, there is plenty to do, and I hope I've persuaded some of you that the history of agency is a promising and even important direction to explore.

NOTES

1 Apart from minor revisions and the inclusion of citations to the literature, this is the text of an invited talk at the 1995 annual meeting of the History of Economics Society.

2 Historiographic reflections that I have come across in the history of economics literature include Blaug's (1978) spirited defence of pure (and retrospective) internalism, Weintraub's (1991) abandonment of his earlier (1979) predilection for Lakatosian rational reconstruction, Hands' (1994a, b) discussions of the utility of a sociology of scientific knowledge approach, as well his discussion of a shift towards taking economics seriously in the philosophy of science (1994c), and a "Minisymposium: Reconstructing Economic Knowledge" featuring essays by Harry Collins, Karin Knorr Cetina and Nancy Cartwright (1991). These reflections all fall within the orbit of the history of ideas.

3 On the history of agency, see also Pickering (1995a, ch. 7, 1995b, forthcoming).

4 I mean this quite literally. Economics does not depend upon the material instruments and experimental set-ups characteristic of the natural sciences; unlike engineers, economists do not build machines; and so on. One exception to this rule concerns the construction of physical analogue models of economic systems in the 1950s: see Richardson (1991, 129–30) and Weagle (1995).

5 Such a purification also took place in the management sciences in the twentieth century.

6 Since writing these words I have read an unpublished paper by Matt Weagle (1995), which does indeed explore the connections mentioned above.
7 Von Neumann has more claims to a central position in the history of agency than anyone else I can think of: his work during and after the Second World War on explosives and atom bombs; automaton theory; the electronic computer and game theory – I believe he even hoped to control the weather.
8 Leonard (1992) rehearses some nice criticisms of game theory from Borel.
9 Thus, for example, Kaplan later discusses a top-secret report on *The Deterrence and Strategy of Total War, 1959–61: A Method of Analysis* completed by Andrew Marshall in 1959 in which: "The logic was presented in the form of Game Theory, with the possible strategies of the U.S. and the U.S.S.R. laid out in giant matrixes. The preferable U.S. strategy was determined by calculating which moves and counter-moves produced the highest value under a broad range of circumstances ..." (214). Since Marshall was one of the first wave of economists hired by the RAND economics division (Leonard 1991, 271) it would appear that the economists did carry through the role that Kaplan has Williams envisaging for them.
10 See Pickering (1995b) for access to recent relevant literature in the history of science and technology.

REFERENCES

Bernal, J. D. (1953a) "Science, industry and society in the nineteenth century," in S. Lilley (ed.), *Essays on the Social History of Science*, special issue of *Centaurus* 3 (1–2), 138–65.
Bernal, J. D. (1953b) *Science and Industry in the Nineteenth Century*, London: Routledge & Kegan Paul.
Blaug, M. (1978) *Economic Theory in Retrospect*, 3rd edn, Cambridge: Cambridge University Press.
Cartwright, N. (1991) "Replicability, reproducibility, and robustness: comments on Harry Collins," *History of Political Economy* 23, 143–55.
Collins, H. M. (1991) "The meaning of replication and the science of economics," *History of Political Economy* 23, 123–42.
Daston, L. (1994) "Enlightenment calculations," *Critical Inquiry* 21, 182–202.
Edwards, P. N. (1996) *The Closed World: Computers and the Politics of Discourse in Cold War America*, Cambridge, MA: MIT Press.
Foucault, M. (1979) *Discipline and Punish: The Birth of the Prison*, New York: Vintage Books.
Gardner, H. (1982) *Logic Machines and Diagrams*, 2nd edn, Chicago: University of Chicago Press.
Gorn, M. H. (1988) *Harnessing the Genie: Science and Technology Forecasting for the Air Force 1944–1986*, Washington, DC: Office of Air Force History.
Hands, D. W. (1994a) "The sociology of scientific knowledge: some thoughts on the possibilities," in R. Backhouse (ed.), *New Perspectives in Economic Methodology*, London: Routledge, pp. 75–105.
Hands, D. W. (1994b) "Restabilizing dynamics: construction and constraint in the history of Walrasian stability theory," *Economics and Philosophy* 10, 243–83.
Hands, D. W. (1994c) "Blurred boundaries: recent changes in the relationship between economics and the philosophy of natural science," *Studies in History and Philosophy of Science* 25, 751–72.
Haraway, D. (1985) "A manifesto for cyborgs: science, technology, and socialist feminism in the 1980s," *Socialist Review* 80, 65–107. Reprinted as "A cyborg manifesto: science, technology, and socialist-feminism in the late twentieth century,"

in D. Haraway, *Simians, Cyborgs, and Women: The Reinvention of Nature*, London: Free Association Books, 1991, pp. 149–81.

Kaplan, F. (1991) *The Wizards of Armageddon*, Stanford, CA: Stanford University Press.

Knorr-Cetina, K. (1991) "Epistemic cultures: forms of reason in science," *History of Political Economy* 23, 105–22.

Latour, B. (1987) *Science in Action: How to Follow Scientists and Engineers through Society*, Cambridge, MA: Harvard University Press.

Latour, B. (1993) *We Have Never Been Modern*, Cambridge, MA: Harvard University Press.

Leonard, R. J. (1991) "War as a 'simple economic problem': the rise of an economics of defense," in C. D. Goodwin (ed.), *Economics and National Security: A History of Their Interaction*, Annual Supplement to *History of Political Economy* 23, 261–83.

Leonard, R. J. (1992) "Creating a context for game theory," in E. R. Weintraub (ed.), *Toward a History of Game Theory*, Durham, NC: Duke University Press, pp. 29–76.

Maloney, J. (1985) *Marshall, Orthodoxy and the Professionalisation of Economics*, Cambridge: Cambridge University Press.

Mirowski, P. (1989) *More Heat than Light: Economics as Social Physics: Physics as Nature's Economics*, Cambridge: Cambridge University Press.

Mirowski, P. (1991) "When games grow deadly serious: the military influence on the evolution of game theory," in C. D. Goodwin (ed.), *Economics and National Security: A History of Their Interaction*, Annual Supplement to *Journal of Political Economy* 23, 227–55.

Pickering, A. (1995a) *The Mangle of Practice: Time, Agency, and Science*, Chicago: University of Chicago Press.

Pickering, A. (1995b) "Cyborg history and the World War II regime," *Perspectives on Science* 3, 1–48.

Pickering, A. (forthcoming) "Practice and posthumanism: social theory and a history of agency," to appear in T. Schatzki, E. von Savigny and K. Knorr-Cetina (eds), *Thinking Practices: The Practice Turn in Social Theory*, Cambridge, MA: MIT Press.

Richardson, G. P. (1991) *Feedback Thought in Social Science and Systems Theory*, Philadelphia: University of Pennsylvania Press.

Romano, R. M. (1982) "The economic ideas of Charles Babbage," *History of Political Economy* 14, 385–405.

Schaffer, S. (1994) "Babbage's intelligence: calculating engines and the factory system," *Critical Inquiry* 21, 203–27.

Secord, J. A. (ed.) (1993) *The Big Picture*, special issue of *British Journal for History of Science* 36(4), 385–483.

Simon, H. A. (1991) *Models of My Life*, New York: Basic Books.

Smith, B. L. R. (1966) *The RAND Corporation: A Case Study of a Non-profit Advisory Corporation*, Cambridge, MA: Harvard University Press.

von Neumann, J. and Morgenstern, O. (1944) *Theory of Games and Economic Behavior*, Princeton, NJ: Princeton University Press.

Weagle, M. (1995) "Computing economic rationality: towards a history of *homo economicus*," draft, University of Notre Dame.

Weintraub, E. R. (1979) *Microfoundations*, Cambridge: Cambridge University Press.

Weintraub, E. R. (1991) *Stabilizing Dynamics: Constructing Economic Knowledge*, Cambridge: Cambridge University Press.

Weintraub, E. R. (ed.) (1992) *Toward a History of Game Theory*, Durham, NC: Duke University Press.

2

THE HISTORY OF CLASSICAL AND FREQUENTIST THEORIES OF PROBABILITY

Philip Mirowski

It is striking that while we are blessed with histories of some of the most arcane and specialized (be that spatiotemporal or intellectual consequence) incidents in the history of economic thought, at this late date there is no synoptic history of some of the key concepts in the discipline, such as "market" or "supply and demand" or "probability." This paper is a first attempt to sketch in some of the early history of that notoriously slippery notion of "probability."

THE CLASSICAL THEORY OF PROBABILITY

Most scholars date the birth of the theory of probability from the Pascal–Fermat correspondence of 1654, although the honors for the first published treatise go to Christian Huygens in 1657. It would be a mistake to view these early discussions as trading in notions we may harbor about "probability"; but examination of what is now called the "classical" approach can begin to sensitize us to the diversity of ideas which led to the expression of randomness by number. While Ian Hacking (1975) has put forward an argument that probability notions were made possible by the breakdown of Renaissance notions of signs and likenesses, and therefore found their first inspiration in the "low sciences" of alchemy and medicine, for the history of economics the historical spadework of Lorraine Daston (1988) is much more compelling, and, so as not to disguise our present motives, much more easily reconciled with the economic concerns so frequently found in the same texts.

Daston claims that probability arose from legal and commercial reasoning prevalent in the commercial centers of exchange along the diagonal "spine of Europe" (from London to Amsterdam to Paris to Northern Italy) in the sixteenth and seventeenth centuries. While this is not quite the same as some Marxist prognostications that probability theory was a function of the rise of capitalism (Maistrov 1974), it does go some distance in explaining the undeniable correlation between the quantification of probability and

19

ruminations over contracts, numismatics, fair monetary settlements, and games of chance. Nevertheless, Daston argues the act of quantification was a byproduct of attempts to codify standards of fairness and good sense, rather than being the *terminus ad quem* of all their endeavors: "The works of the early probabilists were more about equity than about chances, and more about expectations than about probabilities ... classical probabilists quite explicitly translated the legal terms for an equitable contract into mathematical expectation" (Daston 1988, 14). This insight has all manner of philosophical consequences. First, it explains the origins and significance of the central doctrine of the classical theory of probability, namely, the principle of indifference.

The principle of indifference states that all "events" are equiprobable unless there is some reason to think otherwise. This rather innocuous principle is the fount of the entire classical doctrine, as well as the stories told to undergraduates in their beginning statistics courses. What is the probability of throwing "heads" on the single toss of a coin? *If we have no reason to think otherwise*, heads or tails are equally probable; and since heads or tails exhausts the possible set of events or outcomes (when some smart aleck in the back row asks what happens if the coin gets lodged in a crack in the floor and hence lands on its side, and someone else giggles that it is a trick coin, we shall exercise our prerogative as teacher to tell them to shut up), the probability of throwing a head equals one-half.

If we throw the coin twice in a row, and correctly partition the outcomes as HH, HT, TH, and TT (*pace* d'Alembert, who rejected this attribution), the principle of indifference dictates that the probability of throwing two heads in a row equals one-fourth. A moment's reflection will demonstrate that the idea of the additivity of probabilities of mutually exclusive events, $P(HT \cup TH) = P(HT) + P(TH)$ is already "built in" to the principle of indifference. Further contemplation reveals that our rules of calculation also provide us with a definition of "independence": combinations of events which we have no reason to think influence each other's probability can be calculated directly from the probabilities of the individual events by means of a simple multiplication rule; here, $P(H \cup H) = P(H) \times P(H) = 1/4$, a result we had already obtained by applying the principle to the ensemble of tosses. The definition of conditional probability (admittedly a source of greater worry, as we shall discuss below) was regarded as a "loosening up" of the notion of independence; and at this juncture we have conjured nearly the whole of the basic syntax of probability theory from a single principle.

The principle of indifference will hardly qualify as a self-evident truth, as our obstreperous student in the rear so clearly understands; and therefore it becomes interesting to ask why it served so effectively and convincingly as an *a priori* truth in the classical period such that it could give rise to the complex syntax of probability calculations. Daston asserts that it had nothing to do with a capacity to see the world as random, since every single progenitor of the theory was a hard-core determinist. Indeed, in an ironic twist, she claims they had to be determinists to apply mathematics to nature and society, since for them numbers meant necessity.

The conviction of the truth of the principle of indifference derived instead from its origins, that is, from judicial and commercial traditions. While judicial proceedings had long made use of the concept of partial proof, which could be conceptualized as a fraction, the important novel component was the projection of fairness into the realm of the division of contracts or wagers. Simply: if a game were assumed fair and the gamblers on an equal footing, then the probabilities of gain had to be equal. If the parties entering into a contract to fund a merchant's voyage to Denmark were of equal legal status, then their exposure to "risk" must also be equal. Far from being an academic question, courts often found they had to adjudicate division of spoils and liabilities when ships came a cropper from pirates or bad weather. To paraphrase this process, equality of social status was projected into equality of expectation, which, adjusting for possible divergences in monetary stakes, became translated into the presumption of the principle of indifference. Daston is quite clear that this is the reverse of our present perceptions: in the classical era, probabilities were equal because the game was fair (because the parties were on an even footing), and not vice versa.

For the classical probabilists, there was no trace of chance as a phenomenon irreducibly endemic in the world; probabilities just measured ignorance, as they would in a judicial proceeding; providentially there were objective laws which dictated rational behavior in the face of ignorance. Some twentieth-century commentators (Kneale 1949) might simply write this off as a species of "subjective probability," but that would not do justice to the classical figures, not to mention the attendant muddying of subsequent philosophical waters. Rather, it was the projection of the social relations of men upon the objects and events of the world which accounts for the success of the principle of indifference up to 1830 or so. I have discussed elsewhere the idea of Mary Douglas that concepts of the natural world are often stabilized as projections of the social structures in which they are generated (Mirowski 1988, 109ff), as well as the process of the projection of metaphors of the body, value and motion in the reification of invariants as a prelude to the mathematical formalization of a discipline (Mirowski 1989, ch. 3); so we will not belabor the point here, but only register that Daston's description of the origins of classical probability theory is just one more instance of that pattern. Where the natural order of equality and invariance was sanctioned by religion and the guildhall and the courts, there was no call to hunt down some attribute called randomness "in the phenomenon" itself.

One further interesting implication of Daston's thesis is that when this model of enlightened good sense began to bifurcate due to changes in the social order, the principle of indifference subsequently lost its credibility. In particular, the increased differentiation of the merchant from the state resulted in a parting of the ways of what had previously been a single organon: as canons of fairness and justice began to diverge from notions of fiscal prudence, the single conception of equity of expectations gave way to competing and incommensurate notions of rationality (Daston 1988, 68). As the place of rival claimants to market outcomes in a prosperous society was occluded by the possibility of the clash of justice and the wealth of nations, the mathematics of probability came under widespread attack. The most telling example, from Daston's vantage point, is the odd historical fact that the flap over the St Petersburg "paradox," which, as she notes is "trivial in itself," ballooned out of all proportion into a debate over the foundations of probability.

The St Petersburg paradox has been distorted beyond all historical recognition in the economics literature by such authors as Samuelson (1986, 133–64), Baumol and Goldfeld (1968, 13); Schumpeter (1954, 303); Stigler (1965), who have portrayed it as an anticipation of the later "discovery" of neoclassical economic theory.[1] To situate it in its historical context, the Petersburg problem was first and foremost an unpacking of the semantics of mathematical expectation, which had hitherto been used as an uncontentious primitive in the classical tradition. The problem setup was first proposed by Nicholas Bernoulli to Pierre Montmort in correspondence, and then published in Montmort's *Essai d'analyse sur les jeux de hazard* (1713). In this game, Ros(encrantz) gives Guil(denstern) one ducat if the coin falls heads once; two ducats if it falls heads twice in sequence; four ducats for a sequence of three heads . . . and so on. The question posed by Bernoulli was how much should Guil pay Ros to play this game? By the conventional definition of mathematical expectation, the value of the game should be:

$$E = (1)1/2 + (2)1/4 + (4)1/8 + \cdots + \cdots$$
$$= 1/2 + 1/2 + 1/2 + \cdots + 1/2 + \cdots$$

The modern attitude towards the problem is that the series is divergent and is not summable; therefore the expectation does not exist. It was not seen that way at the time, however; generally, it was thought that the series summed to infinity, which is the amount Guil should pay Ros to play a fair game. But, as subsequent commentators never tired of repeating, people did regularly play this game, and they did not pay a bottomless bucket of ducats to do so. Consequently, it was the very idea of mathematical expectation which came under a cloud of suspicion; and, following Daston, when expectation seemed dubious some shadow of doubt also fell upon probability. What was juridically fair was no longer fiscally prudent.

In retrospect, if the anomaly were to be isolated, there were three options to abolish the infinity (Jorland 1987): (a) alter the definition of the probabilities; (b) arbitrarily limit the number of tosses taken into account; or (c) alter the definition of the payoffs. Economists tend to forget that most of the proposals to fix the problem came under the first two headings; they instead focus on one version of the third option proposed by Daniel Bernoulli in 1738.[2] Rather than tinker with the probabilities, Bernoulli posited a distinction between price and moral expectation, so that "any increase in wealth, no matter how insignificant, will always result in an increase of [*utility*] which is inversely proportionate to the quantity of goods already possessed." The *fin-de-siècle* neoclassical will prick up his ears thinking he hears the postulation of diminishing marginal utility of commodities; but care in reading reveals that all calculations still take place in monetary terms, with the mass of goods treated as an undifferentiated "wealth"[3] for the purposes of the argument. There is no moral expectation function with the quantities of individual commodities taken as arguments; no attempt to derive relative price from moral expectation; and no constrained optimization. The sole purpose of this innovation is to place a bound upon the payment terms in the Petersburg sequence, and therefore derive a finite determinate value for the game.

Here (and not for the last time), political economy was invoked to "save" the mathematics of probability theory through an amendment of value theory. The trouble was that neither political economy nor the probabilists (with the important exception of Laplace) showed any interest in this amendment. With a modicum of sympathy, one can readily see why this early union of probability and political economy logarithmic function proved abortive. The choice of a monetary remuneration for moral expectation was left without motivation, and it was soon apparent even in the original discussion that tinkering with this aspect would lead to wide variation in results. If one were allowed minor variations in the game, even this assumption of such a moral expectation would not rule out infinities (Menger 1967). In any event, this "virtual" notion of valuation did not resonate with any well-developed tradition in the political economy at that time, where the law governed character of value was thought to reside in the good rather than in the mind.

But worse than that, if Bernoulli was correct, then all gambling would be irrational, since all games of chance would have a negative moral expectation. While Bernoulli himself saw this as an argument in its favor – "this is Nature's admonition to avoid the dice altogether" – it would inadvertently undermine his entire project, which was to render probability theory the calculus of rational common sense. To effectively posit that the great mass of mankind was stubbornly irrational in their quotidian behavior would demolish the principle of indifference much more dramatically than would one recalcitrant anomaly concerning the existence of an infinite fair valuation. A Pyrrhic budget of paradoxes threatened to ensue. If moral expectation were to be used for the calculation of insurance premia, as Bernoulli advocated, whose logarithmic function would provide the valuation? With some discomfort, Daniel Bernoulli did admit that his cousin

Nicholas had raised just such an objection. Indeed, if gambling were intrinsically irrational, then why should anyone prefer to invest in voyages and other mercantile pursuits in the first place? Given his logarithmic value function, it would take a staggering rate of profit to offset the preferred moral expectation of a sure sum of money in hand. And if that were the case, then most of capitalistic enterprise was irrational – but at this stage in attempts to exorcise the paradox, it was better to just drop the whole idea. And that is precisely what almost everyone did.

It should then prompt us to wonder whether the neoclassicals have been grasping at historical straws when they harken back to Bernoulli for their bloodline, especially when historians such as Jorland (1987, 171) assert that, "Had it not been for Laplace's endorsement of D. Bernoulli's theory, the Saint Petersburg problem would have most likely faded away." The explanation for this neglect was that the appeal to political economy to "save" probability theory gave way to a much more effective appeal to "the natural world" to pull the fat out of the fire, in the form of the Frequentist approach to probability (discussed in the next section). Already in 1776 Laplace was beginning to distinguish between the personal or mental aspects of probability and the external or objective aspects; by the 1830s and 1840s figures such as Ellis, Cournot and Poisson were exploring the implications of this distinction.[4]

Yet before we move on to examine this alternative, it is worthwhile to note that at the very inception of the mathematization of randomness, there was palpable uncertainty over where one might locate the real epistemic invariant in order to discuss rational calculation. While the original juridical context had allowed actors to use probability in pretty much any sense they pleased, the mathematical codification of its rules required one to trace the algebraic structures back to their invariants; at this juncture, the multiple usages translated into multiple candidates. For instance, there was equality of social status, which looked less and less promising in the runup to the French Revolution. There was the invariant of economic *value*; but that also disinterred more problems than it solved. Nothing in the market could be taken naively to be what it seemed, which was the bane of value theory. In the eighteenth century, most seemingly aleatory contracts were in fact disguised loans concocted to circumvent legal ceilings on interest rates (Daston 1988, 169); the hidden motives blocked definitive attributions of rational self-interest. And then there were the attempts to root the invariant in the recesses of the human mind. Both Bernoulli and Laplace had acknowledged begrudgingly that everyone was not alike; but the closer one got to the end of the century, the less willing were readers to pass this by as a second-order complication. As Daston argues, the major trend behind the breakdown of classical probability arguments was the progressive loss of faith in the intrinsic and generic rationality present in every individual's mind. The only remaining road was in fact the one taken: banish the invariant as a totally alien inhabitant of the external natural world. "If we want to discover what is in reality a series of *things*, not a series of our own conceptions, we must appeal to the things themselves to obtain it" (Venn 1962 [1888], 74). In a sense, this was the beginning of the idea of randomness as reified attribute, as opposed to a stress on probability as a modality of rational calculation.

Though these were the primary motivations behind the abandonment of the principle of indifference, philosophers from Keynes to Cohen continued to deploy arguments against it well into the twentieth century; philosophers diligently thrash away in the belief that dead horses often undergo reincarnation. They have certainly been correct to point out the contradictory nature of the principle of indifference, namely, that it is hard to see how supposedly pervasive ignorance can give rise to such precise quantitative knowledge. The reason is, of course, that bone ignorance would imply not only absence of any suitable guidelines in imputing differential probability to different events, but it would also dictate complete and utter inability to enumerate all relevant events or to correctly partition possibilities. Let us return once more to the coin toss. There is a legitimate case to be made that the mere possibility of the coin becoming lodged on its edge in a crack in the floor or disappearing down the air duct should be included as "events"; this would surely undermine the first credo of the probabilist, that the chance of tossing heads is exactly one-half. In our "ignorance," should we allow this amendment or not? Or suppose, just like Rosencrantz and Guildenstern, we have just witnessed ninety-two heads in a row. In our ignorance (and trepidation), should we consider this event unlikely, an omen of the impending intervention of the Author, or simply a reflection of the normal course of events? Many have complained that the entire notion of a "fair game" is circular in a vicious sense in classical doctrine: games are fair unless they are not. This appeal to ignorance leaves us in a worse quandary than when we started out.

There are also some technical objections to the principle of indifference. One is that dependence upon equivalent attribution of probability amongst competing events implies that all numerical probabilities must be rational numbers. Since the suspicion began with Cantor in the later nineteenth century that there were "more" irrationals than rationals in the unit interval, the use of real analysis to discuss the probability calculus harbored a fatal flaw that it would take much time and effort to exorcise.

The other problem revolves around what is now called Bayes' "theorem," often mistakenly conflated with the subjectivist approach to probability. We write "theorem" in scare quotes because, in the version actually attributable to Bayes, it is little more than an inversion of the definition of conditional probabilities: namely, those not directly defined by the principle of indifference. In modern notation, conditional probabilities are defined by:

$$P(B \mid A) = p(A \cap B)/p(A). \tag{2.1}$$

Given that so many contemporary economists seem to think that Bayes' rule is the magic wand which bewitches the problem of induction into dazed innocuousness, it will behoove us to delve a little deeper into its historical context. Recall that the principle of indifference assigns numerical probabilities in the case of equiprobability; outside of the subsequent manipulation of those numbers under the assumption of independence, etc., there still remained the question of where other rather more lumpy odds came from: say, 99/100 or $1/n$ or 1/1001. The answer was provided by the conditional (2.1), patterned upon the accepted rule that pure independence of A *vis-à-vis* B would imply:

$$P(B \mid A) = [P(A) \times P(B)]/P(A) = P(B).$$

The extension of the probability concept to dyadic relations was much more than a generator of more diverse numerical values, however; it also highlighted the critical issue of the relevance of evidence to calculation which had already cropped up in a less insistent way in the issue of the proper partitioning of events. It was one thing to calculate pecuniary expectations; it was quite another to attempt to derive quantitative information about the probability of causes from observed frequencies of events. Of course, the shakiness of the extension of the metaphor of probability to inferred causes did not prevent all and sundry from repeatedly rushing in where angels feared to tread: the issue of inferences about God's original design seemed the eighteenth-century favorite here; though political prognosis might also be grist for the mill. Laplace, for instance, in the first edition of his *Théorie analytique des probabilités* of 1812 sported a prominent dedication to the Emperor Napoleon; while the second edition of 1814 suppressed the dedication but included a new paragraph suggesting that the fall of empires which aspired to universal domination could be predicted by a savant well-versed in the calculus of chance. The reason such gaffes could go unremarked in the eighteenth and early nineteenth centuries was that the principle of indifference effectively blocked any decomposition of the probability concept into distinct legal, economic, epistemic, and aleatory components.

Bayes' theorem arose out of this confusion. The Reverend Thomas Bayes (1702–61) is a bit of a shadowy figure, although we do know he was a Fellow of the Royal Society, a mathematician, and an advocate of the doctrine of divine benevolence (Maistrov 1974, 88ff). "An Essay towards solving a Problem in the Doctrine of Chances" was published posthumously in the *Philosophical Transactions* of the Royal Society in 1763 at the behest of Richard Price. The first direct statement of the definition of the conditional occurs in the first section of the essay, in which it is asserted that "The probability that two subsequent events will both happen is compounded of the probability of the first and the probability of the second on the supposition that the first happens" (Mastrov 1974, 90). By means of a rhetorically effective interlude concerning the tossing of a ball on a table, we are whisked from contemplation of a unitary notion of probability (such as the probability of heads given a throw of tails) in the first section to a dyadic notion in the second section, where the conjunction would link events of substantially distinct character (say, the probability of heads, given knowledge that we obtained the coin from a notorious clipper and sweater of the coin of the realm). Daston (1988, 258) suggests one reason Bayes may have neglected to publish the essay is that he had misgivings about the postulate that permitted him to generalize to such dyadic cases when nothing is known about the prior probabilities of A and B. That postulate is none other than the principle of indifference; a choice which definitively marks Bayes' theorem as an eminently *classical* doctrine.

This may be rendered more apparent if we restate Bayes' rule in more modern trappings. Reproducing his definition of conditionality by writing that the probability of event C is the sum of the dyadic conditionals times the probabilities of each partitioned collateral event B_j:

$$P(C) = P(C \mid B_j) \times P(B_j).$$

Now substitute this definition into the expression (2.1), and we arrive at the modern expression of Bayes' theorem:

$$P(B_i \mid C) = [P(C \mid B_i) \times P(B_i)]/P(C)$$

$$= [P(C \mid B_i) \times P(B_i)]/\sum_j P(C \mid B_j) \times P(B_j) \qquad (2.2)$$

It is common to factor (2.2) into the likelihood of C given the observation of B_i and the "prior" probability of B_i; although it is a bit anachronistic, it can be observed that Bayes himself did something like this, but with the principle of indifference providing the all-important $P(B_i) = P(B_j)$ due to ignorance concerning causes.

Even in the classical period, Bayes' rule meant all things to all people, depending upon the predilections of the beholder. For Bayes, it seemed a method for getting from pure ignorance to something rather more than that. For Richard Price, it was a weapon to wield against the skepticism of David Hume, reinforcing the defense of natural theology (Daston 1988, 267). For Laplace, it more nearly resembled a subtle form of taking an average. From his vantage point, one read (2.2) as one specific conditional divided by all the relevant conditionals. To a modern Bayesian, it is a sausage machine for processing idiosyncratic beliefs into a single seeming consensus. This last interpretation could not even have been imagined in the classical period.

The technical weakness here is that Bayes' theorem does not rectify any of the egregious flaws of the principle of indifference, but rather exaggerates them to the point of parody. If we had felt a bit queasy about the appropriate identification of germane events and their partitions, then extending the concept to dyadic conditional probabilities in situations of total ignorance of the relevance of phenomenon B to phenomenon C surely would stretch credulity to the breaking point. Mechanical procedures for grinding out probability calculations do not and cannot substitute for a theory of probability.

THE FREQUENTIST THEORY OF PROBABILITY

Ian Hacking once wrote (1965, 39): "Only in the imagination do frequencies serve as the sole basis for action." If so, then we live in a world of imagination run riot. For reasons about which we can only speculate, most of the probability theory to which tyros are exposed (usually through classes in introductory statistics) is unabashedly frequentist, as are most of the prognostications of the partisans of "rational expectations" in orthodox economics departments. Your typical physical scientist will generally speak in a frequentist syntax, especially if he/she could not be bothered to think about the foundations of probability. And the incongruous aspect of it all is that the frequentist doctrine is a thoroughly outmoded and discredited basis for probability theory amongst philosophers of all stripes, as well as sophisticated applied probabilists. Perhaps a little history can help us lift the eerie pall of sophistry which drapes this landscape.

We have mentioned the movement to render randomness a reified attribute starting in the 1830s and 1840s, but have not yet asked how such a curious thing could have happened. Following Porter (1986) and Hacking (1982, 1990), we will search for motivations in the relationships of the state and the economy to the populace, in the manner of the previous section. The first place we shall look is towards what Hacking has called "the avalanche of printed numbers," which began with the collection of large-scale bureaucratic statistics in Prussia and France in the 1820s, and was given a boost by the revolutions of 1830 and 1848. However much enthusiasm for the collection of statistics went hand-in-hand with crusades for moral and physical improvement, such as sanitary reform or criminal rehabilitation or the extent of literacy (Cullen 1975), it all ultimately was fallout from the French Revolution. Once the Enlightenment faith in the intrinsic rationality of man was lost, and with it confidence in the natural political order, then the citizenry became a mass of seething discontents and restless rabble, whose existence threatened the integrity of the state rather than constituting it. As early as 1840, Frederic Le Play was defining statistics as "the observation and coordination of facts from the point of view of government ... Politics must unceasingly use statistics as the means by which to regulate its administrative activities" (in Hacking 1990, 136). And whether it was the General Register Office and the Board of Trade in Britain, the Ministère de Justice or the Ministère de l'Instruction Publique in France, or the Royal Prussian Statistical Bureau, that is precisely what they did.

Now, every economic historian worth his or her salt knows the numbers get much better after 1820; but rather than simply taking this as an unproblematic sign of increased rationality, it should be possible to understand this event as part of the constitution of the phenomenon which it initially aimed to gauge. After all, the mere indiscriminate collection of numbers might well be devoid of all significance. For instance, the Swedes collected demographic information on a grand scale nearly a century before our "avalanche," but by all accounts did nothing with it. Being the orderly polity that it was, there was little impetus to search out lawlike frequencies amongst the seething masses. But amongst the restive "lower orders" of the more southerly tier of European states, there now loomed categories never before taxonomized, such as the "sterile but useful class" in France, *Israelites* in Prussia, victims of avoidable railway accidents in London: "As Frege taught us, you can't just print numbers. You must print numbers of objects falling under some concept or another. The avalanche of printed numbers brought with it a moraine of new concepts" (Hacking 1982, 292).

The first among many new concepts was the idea of a freestanding frequency. The *accoucheur* of this concept was most certainly the Belgian polymath Adolphe Quetelet, with his *l'homme moyen* and proclaimed fixed annual proportions of dead letters in the Paris Post Office (Venn 1962 [1888], 29). Ted Porter (1986, 100–9) has admirably told the story of Quetelet and his subsequent influence on Maxwell's gas laws, Buckle's theory of history, Francis Galton's eugenics, and much else besides. In the 1840s we find the idea of a probability as a physical property of some suitably defined empirical population seriously discussed by A.-A. Cournot (1843) and Leslie Ellis (1843); given measured defense by John Venn (first edn 1866); promoted by Georg Helm in 1902; and finally rendered a separate philosophical version of probability theory by Richard von Mises in 1928.[5] Later mathematical elaboration was provided by Abraham Wald and Hans Reichenbach; and one gets the impression that in the middle years of the twentieth century it was the interpretation of choice of the growing army of statistical analysts.

One way of reading the history is to regard the frequentist doctrine as a symptom of the confusion of statistics as a *statist* doctrine with the theory of probability. The shift from a qualitative notion of possibility to a quantitative rational number required the postulation and tabulation of homogeneous categories composed of identical units. After all, is one person's life really so very identical to another's? If mortality is the issue, should people be distinguished by age, or sex, or race, or place of residence, or religion, or a thousand other characteristics? Should fires be tabulated by borough, or construction materials, or type of habitation, or time of year, or sign of the zodiac of the inhabitants?

What we call a nation is really a highly artificial body, the members of which are subject to a considerable number of local or occasional disturbing causes ... It is plain, therefore, that whatever objections exist against confusing together French and English statistics, exist also, though of course in a lesser degree, against confusing together those of various provincial and other components which make up the French people.

(Venn 1962 [1888], 456)

However true in the abstract, no one could effectively resist the engulfing tide of nationalism, and no one mounted resistance to the definition of the nation-state as a homogeneous statistical unit. Once a Frenchman, then always a Frenchman; and, *voilà*, suddenly there is something called a *French* suicide. Other such constructed identities followed apace: tax-defined "incomes," "causes of death" for the bills of mortality, "causes of loss at sea" for insurance projectors, and so on. The statistics came first; the categories were constructed in tandem; and the philosophical justifications of "natural kinds" brought up the rear. Venn (1962 [1888], 55–6) was quite clear on that score:

> for the purpose [of statistics] the existence of natural kinds or groups is necessary ... Such regularity as we trace in nature is owing, much more than is often suspected, to the arrangement of things in natural kinds, each of them containing a large number of individuals ... A large number of objects in the class, together with that general similarity which entitles objects to be fairly comprised in one class, seem to be important conditions for the applicability of the theory of Probability to any phenomenon.

Here, in a nutshell, is the nascent relative-frequentist position. Probability is defined as the limit of a relative frequency of a category of an event to the relevant population of natural kinds in an infinite series of realizations; probability statements attribute an empirical property to the relevant population, which is further asserted to be a real property of their physical makeup. The probability calculus is simply an axiomatic mathematical tool employed in the manipulation of these fundamental probabilities derived from empirical inquiry. As with nearly all popular concoctions, there are at least two flavors retailed under this awning: the Bernoulli–Borel version which stresses strong laws of large numbers, and the von Mises version, which focuses much more directly on the definition of the natural kinds involved (Fine 1973, ch. 4).

The landmark theorem of Jakob Bernoulli, appearing in his *Ars conjectandi* of 1713, might seem to belong under the classical doctrine of probability; but its statistical bent and its subsequent usage deem its center of gravity to be intellectually located in the frequentist camp. Bernoulli asked: What reasons do we possess to think the frequencies of real outcomes will approximate the underlying *known* probabilities, and what is the relationship of this knowledge to the number of instances observed? His answer, letting P stand for the "degree of our certainty" in this regard, p^* be the *a priori*

30

known probability of a chosen event, n be the number of trials of observation, and m/n the observed ratio of the chosen event to number of trials, was a proof demonstrating that:

$$\lim_{n \to \infty} - P(|p^* - m/n|) < \varepsilon \tag{2.3}$$

where ε is any arbitrarily small number. The novelty of this result was appreciable; but its ability to mesmerize has been even more formidable. Clarity in semantics was most certainly violated in a frequentist sense, since "probability" as degree of certainty (P) was conflated in a single expression with probability as a fixed known empirical attribute (p^*), and both subjected to the same formal manipulation. Moreover, Bernoulli was not averse to inverting the meaning of the theorem, by suggesting that it provided a basis for inferring that an observed m/n equals an unknown p^* with a certain "probability" P (Daston 1988, 232); mark well that it sanctions no such thing. It does not take mathematical genius to see that if p^* is really unknown, then we also have no warrant to think that there is a unique stable probability to be found. Nevertheless, in the era of the "avalanche of statistics," such qualms were waved aside as nuisances and quibbles, encouraging further mathematical elaboration of limit theorems.

Simon-Denis Poisson innovated the language of "laws of large numbers" more than a century later to celebrate the avalanche, as well as to extend Bernoulli's theorem to cases of simple binomial distribution where ($p^* + q^* = 1$). Confining his attention exclusively to *a priori known probabilities*, Poisson (1837) imagined a situation where the probability of event E on the first trial, due to cause X_1 equalled p_1^*; the probability of E on the second trial due to cause X_2 equalled p_2^*, and so forth. The average chance of the frequency of E was then equal to:

$$\hat{p} = (1/n)(p_1^* + p_2^* + \cdots + p_n^*)$$

Once this curious setup is admitted, then the proof follows that of Bernoulli, replacing p^* with $\hat{p}$ in (2.3). Poisson also indulged in baseless inversion of his "law," asserting that if $\hat{p}$ started to diverge significantly from previous experience, then there was some warrant to believe that some of the causes $X_1, X_2, \ldots$ had either dropped out or changed. He corresponded with Quetelet along these lines, and obviously believed that his "law" both legitimized and explained many of Quetelet's trumpeted statistical regularities (Daston 1988, 287).

Despite their historical impact, it comes as somewhat of a shock to realize just how very limited are the implications and meaning of the Bernoulli and Poisson theorems. Because of the assumption of the known probabilities, both theorems essentially presume an *a priori* fixed distribution; they then ask what happens when we draw increasing numbers of realizations from that distribution. By definition, if the distribution is single-peaked and well-behaved, the mass of realizations piles up around the mode, and this mass grows faster in proportion than the total realizations as *n* gets large. It is very nearly tautological, and has little to say about any empirical inference, as von Mises (1957, 109) rightly noted:

> The mathematical deductions of Bernoulli, Poisson and Tscheby-scheff, based as they are on a definition of probability which has nothing to do with the frequency of occurrence of events in a sequence of observations, cannot be used for predictions relative to the results of such sequences ... [Poisson] interpreted the probability "nearly 1" at the end of the calculation in a different sense. This value was supposed to mean that the corresponding event ... must occur in nearly all games. This change of meaning of a notion in the course of deduction is obviously not permissible.

Modern commentators in the Delphic mode such as Fine (1973, 96) restate the point as implying that "Probability zero does not necessarily mean a small or negligible set of possibilities"; but we shall bypass such seemingly paradoxical pronouncements for the time being. (Anyone dealing with probability theory must inure themselves to those who talk in riddles.) Instead, we are led in the direction of the work of von Mises, which displaced attention from the limiting process back to the original inspiration of the frequentist doctrine, the categorization of statistical "natural kinds."

Von Mises (1957, 103) wrote: "The essentially new concept of our theory is the collective." The *Kollektiv*, as it became fondly known in the English literature, consisted of an infinite sequence of elements of a set and a countable family of place selection functions, such that the relative frequencies of classes of elements possessed limiting values; that these relative frequencies were all normalized to sum to unity; and that any infinite subsequence chosen by any place selection function also satisfied the first two conditions. The innovation of the place selection functions was the frequentist incarnation of the commonplace postulate of the "impossibility of a gambling system": namely, in a truly fair game, no patterns can be discerned which could be the basis of a superior betting strategy.[6] While that interpretation has its drawbacks, a more transparent construction regards the *Kollektiv* as placing all the stress on the definition of "randomness" as the primitive concept of probability theory. Von Mises was adamant that a random sequence of numbers should be so devoid of all pattern that it could never be the product of any lawlike structure; and yet, in the limit, the frequencies of the individual numbers would converge to fixed values. The activity of place selection, the picking and choosing of numbers out of the sequence, should be so impotent to find any hidden structure that the resulting sequence must itself be effectively indistinguishable from its parent. Strict categorization and invariance under the operation of selection reveals that the issue is still one of the identity of natural kinds, as it was for Venn.

Since von Mises's *Kollektiv* imposed more structure upon the problem than had the Bernoulli or Poisson laws of large numbers, it was thought for a while that it avoided the tautological character of those earlier results. Moreover, its purported empirical character promised to provide the "demarcation criteria" so avidly sought in the 1940s and 1950s to cordon off legitimate science from its mutant pretenders. "Science" for von Mises meant physics; he did not expect to find *Kollektivs* in the social sciences:

> Our probability theory has nothing to do with questions as: Is there a probability of Germany being at some time in the future involved in a war with Liberia? . . . we shall not concern ourselves with the problems of the moral sciences . . . The unlimited extension of the validity of the exact sciences was a characteristic feature of the exaggerated rationalism of the eighteenth century.
>
> (von Mises 1957, 9)

The express reason for this quarantine was that real science dealt in *Kollektivs*, and *Kollektivs* were designedly infinite sequences; there were no such infinite sequences in social life.

Because the role of infinities is the major sticking point in the frequentist doctrine, it is worthwhile to take a moment to see why they are indispensable for this position. Even Venn realized that any empirical regularity in the face of randomness could only be asserted to exist in the "long run," because fixed proportions of events to trials in finite sequences, which then were maintained when the sequences were augmented, suggested deterministic law rather than randomness. Consider (if you will) the following finite sequence:

001001001001001001001001001001001001001001.

The "probability" of the digit 1 is equal to $1/3$; but this is a travesty of the term probability, because we can easily see that the sequence merely repeats the digits 001 indefinitely. On the other hand, consider:

1010000100101010110000101111.

At first blush, it looks much more like a candidate for randomness, and we can estimate from this sample that the digit 1 seems to appear with probability $13/28$; but any particular finite string can always be "explained" by some particular deterministic process that is just not so immediately transparent as in our first example. In this particular string, the sequence is not "random," but rather is the number 203,774,006 expressed in base 2. But hold on, you may cavil, why such an unusual number? The point is not whether you expect it or not (at least in the frequentist gambit), but rather whether you would as readily accept as random the string 203,774,006 as you would 1010000100101010110000101111. (Suppose it were the population of the United States in the year of my birth. Does that render it more or less "random"?)

To hunt for the underlying deterministic law is to deny the importance of probability as an empirical phenomenon; and thus for the frequentist to predicate probability on finite strings that "look" random will not be sufficient. It is only when strings that look random can be indefinitely augmented, and while so doing continue to look random in ways not capable of being extrapolated from the initial string, that we have the curious marriage of irregularity and regular frequency that epitomizes the frequentist doctrine. For the frequentist, either the *Kollektiv* is an infinite process, or it is not a part of the game.

Because the infinite expanse of the *Kollektiv* is the hallmark of the frequentist doctrine, it is all the more daunting that the vaunted infinity is also the Achilles heel of the frequentists. To put it bluntly, it must be an embarrassment to an empirical doctrine that no one has ever seen, heard or touched an infinite *Kollektiv*. To put it somewhat less bluntly:

> an irregular collective cannot be constructed, that is, it cannot correspond to a computable number in the sense of Turing. Existence proofs in mathematics cannot necessarily be made constructive. For irregular collectives, they necessarily *cannot*.
>
> (Good 1983, 84)

Hence the *Kollektiv* can neither be discovered nor constructed artificially; although perhaps it is furtively lurking in the outback with its cousin, the Snark.

Nevertheless, we said at the beginning of this section that imagination given free rein will run riot; and in any event, whole swatches of mathematics are "imaginary" in the best senses of the term. But this fantastic formidable beast, the *Kollektiv*, will never bend to our yoke. As both Fine (1973, 100–13) and Georgescu-Roegen (1967, 248) have argued, the "limiting value" of the *Kollektiv* does not behave like a mathematical limit in the calculus. There is no *a priori* pattern, it cannot be computed, and we have no information as to any rate of convergence. Appeals to the long run become ineffectual, causing all and sundry to cite Keynes's quip that "In the long run we are all dead."

This defect wends its subversive way throughout the rest of the frequentist doctrine: "No relative frequency probability statement, strictly speaking, says *anything* about any finite event, group of events, or series" (Weatherford 1982, 170). In turn, this implies that the champions of an empiricist approach to probability end up admitting that frequentist probabilities can never be known, nor known to exist, nor ever succumb to either confirmation or disconfirmation. The partisans of the doctrine have often worried over the inapplicability of their notion of probability to single or unique events; but we now see that this was just the tip of the iceberg, since most events that one can see, taste or touch are exiled beyond the pale.

The problem here, as elsewhere in other versions of probability theory, is identity and randomness. Von Mises wanted the *Kollektiv* to be random, hence infinitely varied and not subject to any law or pattern; but he also wanted the *Kollektiv* to be a non-arbitrary partition of recognizably similar events that therefore had some rationale for possessing stable probabilities in the limit. How to corral a *Kollektiv*? Presumably we should weed out irrelevant classes of phenomena and subdivide according to available pertinent information. Hence it is not "the coin," the specific well-made coin; not just the specific coin, but the penny; not just the penny, but the unworn penny of recent vintage; not just the unworn penny, but the unworn penny undented by our frequent tosses . . . If we follow this procedure of tracking down the identity to the bitter end, then we have shrunk the *Kollektiv* down to where the probability loses all meaning. (Who cares about the 1989D penny on my dresser anyway?) Every event then becomes "singular." The potential for infinite throws of my specific penny was intended to mask the problem of the incredible shrinking *Kollektiv*; but then we never are assured of observing those infinite tosses of the perfectly identical coin.

Yet not all the objections to the Finitist approach revolve around the infinite character of the *Kollektiv*:

> The interpretation of probability is widely recognized as being controversial and there are many who reject the relative frequency approach on grounds which have nothing to do with issues relating to infinity . . . the finitist [in set theoretic terms] will resist the indiscriminate application of a combinatorial approach to totalities, selections from them and operations on them.
>
> (Tiles 1989, 67)

The reference here is to the axiom of choice in set theory, which has a long history of giving rise to paradoxes, conundrums, and sneaking suspicions that all is not well in the land of metamathematics. To give the merest whiff of the corruption, imagine the problems of a combinatorial approach to probability when a subset of an infinite set can be said to have just as many members as the original set itself. And to give some indication of the wonderful opportunities for self-reflexive paradoxes, recall that von Mises dictated that his place-selection functions could not sort by attribute of the events, but rather must be based on random or irrelevant criteria. This seems to presume a definition of randomness prior to the activity of defining randomness.

If the relative frequency doctrine really is such a house of cards, then what accounts for the fact that it is the perennial favorite of those working scientists who cannot be bothered with philosophical caveats? One is tempted to chalk it up to a pious confession of faith in the "realism" of the external world; but Terrence Fine (1973, 93) has proffered an even better explanation:

> Apparent convergence of relative frequency occurs because of, and not in spite of, the high irregularity (randomness) of the data sequences –

stability of relative frequency is not so much an empirical fact reflective of a law of nature as the outcome of our own approach to data ... Those data sequences to which we commonly apply the relative-frequency argument have failed tests for structure ... the sequences which we select for application of the relative frequency approach have been simultaneously preselected to possess apparently convergent relative-frequencies. It is the scientist's selectivity in using the relative-frequency argument that accounts for his success, rather than some fortuitous law of nature.

Since the point is subtle, it deserves some contemplation. Data which we have deemed deterministic are ruled out *a priori*. Other data which display incomprehensible irregularity are deemed to have not yet been subjected to appropriate categorization, identification or arrangement (i.e., they are not a valid *Kollektiv*), and are also ruled out of court. All that is left are data which display some detectable frequency, though they cannot be reduced to the other two categories. *Voilà!* The world presents us with randomness, since it cannot present us with anything else.

This phenomenon, where we are amazed at the efficacy and cogency of our own constructions because we have forgotten that we made have them, is a theme inadequately developed in the historiography of economics. Time and again one could marvel at the blindness towards the provenance of our own handiwork in the name of some magical "property" of a theorem or an estimator or complex mathematical formalism, when indeed the main role of the probability theory involved seems to be to thrust the rabbit passively back into the hat. Hence it will seem that frequentists have cultivated the maddening habit of leaving their fingerprints all over their constructions, all the while either denying or resenting the fact. For instance, Karl Popper (1976, 154) once bemoaned the spread of subjectivist interpretations of quantum mechanics, and blamed it upon the fact that the relative-frequency theory could not account for the isolated event. Yet the situation was much more fraught with perplexities than that; once the paradoxes of probability were confronted foursquare by physicists, they could not help but notice the role of the observer in the larger scheme of things. It is rather the social scientist (provisionally including here the medical professions and agriculturalists), who in his haste to neutralize the personality of the inquirer and render the object of inquiry a natural entity rushes headlong into concocting a frequentist solution to what must be regarded as an essentially epistemological problem of inference (Hacking 1987, 982).

NOTES

1 The thesis that neoclassical theory was not "discovered" but rather invented by the expedient of the imitation of nineteenth-century energy physics is documented at length in Mirowski (1989). The misrepresentation of various episodes in the

evolution of probability theory to suggest that the neoclassical conception of utility was somehow present in the mathematical literature of the eighteenth century has even found its way into the writings of such historians of science as Hacking (1975, 95); Porter (in von Furstenberg 1990, 49), who should know better, since unlike the economists, they have no stake in the construction of a hallowed pedigree for that doctrine.

2 An English translation of the original Latin document is published in Baumol and Goldfeld (1968, 15–26). It was written while Bernoulli was resident at the New Academy of St Petersburg and published in their *Proceedings*; hence the name of the paradox. This just goes to show how even the naming of a controversy can bias its historical interpretation, especially since Bernoulli's "solution" was not taken up by any subsequent mathematician. Moreover, there is the Whiggish sleight-of-hand of translating *emolumentum medium* in the original document as "utility."

3 For a discussion of the classical language of value as homogeneous substance, see Mirowski (1989, ch. 4).

4 It must further fluster advocates of Bernoulli as a precursor of neoclassical value theory to find one of the actual progenitors of that theory, William Stanley Jevons, still plumping for the principle of indifference long after it was an outmoded doctrine amongst the probabilists; see Jevons (1905, 212).

5 Readers of my *More Heat than Light* (1989) may prick up their ears here, noticing the reappearance of the obscure Helm in this context as well. Their acute sense of subterranean connections does not lead them astray in this instance. Indeed, Helm, one of the premier promoters of "Energetics" in the 1890s, also dabbled in probability theory; but the connection is not merely a coincidence. One can observe in von Mises (1957, 6) that frequentists have tended to compare their doctrine with that of the law of the conservation of energy, because it resembles it in so many curious respects. It is asserted to be empirical but it cannot be empirically discovered; it is claimed to be a corollary of the prohibition of perpetual motion or its correlatives (ibid., 1957, 25–6); it is intimately tied up with the definition of causality; ultimately it rests upon the projection of symmetries and invariances. Indeed, this historical similarity was one of the motivations behind the composition of the present article, providing a signpost indicating the hidden history of the drive to jointly reconceptualize economic value and probability.

6 Jean Ville in 1939 put his finger on a weakness of this particular interpretation, namely, that under this definition of a fair game, it was still perfectly possible for a gambler to start out with positive net winnings and never fall back to zero out to infinity. This curiosum led Ville to develop the theory of martingales.

REFERENCES

Baumol, William and Goldfeld, Steven (eds) (1968) *Precursors in Mathematical Economics*, London: London School of Economics.

Bayes, Thomas (1763) "An essay towards solving a problem in the doctrine of chances," *Philosophical Transactions of the Royal Society* (53): 370–418.

Cournot, A.-A. (1843) *Exposition de la théorie des chances et des probabilités*.

Cullen, Michael (1975) *The Statistical Movement in Early Victorian Britain*, London: Harvester.

Daston, Loraine (1988) *Classical Probability in the Enlightenment*, Princeton, NJ: Princeton University Press.

Ellis, R. L. (1849 [1843]) "On the foundations of the theory of probabilities," *Transactions of the Philosophical Society of Cambridge* (8): 1–6.

Fine, Terrence (1973) *Theories of Probability*, New York: Academic Press.

Georgescu-Roegen, Nicholas (1967) "An epistemological analysis of statistics," *Acta Logica* (10): 61–91.

Gigerenzer, Gerd, Kruger, Lorenz, Daston, Loraine and Heidelberger, Michael (eds) (1989) *The Empire of Chance*, New York: Cambridge University Press.

Good, I. J. (1983) *Good Thinking*, Minneapolis: University of Minnesota Press.

Hacking, Ian (1965) *The Logic of Statistical Inference*, Cambridge: Cambridge University Press.

Hacking, Ian (1975) *The Emergence of Probability*, Cambridge: Cambridge University Press.

Hacking, Ian (1982) "Biopower and the avalanche of printed numbers," *Humanities in Society*, (5): 279–95.

Hacking, Ian (1987) "Probability," in *The New Palgrave*, London: Macmillan.

Hacking, Ian (1990) *The Taming of Chance*, Cambridge: Cambridge University Press.

Heidelberger, Michael *et al.*, (eds) (1983) *Probability since 1800*, Bielefeld: B. Kleine Verlag.

Jevons, William Stanley (1905) *The Principles of Science*, London: Macmillan.

Jorland, Gerald (1987) "The Saint Petersburg paradox, 1713–1937," in Lorentz Kruger *et al.* (eds) *The Probabilistic Revolution*, Cambridge, MA: MIT Press, vol. 1.

Kneale, William (1949) *Probability and Induction*, Oxford: Oxford University Press.

Kruger, Lorentz *et. al.* (eds) (1987) *The Probabilistic Revolution*, Cambridge, MA: MIT Press, 2 vols.

Laplace, Pierre (1951) *A Philosophical Essay on Probabilities*, New York: Dover.

Maistrov, L. E. (1974) *Probability Theory: An Historical Sketch*, New York: Academic Press.

Menger, Karl (1967 [1934]) "The role of uncertainty in economics," in Martin Shubik (ed.), *Essays in Mathematical Economics in Honor of Oskar Morgenstern*, Princeton, NJ: Princeton University Press.

Mirowski, Philip (1988) *Against Mechanism*, Totowa, NJ: Rowman & Littlefield.

Mirowski, Philip (1989) *More Heat than Light*, New York: Cambridge University Press.

Mirowski, Philip (1994) *Edgeworth on Chance, Economic Hazard and Statistics*, Savage, MD: Rowman & Littlefield.

Popper, Karl (1976) *Unended Quest*, London: Fontana.

Porter, Theodore (1986) *The Rise of Statistical Thinking*, Princeton, NJ: Princeton University Press.

Samuelson, Paul (1986) *Collected Scientific Papers*, vol. 5, Cambridge, MA: MIT Press.

Schumpeter, Joseph (1954) *A History of Economic Analysis*, New York: Oxford University Press.

Stigler, Stephen M. (1986) *The History of Statistics*, Cambridge, MA: Harvard University Press.

Tiles, Mary (1989) *The Philosophy of Set Theory*, Oxford: Basil Blackwell.

Venn, John (1962 [1888]) *The Logic of Chance*, New York: Chelsea.

von Furstenberg, George (ed.) (1990) *Acting Under Uncertainty*, Boston, MA: Kluwer Academic.

von Mises, Richard (1957) *Probability, Statistics and Truth*, New York: Dover.

Weatherford, Roy (1982) *Philosophical Foundations of Probability Theory*, London: Routledge & Kegan Paul.

3

CYBERPUNK AND CHICAGO

Craufurd D. Goodwin and Alex Rogers[1]

INTRODUCTION

Parallel to the growth of economics as a rigorous social science, with the generation of theorems, theory testing and increasingly more abstract reasoning, there has existed an underworld of literature that addresses many of the same topics as the professional economist but using different heuristic and rhetorical devices. Typically this literature consists of fiction, poetry, drama, editorializing in the media, and reflective essays of various kinds. Usually, from the professional economists' perspective, these nonscientific works are judged to lack seriousness and standing in debates over principle or public policy. Frequently they are greeted with anger or derision for confusing their audience and for distracting attention from the central issues of economics. Sometimes this literature has been produced by prominent economists themselves through the back door as it were (for example, in the early period by Bernard de Mandeville and in the twentieth century by Kenneth Boulding and John Kenneth Galbraith) but usually it comes from writers variously described as "humanists" or "moral critics." Sometimes the underground writers set out to popularize the principles and policy conclusions of "economic science," as for example Harriet Martineau in her short didactic novelettes. More often they reflect policy dissent, and use a kind of reasoning given relatively little weight in the conventional economic analysis: this is reflected in the attention to human suffering caused by agricultural depopulation in Oliver Goldsmith's "Deserted Village," the concern for environmental pollution and urban degradation of early British industrialization pictured in Charles Dickens's *Hard Times*, and the misery of unemployment during the Great Depression, portrayed in John Steinbeck's *Grapes of Wrath*.

Sometimes this literature reflects a specific heretical ideology such as Marxism or American Institutionalism. More often it reflects sentiments of the wider public or merely the anguish of the particular writer. Many of the most influential works in this nonscientific, moral-critical tradition have been in a genre that is particularly fashionable and influential in its time: for example, Victorian Romantic poetry, the Chicago novels of the 1890s (e.g., *The Pit*, which explored market concentration), the moralizing plays of George Bernard Shaw (e.g., *Major Barbara*), sentimental films from Hollywood such as *Country* (which portrays the effects of competitive markets on marginalized farmers) or *Doctor* (which attacks the role of avarice in modern medicine); (for a more general discussion of "the economic novel," see Taylor 1942). Success in this art form seems to rest upon a clever selection of topics for exploration – those that have wide popular appeal – and use of a medium that reaches a wide audience at the time. One of the most successful expository devices in this underworld literature consistently through time has been the utopia (and its opposite, the dystopia). Edward Bellamy's utopia *Looking Backward 1887–2000* (1888) was the most influential radical tract of its time (over one million copies sold). It pictured a world in the year 2000 in which many of the noxious effects of contemporary capitalism had been eliminated by fundamental changes in the structure of the system. Public ownership of property and equal income distribution had brought heaven on earth; cooperation and benevolence replaced competition and greed. Ayn Rand's novels that picture a utopia based on a minimal state and aggressive self-interest have been almost as popular with conservative thinkers in the years since the Second World War. By contrast, George Orwell's *1984* demonstrated the potential horrors of the powerful state and central planning by carrying the implications of socialist doctrine to negative extremes and the omnipresence of the symbolic "Big Brother."

A distinctive characteristic of utopias and dystopias is their similarity to the long-run models of the professional economist. They too are models and rest on simplifying assumptions that are projected into the future. For this reason, utopias and dystopias are relatively easy for writers with some training in economics to appreciate, either as authors or audience. Indeed, some of the most celebrated economic models are directly parallel in form. Bellamy's utopia is more than reminiscent of J. S. Mill's conception of the stationary state. Orwell's socialist dystopia is close in structure (but very different in implication) to Karl Marx's crisis of capitalism in which contradictions ultimately render private property socially insupportable.

By and large, professional economists have dismissed the commentary on economic principles and economic policy that appears in this nonprofessional literature, when they have taken notice of it at all, as mere background "noise" to "serious" professional debates and of no interest to the science. This parody of economics, they say, stands as alchemy to chemistry, as phrenology to psychology. Sometimes the hostility of the profession has become intense and vindictive, especially if the outside commentator has been able to attract a substantial audience. When the art historian John Ruskin published his commentary on political economy "Unto This Last" in the *Cornhill Magazine*, his economist critics threatened never to publish in that journal again.

If the profession dismisses this nonprofessional literature, why then should historians of economics attend to it? There are several compelling reasons. First, like it or not, this literature constitutes an important part of the milieu in which economic science is practiced. Economists are not immune to their environment, and if their creativity is being probed, this conspicuous element in their surroundings must be taken into account. Second, the nonprofessional literature that deals with economic issues is an important determinant of the reception given to professional ideas. If the history of economics is taken to include the use as well as the generation of economic ideas, then this element in the context of use needs to be well understood. Third, this creative literature on economic subjects, while often reflecting a misunderstanding of "sound" economic principles of the time, has, nevertheless, been prescient in perceiving facts and relationships that would be accepted by later professional economists. For example, in this literature in the nineteenth and early twentieth centuries can be found discussions of market externalities and of complex human behavior that would be dealt with only considerably later by the profession. An understanding of this occasional perception of the Emperor's nakedness, then, has relevance both for past and current economic science. Finally, while some of this nonprofessional literature has "led" the science, most of it merely reflects the fears, the hopes, and the sentiments of the wider population. These may represent more ignorance than enlightenment, more error than truth, but they are the context in which science evolves and, together with public opinion polls, they are one useful gauge of civil society.

Historians of economics have to date ended their examination of humanistic commentary on economics mainly with the 1930s (e.g., see Grampp 1973), perhaps because they believe that afterwards the science became effectively impervious to outside influence, and perhaps because imaginative literature, more than the conventional professional product, is difficult to appreciate and place in perspective in one's own time.

This paper explores a body of literature from the 1980s referred to as "cyberpunk" that both draws heavily on modern economic ideas and deals with them in a way that is reminiscent of but distinctly different from the earlier humanistic commentary. This literature provides a dystopian vision of the future of a liberal free-market society to contrast with Rand's utopias on the same theme, and to complement Orwell's socialist dystopia.

In the next section we explain what this literature contains, then we suggest what it signifies for the history of economics, and finally we ruminate about its impact on contemporary society.

A NEW BRAND OF SCIENCE FICTION

Who are the cyberpunk writers? The originals – Rudy Rucker, Lewis Shiner, John Shirley, and Bruce Sterling – were a small coterie of contributors to

Cheap Truth, a freely distributed, uncopyrighted science-fiction magazine that ran from the mid-1970s to the early 1980s. In 1984, William Gibson wrote the canonical work *Neuromancer*, which has become the manifesto of the movement. By the late 1980s, Gibson, Sterling, Rucker, Shiner, and Shirley, along with Walter Jon Williams and Pat Cadigan, had become the cyberpunk core. Gibson's novels and short stories still best illustrate the genre.[2]

Cyberpunk is a science fiction category with certain well-defined characteristics, the most prominent of which is commitment to an exploration of and inquiry into the social consequences of information technologies.[3] Bruce Sterling explains in his introduction to the 1986 cyberpunk anthology *Mirrorshades* that cyberpunk authors are the first generation of science fiction writers to grow up in a science fictional world. Their concept of the future relies much more heavily on developing a projection from the present and on the world already around them than imaginative speculations of their "hard SF" predecessors (Sterling 1986, xi). Others, too, view cyberpunk as a reflection of the present. William Gibson has said in regard to his work *Neuromancer*, "What's most important to me is that it's about the present. It's not really about an imagined future. It's a way of trying to come to terms with the awe and terror inspired in me by the world in which we live" (in Rosenthal 1991, 85). Fredric Jameson writes: "Perhaps what is implied is simply an ultimate historical breakdown, and that we can no longer imagine the future at all, under any form, Utopian as well as catastrophic. Under these circumstances, a formerly futurological Science Fiction (such as 'cyberpunk' today) turns into mere realism and an outright representation of the present" (ibid., 87).

The Cyberpunk Frequently Asked Questions (FAQ) list, available on the Internet, describes the cyberpunk world as populated by "marginalized people in technologically enhanced cultural 'systems'."[4] The people are "marginalized" because they have no control over their own lives; the "systems" that control them are usually either a dominating corporation or a fundamentalist religion. In either case, the participants in these systems have neither the freedom of expression nor action enjoyed by people today. Instead, through the use of invasive technologies, the "systems" manipulate not only the behavior but also the thoughts of their dependents. Advanced information technologies create imaginary virtual worlds, in which the people live, so real that they are indistinguishable from the physical world. In addition, "this technological system [sometimes] extends into its human 'components' as well, via brain implants, prosthetic limbs, cloned or genetically engineered organs ... [h]umans themselves become part of the 'Machine.' This is the cyber aspect of cyberpunk" (FAQ). The genre's protagonists are drawn from those who not only live outside the system but also fight it, generally using the system's technologies against it. From a societal perspective, the heroes are the outcasts, the criminals, and occasionally the visionaries, none of whom conform to social norms. The protagonists, therefore, form the basis for the "'punk' aspect of cyberpunk" (FAQ). Finally, stylistic features separate cyberpunk writings from other works with similar themes. Their tone is dark and pessimistic; the narrative pace is relentless; few if any pauses in the action occur; purely descriptive scenes are rare. Moreover, readers are often bewildered by the changing scenes and the dysfunctional moral compass that guides the characters through the cyberpunk world. Though fighting against the "system" might protect a character's individuality, it does not make him or her a "good" person. Traditional notions of right or wrong have little relevance in cyberpunk literature.

Gibson's cyberpunk world is placed at some unspecified time in the future Information Age. He never directly explains the history of how that world develops, but from the clues he does give, we have created our own interpreted history of Gibson's future. At some point, many many years before *Neuromancer* begins, multinational corporations started using the then-new information technologies to decrease their reliance on geographically centralized headquarters. By making use of fiber optic and cellular connections, the corporations have spread their top managers across the world, yet they still "meet" to discuss long-range strategies and problems. The need to make these meetings as efficient and comfortable as possible spurs the growth of a worldwide information network called by Gibson either "the Matrix" or "cyberspace."

While multinationals learn how best to use cyberspace, two other developments take place. Private commercial ventures wholly owned by large extended families called "clans" organize and prosper. For a brief period these clans dominate the financial scene. The profits generated by that dominance enable the clans to establish hugely expensive orbital and lunar colonies while simultaneously making massive investments in artificial intelligence technologies. Toward the end of the reign of the clans, family-led designers create sentient computers to which international authorities grant conditional citizenship. As the clans expend their resources, Japanese *zaibatsus*, large corporations which guarantee lifelong employment and create distinct corporate cultures, recognize a fundamental shift in how technology affects society. In essence, they are the first to appreciate the imminent change to an economy with near-perfect information. Having long excelled at planning well into the future, the *zaibatsus* organize themselves in order to capitalize on the changes they know will soon come.

Clan leadership proves transitional and the family ventures grow excessively unwieldy, while the owners themselves become distant from world affairs and their own business concerns. Having amassed fortunes large enough to sustain them indefinitely, the clan leaders withdraw from the business world, leaving a vast power vacuum and creating an atmosphere of extreme uncertainty. The late Howard Hughes might serve as a model for

these elusive and eccentric clan leaders. Because neither national govern-
ments nor the clans can any longer protect their citizens nor control an
increasingly unstable world, popular support for the *zaibatsus* peaks.

Offered lifelong stability as well as a secure environment, workers flock to
the *zaibatsus*. Eventually, after another long interval workers begin to identify
themselves by *zaibatsu* first, nationality second (Gibson 1986a, 121). Nations
grow so dependent on *zaibatsus* that, in effect, they cease to have much
independent influence on what happens within their borders. Moreover, as
other multinationals see the *zaibatsu* model working, they reorganize themselves into *zaibatsu*-like structures. The dollar, the mark, the pound all vanish,
leaving only the yen. By the time of the cyberpunk "present," Japanese
money, Japanese culture, and Japanese discipline dominate all other alternatives.[5] Gibson's trilogy takes place in this *zaibatsu*-run world.

Little of nature and less of appreciation for it survive the agglomeration
of large cities into megalopolises in the cyberpunk world. The most prominent megalopolis in Gibson's trilogy is the Sprawl, a city stretching from New
York to Atlanta. For most, living in the Sprawl takes place indoors under the
auspices of the *zaibatsus* within institutions called arcologies which serve as
both living spaces and cultural identifiers.[6] The *zaibatsus* operate the arcologies for their employees, and though the universal currency among arcologies
is the "nuyen," *zaibatsus* mostly pay their employees in "credits" which have
value only within a firm's arcology. Much as the company store tied miners
to the mines, *zaibatsus* bind their workers to the company-owned arcology in
order that their employees may "benefit" from the particular climate and
atmosphere the managers discover will make their inputs most productive.
The large urban cities do not contain all the arcologies – those firms engaged
in highly sensitive research isolate themselves outside the cities for better
protection against penetration. Typically, each *zaibatsu* owns many arcologies.
The structure and organization of several arcologies run by the same *zaibatsu*
will have more characteristics in common than differences.

Those in Gibson's world who do not live in the arcologies exist in literal
underworlds, the seamy, violent antithesis of the calm, antiseptic world of
corporate life. In *Neuromancer*, Night City is one such place. It "was like a
deranged experiment in social Darwinism, designed by a bored researcher
who kept one thumb permanently on the fast-forward button" (Gibson
1984, 7). Though Night City's denizens pursue thoroughly disreputable activities, places like Night City play a vital role in the economy (Gibson 1986a,
34). The *zaibatsus* tolerate the Night Cities not for their inhabitants "but as a
deliberately unsupervised playground for the technology itself" (Gibson
1984, 11). The need for a "technology testing ground" comes from the
nature of the technology. Much of it involves intrusive procedures which
might have deleterious effects on subjects. Night City provides humans willing to risk death or permanent dysfunction in order to survive.

Why would anyone choose the uncertain, dangerous life of the Night

Cities over the comfortable safe life of the arcologies? The answer lies in the nature of the population. Gibson's world contains institutional extremes where arcologies represent absolute order and the Night Cities absolute chaos. The characters, too, rest at polar extremes. There are only the rich and the poor, denizens above and prisoners below. No middle ground is left (Gibson 1993, 146). To understand the choice between order and chaos, one must examine the characters which populate cyberpunk and the conditions under which they live.

A grim, harsh atmosphere and tone pervade cyberpunk. The future holds many marvels, but for the common man, change comes at a bewildering pace and brings little reward. Few aspects of the cyberpunk world run at normal speed; "standing still" means death. "Stop hustling and you sank without a trace" (Gibson 1984, 7). Hopelessness and insecurity pervade Gibson's work. For the individual, striving against the *zaibatsus* leads only to the loss of what little self-control remains in a world of externally imposed order – a world where order derives from control over the flow of information; all kinds of data increase the *zaibatsus*' dominance:

> We're an information economy. They teach you that in school. What they don't teach you is that's impossible to move, to live, to operate at any level without leaving traces, bits, seemingly meaningless fragments of personal information. Fragments that can be retrieved, amplified.
> (Gibson 1986b, 39)

In the cyberpunk world, no matter what actions people take, they cannot help but leave a "data shadow," an information afterimage which allows corporations to create holistic profiles of their employees and consumers. With the help of artificial intelligence (AI) these corporations build models which contain insights into people's characters that the subjects themselves do not even have (Gibson 1986a, 141). Most people in Gibson's world have no control over, or even influence on, the institutions which dominate their lives.

Virtual reality, however, offers the illusion of freedom, a means to escape despondency. In a very real sense, the virtual reality capabilities of the cyberpunk future offer a true opiate to the masses: through the exercise of their fantasies, people are given the ability to live other people's lives and to create virtual situations in which they are under the illusion that they control, even dominate, their surroundings. Social station, physical attributes, even gender can be changed within these virtual scenarios. People in Gibson's cyberpunk world cope with real despondency by escaping to artificial reality.

A few participants in the cyberspace world have not succumbed to their bleak surroundings. These "heroes" do not accept the confining circumstances of their world. Most often, they are cyber-jockeys, computer wizards able to manipulate cyberspace to achieve their own unusual ends. They are "thie[ves] work[ing] for other, wealthier thieves, employers who provided the exotic software required to penetrate the bright walls of corporate systems, opening windows into rich fields of data" (Gibson 1984, 5). Although the cyber-jockeys steal information from one *zaibatsu* and release it to another, the *zaibatsus* themselves hire many such employees. In essence, the *zaibatsus* engage in a continuing game of elaborate deception wherein they try to steal from one another. These heroes survive by violating the sanctity of proprietary information. They parasitically leech off of society. The *zaibatsus* face the "prisoners' dilemma": all corporations would be better off if cyberspace cowboys were eliminated, yet so long as the incentive to cheat on any collusive arrangement exists, the "cowboys" will remain an unwelcome but predictable feature of corporate reality.

Other noncowboy characters who operate outside the system are also threats to corporate life. Turner, a character in Gibson's *Count Zero*, is an extraction artist. Rather than steal data, he steals people. Often, even the most successful in the cyberpunk world are little more than indentured servants to the corporation. Contracts between scientist and laboratory are lifetime arrangements which can never be legally terminated by the scientist (Gibson 1986a, 129). Turner "steals" these employees when contracted to do so by a competing *zaibatsu*. The pattern here, too, follows that of the cyber-jockeys: the *zaibatsus* do not like the existence of people like Turner but they have no choice other than to tolerate and employ them.

The cyberpunk hero does not usually have the moral virtues normally associated with heroes. In fact, the cyberpunk hero often engages in criminal activities. The cyberspace wizards prosper by breaking into computer systems to steal data; extraction artists physically spirit disgruntled wizards from one *zaibatsu* to another, breaking the employee's contract with the first employer. Cyberspace heroes are applauded not for their actions but for their attitudes. For cyberpunk authors, the hero is the loner who fights the system, who wants something more than merely to pay homage and kowtow to the corporation. Both cyberspace wizards and extraction artists have the same essential quality. They might ultimately work for the system that they, at their core, loathe, but they do so in a way fundamentally antithetical to the ordering principles on which the *zaibatsu*-led society rests. They self-contract their services, moving from employer to employer and holding no strong loyalty for any one. More importantly, they introduce chaos and uncertainty into the otherwise placid world scene.[7] The *zaibatsus* are unquestionably predatory in character, but much of their success comes from the use of people like Turner or Case (the protagonist in *Neuromancer*), and their powerful position comes as a direct result of information technologies.

The new technologies of the cyberpunk future are extraordinarily varied. They range from advances in genetic engineering, biochemical research, and cybernetics to the creation of designer drugs and improvements in virtual reality. In one form or another, however, every new technology is to some extent intrusive. Just as better information technologies led to the rise of *zaibatsus*, which proved inimical to individual liberty, so too do the technologies themselves, regardless of their long-range consequences, threaten individual liberty. In cyberpunk, technology is never neutral. The existence of the new information technologies is so inimical to the individual that it can only be classified as evil.

The two most significant technological advances, cyberspace and simstim, are both applications of information technology. In *Neuromancer*, Gibson (1984, 51) defines cyberspace as

> A consensual hallucination experienced daily by billions of legitimate operators, in every nation, by children being taught mathematical concepts ... A graphic representation of data abstracted from the banks of every computer in the human system. Unthinkable complexity. Lines of light ranged in the nonspace of the mind, clusters and constellations of data.

Simstim stands for "simulated experience" and is the common man's entry into virtual reality.

Both these technologies have intrusive qualities. A person enters cyberspace through a "deck." By connecting the deck directly to one's nervous system, the user enters cyberspace. Injuries sustained in that electronic world may very well have real, physical consequences. To use simstim, a person must have a jack, an entry port, surgically implanted in the head. With that jack, one may insert discretely purchased scenarios or connect to one of the virtual soap operas broadcast much as television is distributed today. In either case, the simstim user fully experiences the life of the person in the scenario. It is the perfect, complete escape.

Much of the interaction in the cyberpunk world takes place in cyberspace. Commerce, friendly discussions, business meetings, and other similar activities occur virtually. Cyberspace has removed geographical constraints on action – anything that can be done in the real world can also be done in cyberspace. In fact, corporations rely on cyberspace to such an extent that they are loath to enter the few remaining markets where cyberspace connections have not yet been developed (Gibson 1986a, 120–1). A complete information economy manifests itself in the Matrix, in cyberspace where ultimately even the participants, while they are on-line, are nothing more than 1s and 0s stored in some machine somewhere. Cyberspace is the *sine qua non* of the cyberpunk world. From information technology did the *zaibatsus* gain power; through it, they maintain their position.

CYBERPUNK AND ECONOMIC THOUGHT

Why is the title of this paper "Cyberpunk and Chicago"? Because this literature is entwined very closely with the two Chicago traditions in economics, first the turn-of-the-century radicalism associated with Thorstein Veblen and the Chicago novelists, and second, the neoliberal free market economics epitomized by Milton Friedman's popular book *Free to Choose* (1980) and the policy pronouncements of the other Chicago Nobelists, especially George Stigler and Gary Becker. The overwhelming message of the later Chicago is meliorist. Free markets maximize human welfare – and by and large the freer the better. To the extent that the condition of perfect markets is obtained, the allocation of resources is optimized. In particular, the new "economics of information" reflected in Chicago doctrine by the 1980s promised great strides toward the theorist's Elysium of greater consumer welfare.

Cyberpunk came on the scene just when modern Chicago was at its zenith in the mid-1980s. By that time, neoclassical microeconomics seemed to have both Keynesian macroeconomics and socialist-style state planning firmly on the run. Its admirers were ensconced in the White House, 10 Downing Street, and lesser political residences around the world. Its missionaries, such as Arnold Harberger, were going forth into the developing world and, yea, into the deepest recesses of the communist world, as well as into the World Bank and Fund. What arguments could possibly remain for a vigorous role for government in the economy?

The cyberpunk authors were certainly not intellectually equipped to answer this question head on. As far as we know, none has had any advanced study in economics. Yet we know, they recoiled at the policies of Reagan and Thatcher and must have felt viscerally that a contrary case could be made. They did recognize that by the 1980s the problem of corporate control had been vastly complicated by the global reach of the corporate units to be constrained; and it was far from clear that individual nation states could intervene successfully on their own.

There is much in cyberpunk that is familiar from the corpus of radical economics over the last century and a half. It must be presumed that the cyberpunk authors were familiar with this general body of thought. From Marx comes the notion that technological change empowers the dialectic in society. Ideas and institutions will evolve inevitably, in response to changes in the forces of production. But following contemporary economics, the context is modernized to feature change in information technology, rather than in machines, as the instigating force. From Marx also comes the emphasis on contradictions, or flaws in the economy. Indeed, the cyberpunk economy is the manifestation of these contradictions carried to far extremes. The widespread dispensation by corporations to their work force of various narcotics, including the ultimate escape into simstim, is a modern version of Marx's religion, the opiate of the people. Conflict among the *zaibatsu*s seems bound ultimately to lead to some crisis in the cyberpunk world; yet there is no Marxian prospect of happiness after the revolution.

But more can be found in cyberpunk from the old Chicago of Thorstein Veblen and *The Theory of the Leisure Class* (1904) even than from Marx. From these Institutionalists comes a portrayal of human beings as easily manipulated by suppliers of goods and services (unlike the confident consumers of

48

the later Chicago world) and an economy dominated by large amoral corporations. William Gibson's *zaibatsu*s have the distinct flavor of the Railroad Trust in Frank Norris's *Octopus* (1901). The complex psychological drives of the leaders of the evolving multinationals, not simple profit-maximization, are the determining force in cyberpunk as they are for pecuniary elites in Veblen and the later technostructure of Galbraith. The individual consumer and the worker in both the cyberpunk and Institutionalist systems have little true free will. Freedom to choose is a sham. Indeed, manipulation of individuals by those who control the cyberpunk world is highlighted by contrast with the freewheeling outlaws of the underworld. In the cyberpunk future the only real freedom exists for the criminals.

In the venerable tradition of humanistic critiques of conventional economic doctrine, cyberpunk provides a cynical reinterpretation of notions popularized during the 1980s by Friedman and others. Just as Dickens and Shaw mocked claims for capitalism in the nineteenth and early twentieth centuries, and Orwell heaped scorn on the claims of central planners, Gibson and his compatriots construct a dark dystopia to cast doubt on the extravagant promises of the "neoliberal" thesis of their time. They do this with considerable sophistication, including portrayal of features of a future economy that were under discussion among professional economists such as a cashless society (see Cowen and Kroszner 1987). In the cyberpunk world people make purchases with a moneychip.

But the secret of cyberpunk is not the packaging of old wine in new bottles. This function would not have sold several million copies of their works to date. Cyberpunk has played effectively on the fears and prejudices of its contemporary readers. It provides a picture of the future which contains some elements that are perceived fearfully today, and suggests explanations for others which are only just on the horizon but already fill many readers with dread. The racial prejudice of Americans is touched upon in the caricature of the Japanese as the agents of dominance. That symbol of American power and pride, the dollar, is entirely supplanted by the Japanese "nuyen." Pollution of nature by large corporations, like the oil spill from the *Exxon Valdez*, is projected to a point where everyone must live indoors. The large corporations extend their power over individuals by perfecting various intrusive technologies, and in order to test dangerous new products (like Dow Corning's breast implants) they maintain "Night Cities" of free-spirited but compliant experimental subjects. Through their control over information they remove the possibility of individual privacy. At a deeper level, there is play on the unease that many Americans harbor about the seemingly empty lives led by their children and neighbors, drugged by endless television and stronger intoxicants. Cyberpunk both extrapolates this trend and provides an explanation of it. In this state of corporate-controlled collective dissipation, they find a total absence of the virtues Americans traditionally hold dear: patriotism, honor, exercise of individual free will, and

CRAUFURD D. GOODWIN AND ALEX ROGERS

loyalty to one's fellows. Only those frightening fundamentalist religions that appeared as significant forces on the political scene in the 1980s have gained even greater strength in the cyberpunk future.

Finally, cyberpunk deals, albeit obliquely, with the decline of an independent middle class in a capitalist society – a phenomenon that has terrified many of their readers old and young in the 1990s. In the cyberpunk world technological change has virtually obliterated the middle class and placed all power in the hands of executives of large corporations, by whose whims ordinary citizens virtually live or die. Although the process of destroying a social class has a distinctly Marxian ring, it is now the bourgeoisie, not the proletariat, that is on the block.

CYBERPUNK AND THE REAL WORLD

What possible impact could the fancies of science fiction writers have on thinkers, and doers concerned with real problems? We suggest that cyberpunk's significance comes in three areas. First, it has resurrected unfashionable economic ideas, discussed in the last section, and repopularized them. Second, it has introduced many of the terms now used in popular parlance to describe America's information future. Finally, and most ambiguously, aspects of the Clinton Administration's approach to regulating the National Information Infrastructure (NII) seem to include some of cyberpunk's core concerns.

Radical ideas certainly did not disappear from the American political consciousness in the 1980s; but they were undeniably in retreat. Marxist notions had to deal with the suggestion that they were the doctrinal basis for collapsing social systems in the real world. Collectivist theory was as much a loser in the Cold War as the Soviet Union. At the same time, softer, New Deal-style reformism was derided by its critics as "tax and spend liberalism." The apparent failures of many Federal programs based on this doctrine – the war on poverty, public education, farm subsidies – all made the ideas of Institutionalism from Veblen through Berle and Means to Galbraith seem discredited and a little musty – like "your father's Oldsmobile." Even the new twists of Robert Reich and Lester Thurow did not change the image. What cyberpunk did was make these ideas live again, to make them hi-tech and *à la mode*, to reach a new generation through associations that they well understood.

When ideas that are conventional or radical become embedded in the popular culture it is extremely difficult to discern their origin or source of strength. It may be enough, perhaps, in this case to give only one example of how conventional elements of radicalism remain in the rhetoric of protest in America of the mid-1990s dressed up in their new cyberpunk clothes.

On April 24, 1995 the *New York Times* received a letter from "Terrorist group FC" that claimed responsibility for a series of bombings attributed by the Federal Bureau of Investigation to a single person or a group known as Unabom. The letter (*NYT*, April 26, 1995, p. A16) has been heavily censored by the FBI in its published version, but parts that are now available reflect very closely critiques of social change that are clearly evident in cyberpunk. Authors of the letter condemn corporate manipulation of human attitudes, environmental degradation, and academic research on topics of alleged corporate interest such as behavior modification, genetics, and computer science. The letter says:

> we attacked Burston-Marsteller less for its specific misdeeds than on general principles. Burston-Marsteller is about the biggest organization in the public relations field. This means that its business is the development of techniques for manipulating people's attitudes ... We have nothing against universities or scholars as such. All the university people whom we have attacked have been specialists in technical fields. (We consider certain areas of applied psychology, such as behavior modification, to be technical fields.) We would not want anyone to think that we have any desire to hurt professors who study archaeology, history, literature or harmless stuff like that. The people we are out to get are the scientists and engineers, especially in critical fields like computers and genetics.

In the same way as cyberpunk authors, the Unabomers condemn a world dominated by large corporations even though they are unable to prescribe an alternative. They claim to reflect a wide body of ideas shared by anarchists and environmentalists:

> We call ourselves anarchists because we would like, ideally, to break down all society into very small, completely autonomous units. Regrettably, we don't see any clear road to this goal, so we leave it to the indefinite future. Our more immediate goal, which we think may be attainable at some time during the next several decades, is the destruction of the worldwide industrial system. Through our bombings we hope to promote social instability in industrial society, propagate antiindustrial ideas and give encouragement to those who hate the industrial system ... For security reasons we won't reveal the number of members of our group, but anyone who will read the anarchist and radical environmentalist journals will see that opposition to the industrial-technological system is widespread and growing.

The Unabomer demands are not for ransom or for other familiar quid pro quos but rather for wide dissemination of their "anti-industrial" ideas, for access to communications:

> The people who are pushing all this growth and progress garbage deserve to be severely punished ... It may be just as well that failure of

our early bombs discouraged us from making any public statements at that time. We were very young then and our thinking was crude. Over the years we have given as much attention to the development of our ideas as to the development of bombs, and we now have something serious to say. And we feel that just now the time is ripe for the presentation of anti-industrial ideas.

No matter whether this letter does indeed come from the Unabomers, or whether it is directly influenced by cyberpunk, it is consistent with the radical doctrine that reflects and is sustained by cyberpunk.

Apart from its relationship to radical doctrine, cyberpunk has introduced part of the vocabulary used to describe America's information future. Publications routinely use the phrase "cyberspace" – first used in Gibson's *Neuromancer* – to describe on-line environments. One magazine, *Newsweek*, reveals several examples. Each week, *Newsweek* runs a section called "Cyberscope" in which it discusses new and interesting features of the global network of networks called Internet. The choice of titles is revealing for two reasons. The prefix "cyber" shows up in two English words, "cybernation" and "cybernetics" (*OED*). Cybernation is the theory, practice, or condition of control by machines; cybernetics is the theory or practice of control in living organisms or machines. Their shared etymological parent, κυβερναν means "to steer." Unless *Newsweek* has made the affirmative decision to suggest that their "Cyberscope" section concerns the manner in which the Internet steers and controls American society, their choice of title had to have a different origin. Since cyberpunk represents the only widespread use of the prefix "cyber-" in science fiction, and cyberpunk has proved itself a commercially successful genre, we infer that *Newsweek* chose its title based on the likelihood that their readership would either recognize the phrase or think it a "cool" way of describing the topic. Other evidence exists that the magazine has appropriated the word "cyberpunk" and started to use it to describe real-world people and events. In its Year-in-Review issue for 1994, *Newsweek* described Newt Gingrich as "a political cyberpunk."

Cyberpunk itself uses the κυβερναν root in its proper form. As described earlier in this paper, the Cyberpunk FAQ presents the "cyber" aspect of cyberpunk as not only the mechanical prostheses and electronic implants which invade characters of the cyberpunk world but also the presence of a technological system which dominates and controls everyone who lives within it. The "cyber" aspect of cyberpunk conveys a negative image and non-science-fiction publications have started using the term to describe negative real-world stereotypes in a manner not foreseen in the literature. Two *New York Times* authors, Katie Hafner and John Markoff, wrote a book in 1990 titled *Cyberpunk: Outlaws and Hackers on the Computer Frontier*, and as author Bruce Sterling explains, FBI agents routinely attend cyberpunk conventions fearing that attenders will conspire to foment electronic mischief (Fischlin, *et al.* 1992, 5).

Though cyberpunk manifests itself in word choice, the ideas it reflects also appear in the policy debate over America's information infrastructure policy. Cyberpunk posits a world in which information technology dominates the common man, controlling, at some level, his every movement. At least some of the current policy proposals for the National Information Infrastructure (NII) explicitly work to include citizens in, rather than separate them from, the developing electronic world.

The Clinton Administration has successfully made the phrase "information superhighway" the most popular metaphor for America's information future. Since the Administration supports giving every citizen the right to use and add information to the NII, the highway metaphor proves very advantageous: all citizens can freely use the interstate highway system, and municipalities make every effort to provide some way to reach the highways from their towns. Similarly, the Clinton Administration has put much effort into promoting universal service and a universal access program which would require every American to have not only access to the information superhighway but also the capacity to make their own information available to all other users of that highway. Whether or not the highway metaphor suggests most closely what a NII will be, is no longer significant. The public has accepted the phrase "information superhighway" and its implications.

The Administration describes the NII in its white paper titled *An Agenda for Action* in the following manner

> The National Information Infrastructure will consist of (1) thousands of interconnected, interoperable telecommunications networks, (2) computer systems, televisions, fax machines, telephones, and other "information appliances," (3) software information services, and information databases (e.g., "digital libraries"), and (4) trained people who can build, maintain, and operate these systems. In the future, the NII will enable all Americans to get the information they need, when they need it and where they need it for an affordable price.[8]

Using the highway metaphor, we can relate each of the Administration's four points to some physical characteristic. The "thousands of interconnected, interoperable telecommunications networks" refer to the physical roads which comprise the interstate system. The "computer systems, televisions, fax machines, telephones, and other 'information appliances'" are analogous to the cities which are destinations on the highway. The "software information services, and information databases" parallel the cars which make travel possible, and the "people who ... operate these systems" are us, the drivers of the cars, the users of the interstate system.

While few would question that the highways themselves and their endpoints (cities) constitute the infrastructure of the interstate highway system, fewer still would agree that cars and their drivers are an equal component of that system. By including people in the definition of "Information

CRAUFURD D. GOODWIN AND ALEX ROGERS

Infrastructure," however, the Administration is trying to ensure that as we progress toward an information future, people do not become superfluous bits within the system but rather remain an integral part without which the whole system loses its meaning.

The Administration has chosen to focus so much of its energy on the information superhighway because it does not want the grim, impersonal cyberpunk future to come to pass. A wide spectrum of officials within the Administration are known either to have read about or to have dealt with similar themes.[9] Moreover, many of the themes expressed in Administration rhetoric give strong circumstantial evidence that they are derived from the "information" problems of which cyberpunk authors write. Michele Farquhar (1993, 1) notes in her capacity as Chief of Staff and Director in the Office of Policy Coordination and Management for the National Telecommunications and Information Administration (NTIA) that

> [t]here is no more compelling reason for this administration to take the development and enhancement of a National Information Infra- structure so seriously – [than] the concern that full and productive participation in the society of the future will depend not just on monetary wealth, but just as much on access to information.

The Clinton Administration believes that information technology will deter- mine the way commerce takes place and how society evolves. The proposed universal service and universal access programs are designed to forestall the impersonal, technocratic evils of the cyberpunk world. Rather than let Gibson and others play Cassandra to America's unwary Troy, the Administra- tion hopes to make cyberpunk predictions as valid as the medieval millennialists who proclaimed that the year 1000 would hear the sounding of the final trumpet. As Orwell galvanized a generation against Big Brother, so too has cyberpunk seemed to energize the Clinton Administration to promote universal service and universal access programs as necessary features of America's information future.

NOTES

1 We are grateful to colleagues for comments on an earlier draft of this paper, espe- cially Jeff Biddle, James Wible, and Sam Bostaph.
2 A number of recent appraisals by literary critics accept Gibson's central role. Istvan Csicsery-Ronay argues that Gibson is "original and gifted enough to make the whole movement seem original and gifted." Nicola Nixon (1992, 221–2) calls Gibson the "king of cyberpunk."
3 The alt.cyberpunk FAQ (Frequently Asked Questions), available at http:// tamsum.tamu.edu/~ers0925/alt.cp.faq.html, notes that Gardner Dozois, an editor of *Isaac Asimov's Science Fiction Magazine* during the early 1980s, first used the phrase "cyberpunk" to denote a body of literature. He, in turn, is thought to have taken the word from Bruce Bethke's short story, "Cyberpunk."
4 Compiled by Erich Schneider. Available by anonymous ftp from bush.cs.tamu.edu:/

54

pub/misc/erich/alt.cp.faq. A FAQ is generally taken to be the consensus opinion of all regular participants in any newsgroup. This FAQ comes from the alt.cyberpunk newsgroup. Thus, this description reflects the opinions of those on the Internet who most actively discuss issues of interest surrounding cyberpunk themes.

5 Gibson (1989b, 107) writes in the short story "New Rose Hotel": "Imagine an alien ... who's come ... to identify the planet's dominant form of intelligence ... What do you think he picks? ... The zaibatsus, Fox said, the multinationals ... The structure is independent of the individual lives that comprise it."

6 The arcologies are one aspect of the "system" described above.

7 Admittedly, even without the outsiders the *zaibatsus* would fight against one another. The difference created by the rebels is that without their presence the violence and aggression would take more predictable and less devastating paths, for in the long run, the interfirm battles depress profits. Only the presence of the unpredictable prevents *zaibatsus* from lowering their defenses and colluding to increase stability.

8 The National Information Infrastructure Frequently Asked Questions List from the IITF gopher, question 1.

9 This conclusion is strengthened by an informal survey we conducted on the Americans Communicating Electronically listserv, whose membership includes high Administration officials ranging from an Assistant Secretary of Commerce to deputy directors of the National Economic Council to officials from a wide variety of other agencies.

REFERENCES

Cowen, Tyler and Kroszner, R. (1987) "The development of the new monetary economics," *Journal of Political Economy* 97: 567–90.

Farquhar, Michele (1993) "The Administration's vision for developing a National Information Infrastructure," Conference on Electronic Superhighways sponsored by Telecommunications Reports, Washington, DC, December.

Fischlin, Daniel, Hollinger, Veronica and Taylor, Andrew (1992) " 'The charisma leak': a conversation with William Gibson and Bruce Sterling," *Science Fiction Studies* 19(1): 1–16.

Friedman, Milton (1980) *Free to Choose: A Personal Statement*, New York: Harcourt Brace.

Galbraith, John Kenneth (1967) *The New Industrial State*, Boston, MA: Houghton Mifflin.

Gibson, William (1984) *Neuromancer*, New York: Ace Science Fiction.

Gibson, William (1986a) *Count Zero*, New York: Arbor House.

Gibson, William (1986b) *Burning Chrome*, New York: Ace Science Fiction.

Gibson, William (1988) *Mona Lisa Overdrive*, New York: Bantam Spectra.

Gibson, William (1993) *Virtual Light*, New York: Bantam Spectra.

Grampp, William (1973) "Classical economics and its moral critics," *HOPE* 5 (Fall): 359–74.

Nixon, Nicola (1992) "Cyberpunk: preparing the ground for revolution or keeping the boys satisfied?" *Science Fiction Studies* 19(2): 219–35.

Norris, Frank (1901) *Octopus*, New York: Grosset & Dunlap.

Rosenthal, Pam (1991) "Jacked in: Fordism, cyberpunk, Marxism," *Socialist Review* 21(1): 79–104.

Sterling, Bruce (1986) Introduction to *Mirrorshades: The Cyberpunk Anthology*, ed. Bruce Sterling, New York: Ace.

Taylor, Walter Fuller (1942) *The Economic Novel in America*, Chapel Hill, NC: University of North Carolina Press.

Veblen, Thorstein (1904) *Theory of the Leisure Class*, New York: Scribners.

4

HETEROGENEOUS LABOR IN A SIMPLE RICARDIAN MODEL

John B. Davis and Amitava Krishna Dutt[1]

INTRODUCTION

The simple model that derives from Ricardo's *Principles of Political Economy and Taxation* assumes a three-class economy with landlords who own land, workers who provide labor, and capitalists who accumulate capital (as a wages fund or in the form of fixed capital). In the simple model, diminishing returns to labor arise due to the heterogeneity of land: as the margin of cultivation is extended, labor is used on progressively less-fertile land, which makes labor less productive. The rent, which is determined so that the marginal land earns no rent, goes to landlords by virtue of their monopoly over land ownership. This model, used extensively in the literature (see, for instance, Kaldor 1956; Pasinetti 1960; Samuelson 1959, 1988; Casarosa 1978; Hicks and Hollander 1977) has increased our understanding of the dynamics of growth and distribution first developed informally by Ricardo.

Davis (1993), in examining the implications of Ricardo's addition of a chapter on machinery introduction to the third edition of the *Principles*, has suggested a modification of Ricardo's original framework in which the role of land and labor as causes of differential productivity and rent are reversed. According to Ricardo's machinery analysis, in the extreme case when machinery is perfectly substitutable for labor, wages cannot rise, and land thus ceases to play an important role in the economy. Suppose, then, that just as there are different soil fertilities, there are also different qualities of workers, which may also be ranked from most to least productive. Then, on Ricardo's reasoning, inframarginal, higher-quality workers would receive rents by virtue of their monopoly ownership of their skills, while the lowest-quality workers would find themselves at the margin in the labor force earning no rents. This modified model is still Ricardian, because it relies on an inverse relation between rents and profits, but it departs from Ricardo's original class setting by translating the contest between landlords and capitalists into a more modern one between workers and capitalists.

We think this analysis is very much in the spirit of Ricardo's original view, and thus is an opportunity to, as it were, let Ricardo speak about those

56

features of modern economies that closely resemble features of the economy that he himself examined. In this way we of course hope to show the continuing relevance of Ricardo's thinking to modern concerns. But a further goal of the paper is to apply a form of counterfactual analysis to the history of economic thought to elicit bedrock themes in an historical figure's thought. That is, by applying Ricardo's rent theory to different qualities of workers rather than different qualities of land, we show what features of Ricardo's thinking are essential to his reasoning about growth and distribution in contests between capitalists and resource owners, whatever the nature of the resources under the latter's control. This form of counterfactual reasoning contrasts with traditional comparative static analysis, in that rather than vary a system parameter, we vary the context in which the system operates. We believe this method of investigation valuable for history of economic thought analysis, and one which acts to remove dividing lines between the history of economic thought and economic analysis *per se*.

The paper, then, develops a simple Ricardian model in which the differential productivity of labor arises due to differences in the quality of workers, and in which inframarginal workers appropriate the Ricardian extensive rent. It is our belief that this model is relevant for advanced capitalist economies in which the agricultural sector plays a relatively small role in economic activity, in which land rent is a small fraction of total income, and in which there are significant differences between workers of different types. We also depart from another major assumption of the original Ricardian model which does not appear appropriate to modern conditions; that is, the Malthusian relation between population (and labor supply) growth and the wage rate, in an effort to further adapt Ricardo's thinking to the contemporary world. In our analysis, inframarginal workers earn rents in addition to wages, but this makes them no more likely to reproduce their ranks than marginal, no-rent workers.

One way of understanding our analysis is in terms of the difference between formal and informal sectors in developed market economies. In the formal sector workers are supported by a wage fund determined by the past accumulation of capitalists. Workers in the informal sector, on the other hand, depend upon a variety of subsistence activities that in many instances make use of markets, though no accumulated wage fund is involved. We think this way of approaching Ricardo does more justice to his thinking than crude Malthusian interpretations of worker subsistence that seem to suggest that workers are always on the edge of survival. On our understanding, workers may be drawn from the informal sector into the formal sector when capital accumulates faster than population growth. In addition, this approach suggests that workers in the informal sector have only fewer skills than do workers in the formal sector, so that the dividing line between the formal and informal sectors only picks out one point on a skill–productivity continuum.

Heterogeneous labor models already exist in both the neoclassical and neo-Marxist literatures. Neoclassical theorists have developed adverse selection models in connection with efficiency wage and dual labor market theories to show how some workers are paid above competitive wages because of qualities as workers that make them more valuable to firms (Bulow and Summers 1986; Weiss 1991). Neo-Marxist models date back to debates in the 1970s over the labor theory of value, and whether Marx's theory of exploitation can be developed to explain unequal rates of exploitation across different class fractions (Morishima 1978; Bowles and Gintis 1978). The Ricardian model developed here, however, makes a contribution distinct from both of these approaches in its focus on growth and distribution. We think that the importance of these issues justifies both the re-examination of Ricardo's original argument along the lines suggested by the added machinery chapter, and the application of the model to contemporary policy concerns.

The model is presented in the next section, and then elaborated in two versions: first, for a world with unemployment, and second, for a world with full employment. In the subsequent section we consider important policy implications for both versions of the model by looking at the effects of two possible developments that might be the outcome of social policy: first, changes in the inequality amongst workers that may arise from policies that influence worker endowments in human capital, our proxy for quality; second, changes in the rate of population growth that may arise from policies that influence migration or natural population growth. The paper is thus Ricardian in not only using Ricardian assumptions to model the economy, but also in succumbing to the Ricardian vice of drawing policy conclusions from simple analytical constructions. The concluding section comments on the extension of Ricardo's growth and distribution thinking to the modern world.

A SIMPLE MODEL

Consider a closed economy which produces one good with only one factor of production, labor. Labor is heterogeneous in the sense that different types or qualities of labor have different levels of productivity. This heterogeneity may be thought to arise because of differences in the endowments of something we call, for lack of a better expression, human capital. We suppose that, upon entering the labor force, workers' endowments are essentially fixed. Differences in worker endowments we attribute to differences in families' abilities to support education and training. Such differences may range from differences in acquired skill and ability to differences in such things as tendencies toward absenteeism and job commitment. Whatever these qualities may be, moreover, the distribution of qualities of labor is taken to proxy the distribution of wealth across families.

For simplicity, we assume that $y(n)$, the productivity of the nth worker, is given by the simple linear function

$$y(n) = \alpha_0 + \alpha_1 v(n) \tag{4.1}$$

where α_i are positive constants. We assume that workers can be ranked from most productive to least productive according to their respective endowments of human capital in descending order, as follows:

$$v(n) = \beta_0 - \beta_1 n \tag{4.2}$$

where the β_i are positive constants and n is the worker index. Linearity in the ranking of skill levels is a simplification which can be eased without significant changes in the analysis. Using equations (4.1) and (4.2), the marginal product function for this economy is thus seen to be given by

$$y(n) = (\alpha_0 + \alpha_1 \beta_0) - \alpha_1 \beta_1 n \tag{4.3}$$

This is shown as the downward-sloping line in Figure 4.1.

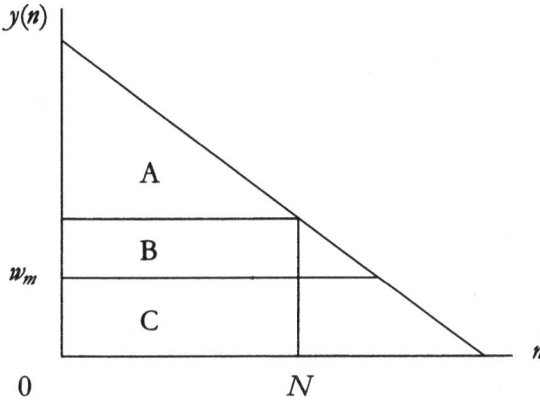

Figure 4.1

For any given level of employment, N, the Ricardian (extensive) rent accruing to worker n is given by

$$r(n) = y(n) - y(N) \tag{4.4}$$

The wage received by worker n is given by

$$w(n) = r(n) + w_m \tag{4.5}$$

where w_m is the wage received by the marginal worker, N. The total wage received by all workers is given by

$$W(N) = \int_0^N w(n) \, dn \tag{4.6}$$

which, using equations (4.3) through (4.5) is given by

$$W(N) = \frac{1}{2} \alpha_1 \beta_1 N^2 + w_m N \tag{4.7}$$

Total profit when N workers are employed is given by

$$P(N) = \int_0^N y(n)\, dn - W(N) = [\alpha_0 + \alpha_1\beta_0 - \alpha_1\beta_1 N - w_m]N \qquad (4.8)$$

In Figure 4.1, the total wage bill is given by the sum of areas A and C, and total profit is given by area B.

Workers consume all of their income, while capitalists who receive profits save a fraction, s, of their profits. All saving is automatically invested in this Ricardian Say's Law world.

At a point in time – which we call the short period – we take the wages fund, W, to be given as a result of past accumulation. The wages fund approach can be interpreted to be a simple characterization of credit constraints in modern economies. In the long period the change in the wages fund is determined by the level of investment in the economy, so that

$$\frac{dW}{dt} = sP(N) \qquad (4.9)$$

We now consider two versions of the model. In one, we assume that the wage of the marginal worker, w_m, is given,[2] and the level of employment, N, is determined to use up the entire wages fund. We assume that the supply of labor is always greater than N, and call this the model with unemployment. In the other version, the level of employment, N, is given at a point in time, and the wage schedule varies to clear the market for labor, given the wages fund. We call this the full-employment model.

In the unemployment model we use equation (4.7), with fixed values of W and w_m, to determine the short-period equilibrium value of N, given by

$$N = \frac{\sqrt{(w_m^2 + \alpha_1\beta_1 W)} - w_m}{\alpha_1\beta_1} \qquad (4.10)$$

If we substitute this value of N into equations (4.8) and (4.9) we obtain an equation of motion for W which states that dW/dt depends only on W and the parameters of the model. This equation traces the evolution of W over time and shows that the economy attains a stationary state (or long-period equilibrium) at which $dW/dt = 0$, which implies, from equations (4.8) and (4.9) that the stationary-state value of N is given by

$$N = \frac{\alpha_0 + \alpha_1\beta_0 - w_m}{\alpha_1\beta_1} \qquad (4.11)$$

This value is shown in Figure 4.2 by the level of n at which the w_m line intersects the marginal product schedule, denoted by N_s.[3]

The stability of this stationary-state equilibrium is ensured by the fact that at equilibrium, $d(dW/dt)/dW = s(dP/dN)(dN/dW) < 0$, $dN/dW > 0$ from equation (4.10), and $dP/dN < 0$ at equilibrium. At long-run equilibrium profits are squeezed to zero, and accumulation comes to a halt.

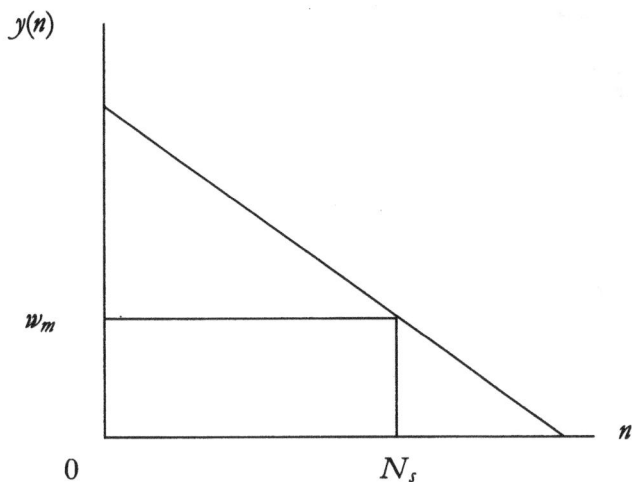

Figure 4.2

In the full-employment model, in the short period w_m is determined from equation (4.7), given values of W and N. The equilibrium value of w_m is given by

$$w_m = \frac{W}{N} - \frac{1}{2}\alpha_1\beta_2 N \tag{4.12}$$

Substituting this into the expression for profits, given by equation (4.8), we obtain

$$P(N) = \alpha_0 + \alpha_1\beta_0 - \frac{1}{2}\alpha_1\beta_1 N^2 - W \tag{4.13}$$

which we assume to be positive for the initial level of W. We assume that the supply of labor, given by N, does not change over time. The wages fund changes over time in the manner shown by the equation of motion for W given by substituting equation (4.13) into equation (4.9). Since N is constant, W rises over time till $P(N)$ becomes zero, which occurs when

$$w_m = \alpha_0 + \alpha_1\beta_0 - \alpha_1\beta_1 N \tag{4.14}$$

which is the stationary-state wage of the marginal worker.

SOME IMPLICATIONS OF THE MODEL

This section examines important policy implications for both versions of the model advanced in the previous section in regard to developments that might be the outcome of social decisions that affect worker inequality and levels of migration.

Effects of a change in inequality amongst workers

Inequality amongst workers is due to differences in their endowments of human capital, which in turn we have taken to be due to differences in family wealth and ability to support education and training. We can accordingly examine changes in worker inequality by allowing for changes in the distribution of endowments among workers that are the product of policies that differentially affect families' wealth levels and ability to educate and train children. For example, changes in tax laws and government-supported college loan programs may directly affect the distribution of endowments among workers. But more generally, policies that affect incomes may also affect the resources that families are able to commit to training and education.

We model changes in inequality amongst workers by changing the slope and intercept of the $v(n)$ curve. To keep total endowments constant when we change only the degree of inequality we must rotate the curve in a manner which satisfies some conservation principle. A natural way to parameterize the degree of equality with N_1 workers is with the parameter θ in the equation

$$v(n) = (\beta_0 - \theta) - \left(\beta_1 - 2\frac{\theta}{N_1}\right) n \qquad (4.15)$$

where increases in θ denote increases in equality. This keeps constant the total endowment of human capital for the N_1 workers.

The effect of such a change in the $v(n)$ function is to change the marginal product curve given by $y(n)$. For the full-employment model the effect is straightforward. As shown in Figure 4.3, the marginal product curve rotates

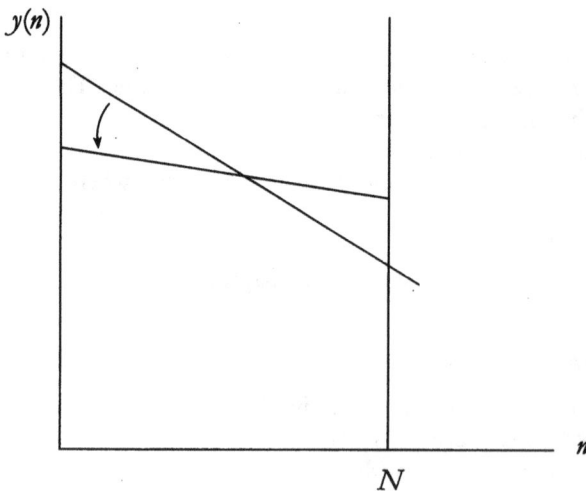

Figure 4.3

downward, keeping the area under it constant for N workers. Total product remains unchanged while the distribution of wages adjusts towards greater equality, mirroring the change in the distribution of endowments.

The effect in the model with unemployment is more interesting. Here, since the level of employment can and does change, it is necessary to decide on the appropriate number of workers for which the total endowment is to be held constant. In this case it is appropriate to hold total endowments constant for the total number of workers who will be employed in at least one of the two periods, before and after the change in distribution (in long-period equilibrium).

The first point to note here is that any change in the $v(n)$ curve which increases the endowment of human capital of the marginal worker will change the $y(n)$ curve in such a way that it will intersect the w_m line at a higher N. This implies that the level of employment with a greater degree of equality will be higher, at N_2 in Figure 4.4, than at N_1, the initial equilibrium.

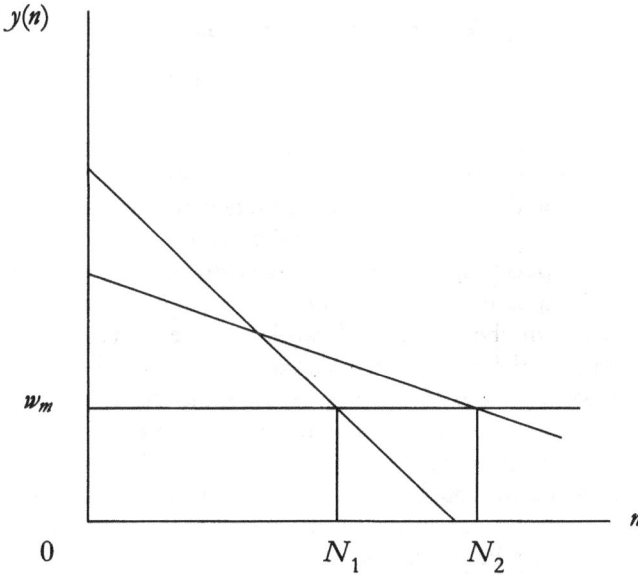

Figure 4.4

This also implies that the $y(n)$ curve should be rotated so that the area under the two marginal curves between 0 and N_2 must be the same, to keep the total endowments of N_2 workers constant.

The short-period impact of a rise in equality measured by a rise in θ will be a rise in the level of employment. This occurs because the wages fund required to hire N_1 workers with the new $y(n)$ line is less than with the old, since the area under the new curve up to N_1 is smaller than under the original curve (this is because the areas under the curves are the same if one goes to the level N_2, as pointed out in the previous paragraph), and also since there will be a profit component under the new curve, which was not the case with the old curve (because we were initially at a stationary state with zero profits). Since profits emerge, capitalists will accumulate and employment will increase over time till the new stationary state is attained at N_2.

Compared to the initial stationary state there will not only be a rise in employment and thus a fall in unemployment, but also a rise in total output. This can be seen from the fact that the area under the original curve between 0 and N_1 is less than the area under the original curve between 0 and N_2 which is equal to the area under the new curve between 0 and N_2. The reason for the increase in output is that workers who were previously unemployable because of their low endowments of human capital, given the institutionally given minimum wage w_m, are now employable because of their higher productivity and contribution to the increase in total output. Distribution and the total level of activity are thus positively related.

Effects of population growth

The effects of population growth can also be examined in the model. We think of population growth as being due to either migration policy or policies aimed at altering natural population growth. The former case can have both short-run and long-run impacts; in the latter case we consider long-run impacts, and assume that new people become new workers. The analysis of population growth in our framework requires us to consider not only the growth of total population, but also possible changes in the structure of the population in terms of endowments. A neutral assumption would be a proportional increase in the number of workers of each type. Thus if we imagine that initially there were k workers of each type, and allow the number of each type of worker to increase by the same amount, the $v(n)$ curve would become flatter, rotated around the vertical intercept. This can be formalized in terms of a fall in the coefficient β_1; the total number of workers in the economy would rise by the same rate at which β_1 falls.

In the case with full employment, total employment and total output increases with the rise in population at the stationary state. Since output is constrained by the labor supply, it should not be surprising that an increase in labor supply also increases output.

In the case with unemployment, a rise in population increases output and employment in the short period as well as in the long period, as shown in Figure 4.5. Because of the shift in the $v(n)$ curve, the $y(n)$ curve shifts in a similar manner. The initial wage fund, ABN_1O, is bigger than the wage fund required to hire N_1 workers after the shift, given by $ADE + w_m BN_1O$ (since $ADE < ABw_m$). Thus in the short period more workers than N_1 can be hired with the initial wage fund (although this must be less than N_2 since $ABN_1O < AFN_2O$). Since positive profits emerge in the short period, capital

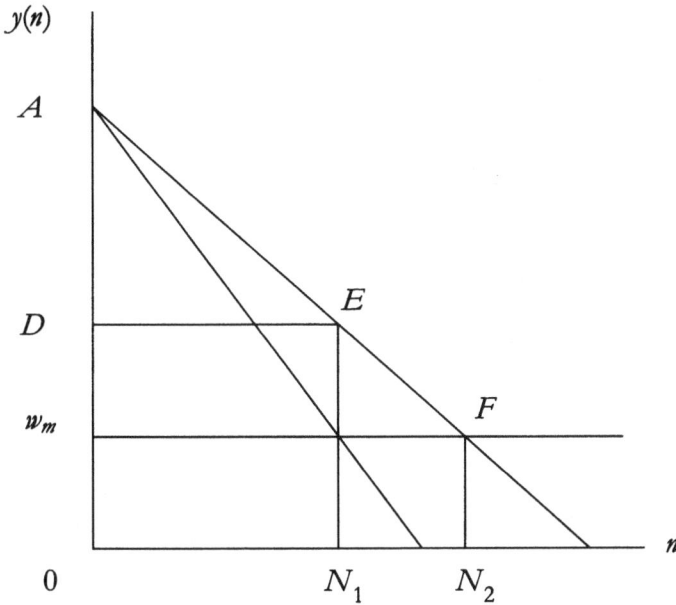

Figure 4.5

in the form of the wages fund will be accumulated in the long period, so that employment will increase to N_2 in the new stationary state. The original workers, who experience a decline in their wage in the transition phase (and in some cases a loss of jobs), receive the same wages as they did earlier at the new stationary state. Thus even in a model in which labor is not constrained by labor supply (since there is unemployed labor), an increase in population will increase total output. This result does not depend on our assumption that the supply of each kind of labor increases equiproportionately; all we require is that the supply of labor of the types which were previously employed increase.

CONCLUSION

Our simple Ricardian model which interchanges the roles of land and labor in the original Ricardian model provides a potentially useful way of modeling an economy with labor heterogeneity. Although we have considered a very simple version of the model with only one factor of production, and examined only a few of its implications, we find that the model does produce some interesting results regarding the relationship between output and distribution and regarding the effects of changes in inequality and population growth in economies with unemployment and institutionally determined minimum wages. Specifically, policies that reduce the inequality amongst workers, such as might come about from tax law changes or increased support for college loan programs, and policies that affect labor supply, either naturally or through migration, both increase employment and output. In the case of policies affecting labor supply, this is true in both the short run and the long run, though wages and perhaps employment for already-employed workers may fall in the transition period before returning to their original level in the new stationary state.

Of course, in the first two editions of his *Principles* Ricardo was not directly concerned with employment and unemployment, and his attention to the subject in the chapter on machinery introduction in his third and last edition was limited. Yet in addition to his well-known advocacy of corn law repeal, he was also an active defender of parliamentary reform and the secret ballot, and, according to recent commentators, made a "quite sophisticated argument for democratic citizenship as a prerequisite for economic progress" (Milgate and Stimson 1991, 18). This suggests that he took seriously policies that might enhance employment and the conditions of workers, and lends support for the heterogeneous labor modification and extension of his model of growth and distribution developed here. We believe that this development of the model helps to open contemporary Ricardian approaches to important social policy issues, and demonstrates how Ricardo's ideas continue to be relevant when introduced into new contexts.

NOTES

1 The authors are grateful to Allin Cottrell and Spencer Pack for comments on an earlier version of this paper.
2 This model is more Ricardian (see Pasinetti 1960) in nature than the subsequent one. Some Ricardian models, however, take the level of employment to be given at a point in time, and allow the short-period wage to be determined (at a level different from the subsistence one) by supply and demand (see Casarosa 1978, and Hicks and Hollander 1977). Malthusian population dynamics then take over in the long run, ensuring that the wage rate is at the subsistence level in the long run. Since in our framework we are assuming away Malthusian dynamics, we follow the fixed-wage approach. The alternative model allows the wage to be determined by supply and demand.
3 We assume that the supply of labor is large enough so that full employment is not reached at a level below this amount; alternatively, we assume that labor supply rises endogenously through some unspecified mechanism.

REFERENCES

Bowles, S. and Gintis, H. (1978) "Professor Morishima on heterogeneous labour and Marxian value theory," *Cambridge Journal of Economics* 2 (September): 311–14.
Bulow, J. and Summers, L. (1986) "A theory of dual labor markets with application to industrial policy, discrimination and Keynesian unemployment," *Journal of Labor Economics* 4: 376–415.

Casarosa, C. (1978) "A new formulation of the Ricardian system," *Oxford Economic Papers*, March.

Davis, J. B. (1993) "Ricardo's theory of profit and the third edition of the *Principles*," *Journal of the History of Economic Thought* 15 (Spring): 90–106.

Hicks, J. R. and Hollander, S. (1977) "Ricardo and the Moderns," reprinted in J. Hicks, *Classics and Moderns: Collected Essays on Economic Theory*, vol. III, Cambridge, MA: Harvard University Press, 1983.

Kaldor, N. (1956) "Alternative theories of distribution," *Review of Economic Studies*, 23(2): 83–100, reprinted in N. Kaldor, *Essays on Value and Distribution*, London: Duckworth, 1960.

Milgate, M. and Stimson, S. (1991) *Ricardian Politics*, Princeton, NJ: Princeton University Press.

Morishima, M. (1978) "S. Bowles and H. Gintis on the Marxian theory of value and heterogeneous labour," *Cambridge Journal of Economics* 2 (September): 305–9.

Ricardo, D. (1821) *On the Principles of Political Economy and Taxation*, ed. P. Sraffa, Cambridge: Cambridge University Press, 1951.

Pasinetti, L. L. (1960) "A mathematical reformulation of the Ricardian system," *Review of Economic Studies* 27 (February): 78–98, reprinted in L. Pasinetti, *Growth and Income Distribution: Essays in Economic Theory*, Cambridge: Cambridge University Press, 1974.

Samuelson, P. A. (1959) "A modern treatment of the Ricardian economy: I. The pricing of goods and of labor and land services," *Quarterly Journal of Economics* 73 (February): 1–35, reprinted in J. Stiglitz (ed.), *Collected Scientific Papers of Paul A. Samuelson*, vol. 1, Cambridge, MA: MIT Press.

Samuelson, P. A. (1988) "Mathematical vindication of Ricardo on machinery," *Journal of Political Economy* 96(2): 274–82.

Weiss, A. (1991) *Efficiency Wages, Models of Unemployment, Layoffs, and Wage Dispersion*, Oxford: Clarendon Press.

5

INTERNATIONAL TRADE, MACHINERY, AND THE REMUNERATION OF LABOR

A reexamination of the argument in the third edition of Ricardo's *Principles of Political Economy and Taxation*

Robert E. Prasch[1]

INTRODUCTION

It is widely understood in the literature that David Ricardo was among the first economists to identify and employ the economic principles which lay behind the theory of comparative advantage (Gomes 1987, 141–4; Schumpeter 1954, 607–8). The bulk of this work appears in Chapter 7 of his justly famous treatise, *The Principles of Political Economy and Taxation*, which first appeared in 1817. Ricardo lightly revised his successful treatise for the second edition in 1819. However, it was his revisions to the third, 1821 edition, that caused the most controversy. This third edition of the *Principles* became renowned, perhaps even notorious, for the fact that its author added a chapter, entitled "On Machinery," as the new thirty-first chapter of the book. This chapter would be recognized for Ricardo's unanticipated modification of his views on the "question of machinery." One hundred and thirty years later, in his introduction to *The Works and Correspondence of David Ricardo*, Piero Sraffa described this new chapter as "The most revolutionary change in edition 3" (Sraffa 1951, lvii).[2] Needless to say, Ricardo's revised view dismayed some of his most ardent supporters such as John Ramsey McCulloch.[3]

That this new chapter was a distinct change of opinion is clear from Ricardo's explicit announcement of his new position:

> It is more incumbent on me to declare my opinions on this question, because they have, on further reflection, undergone a considerable change; and although I am not aware that I have ever published anything respecting machinery which it is necessary for me retract, yet I

have in other ways given my support to doctrines which I now think erroneous; it therefore becomes a duty in me to submit my present views to examination, with my reasons for entertaining them.

(Ricardo 1951 [1821], 386)

Ricardo then presents his new, remarkable findings: "These were my opinions, and they continue unaltered, as far as regards the landlord and the capitalist; but I am convinced that the substitution of machinery for human labour is often very injurious to the interests of the class of labourers" (ibid., 388). Thus far these details concerning Ricardo's change of heart on the machinery question are well known, and recounting them will not pose a serious conundrum to the established literature on Ricardo (St Clair 1957, ch. 12; Hollander 1971; Eltis 1985; Meacci 1985; Davis 1989).

However, upon reflection, the following problem arises: can we reconcile Ricardo's new-found ambivalence towards the substitution of machinery for labor with his apparently undiminished enthusiasm for free trade? Prior to the third edition, Ricardo opined that the introduction of machinery would have the same positive effect on labor as a turn to free trade. As the following quotation demonstrates, the arguments were virtually identical: "The effects [of free trade] on the interests of this class, would be nearly the same as the effects of improved machinery, which it is now no longer questioned, has a decided tendency to raise the real wages of labour" (Ricardo 1951 [1815], 35).

In reflecting on the machinery chapter, a number of scholars have concluded that Ricardo's revised position is not fully integrated with some of the preconceptions and arguments that typify the rest of his *Principles* (Blaug 1958, 70–1; Davis 1989, 472–80). However, if Ricardo came to be convinced that machinery potentially causes unemployment, could he have considered the possibility that he had stumbled upon a more general problem – one that applies equally to international trade? The record indicates that if Ricardo felt that this was the case, he did not put his doubts into print or in his letters. Nevertheless, this paper will argue that, in light of the revisions that Ricardo made to the third edition of his *Principles*, it is *possible* to read a good deal of ambiguity into Ricardo's chapter, "On Foreign Trade."

Regardless of the ambiguity, it should be remembered that Ricardo remained a supporter of free trade and the unregulated adoption of machinery (Ricardo 1951 [1821], 396–7). From the written record it is clear that Ricardo did not think that international trade threatened labor in the same way that machinery did. What may be more controversial is the possibility that the reason behind Ricardo's seemingly complacent position was a theoretical construction, the wage-fund doctrine, that modern economists would be unlikely to identify as a convincing basis for a coherent economic argument.[4]

ROBERT E. PRASCH

THE ROLE OF INTERNATIONAL TRADE IN THE ACCUMULATION OF CAPITAL

While a number of chapters within the *Principles* explored the problem of foreign trade, the most significant and complete analysis appears in Chapter 7, "Of Foreign Trade." In this chapter Ricardo argues that goods are exchanged on the basis of relative, or comparative, cost as opposed to absolute cost. Consistent with some earlier arguments in the *Essay on Profits* (1815), international trade is thought to provide the trading country with a number of advantages: (a) an increased variety and quantity of goods (Ricardo 1951 [1815], 25–6; 1951 [1821], 133); (b) a lower cost of "provisions." This, in turn, lowers the cost of labor, thereby increasing the rate of profits (Ricardo 1951 [1815], 16n, 22, 25, 26n; 1951 [1821], 132; 1951 [1822], 237).

Now it is clear that our contemporary theory of comparative advantage, which is based on an underlying model of welfare economics, is parallel to the first part of Ricardo's defense of free trade (Schumpeter 1954, 610). However, this "welfare-enhancing" attribute of trade was not of primary theoretical or policy interest to Ricardo. His attention was directed toward distribution, and its effect on accumulation. This concern is reflected in Ricardo's theory of profits, and in his doctrine that the level of wages and the level of profits are inversely related to each other (Ricardo 1951 [1821], 115, 132; 1951 [1822], 215, 237; St Clair 1957, ch. 10).

As noted, these propositions were developed in the course of Ricardo's *Essay on Profits* (1815). The theoretical framework of the *Essay*, with its characteristic link between trade policy and the profits–wages trade-off, was inspired by heated parliamentary debates over what were known as the Corn Laws (Dobb 1973, 65–73; O'Brien 1981, 359–61). According to Mark Blaug, "Ricardo's theoretical system emerged directly and spontaneously out of the great corn laws debate of 1814–16" (Blaug 1958, 6).[5]

Ricardo was convinced that the rate of profit would be lowered by the increasing cost of labor. In turn, the wages of labor, while subject to supply and demand in the short term, were determined by the cost of provisions over the long term (Ricardo 1951 [1821], 97). This latter constraint is, of course, the classical notion of the "natural wage" (Peach 1993, 103–31; O'Brien 1981, 365–70). Now the value of this natural wage was, to Ricardo, in large part determined by the cost of agricultural produce (Ricardo 1951 [1822], 236). We should note that tying the wages of labor to the cost of "corn" was not a uniquely Ricardian position. According to Blaug (1958, 6–7):

> restrictions on the importation of grain cause the price of wheaten bread to rise and . . . the price of this food article regulates the money wages of labor and the general rate of profit. Whatever the doctrinal precedence for such a view, this was nothing more than the common belief of the commercial classes of the day.

Ricardo thought that over the long term the cost of provisions would rise due to the increased scarcity of quality farmland that accompanied prosperity and increased population: "[I]n the progress of society and wealth, the additional quantity of food required is obtained by the sacrifice of more and more labour" (Ricardo 1951 [1821], 120). The landlord enjoyed an enhanced rent from his land if, with the "progress of society," agricultural goods were in high demand and quality farmland was thereby rendered scarce: "The rise of rent is always the effect of the increasing wealth of the country and of the difficulty of providing food for its augmented population" (ibid., 77).

However, the landlords, as a class, did not have to await the relatively slow progress of accumulation, and the consequent pressures of population, to acquire higher rents. They could induce a higher rent on land through the "artificial" policy of agricultural protection (Ricardo 1951 [1822], 237–8). This was the economic basis for the landlord's class interest in a tariff levied upon agricultural imports – a policy that Ricardo thought to be an unnecessary transference of purchasing power from the capitalists to the landlords. To Ricardo, a freer importation of agricultural goods would be sufficient to lower labor costs and thereby allow a rise in the rate of profit. Increased profits would induce an enhanced rate of capital accumulation (Ricardo 1951 [1815], 35–7).[6]

The point is that international trade, if it takes place in the form of an importation of consumption or subsistence goods for the lower classes, will lower the cost of providing for the wages of labor. Ricardo thought that such a policy would allow England to continue to accumulate capital despite the potential difficulties suggested by the tendency towards rising wages and falling rates of profit, which were the direct consequence of economic growth.[7] Given this conclusion, the question that confronts us is as follows. If the primary goal of a free trade policy is to raise the profit rate – and if it is the case that the only way to accomplish this is to lower the wage rate – is it the case that, within the Ricardian system, free trade is potentially detrimental to the interests of labor?[8] The Ricardo of the *Essay on Profits* (1815) and the first two editions of the *Principles* clearly did not think so. What about the Ricardo of the controversial third edition?

We do know that the preponderance of evidence demonstrates that Ricardo was not one to represent himself dishonestly or hold dogmatically to a theory (Mongiovi 1994, 262).[9] I would suggest that this attitude is also true with regard to his positions on policy. The chapter "On Machinery" is clear evidence of Ricardo's honesty. Indeed, his friend and correspondent McCulloch felt it was overly straightforward (McCulloch to Ricardo, June 5, 1821, in Ricardo 1952, 382). Ricardo's lack of dogmatism can be discerned from his observation that under a number of conditions free trade could make a country worse off. Such a misfortune might occur in one of two ways. The first, and simplest, example is in the event that a country is subjected to colonization. In Ricardo's words: "It is evident, then, that the trade with a colony may be so regulated that it shall at the same time be less beneficial to the colony, and more beneficial to the mother country, than a perfectly free trade" (Ricardo 1951 [1821], 343). The second trade mishap that concerns Ricardo is more interesting, given the structure of modern markets. He is convinced that capital exports would be economically disastrous for a country, and makes his concern explicit on several different occasions (Ricardo 1951 [1815], 16n; 1951 [1821], 83, 271; 1951 [1822], 237).[10]

INTERNATIONAL TRADE AND ITS THEORETICAL RELATION TO THE MACHINERY QUESTION

There is another aspect of Ricardian trade theory which has not received an adequate examination in the literature. This is Ricardo's frequent insinuation, even statement, that trade has the capacity to act "like machinery" in its impact on the profit rate, capital accumulation, and the economy. In his earlier essays, but also within the *Principles*, Ricardo frequently and explicitly makes this comparison. Of most relevance to this paper are the ten separate references to machinery which remain in the seventh chapter (entitled "On Foreign Trade") of the controversial third edition of the *Principles* (Ricardo 1951 [1821], 131, 132(3), 133, 141, 142(2), 145(2)).

I bring the reader's attention to these references since we know, from the editorial footnotes to Piero Sraffa's excellent edition of the *Principles*, that Ricardo made a number of minor changes in this crucial chapter as part of his overall revisions for the third edition. It follows that Ricardo *deliberately and consciously* decided to leave in all references to machinery in this new edition despite his radical reassessment of his views on the politically potent machinery question. I would argue, on the basis of this important set of editorial facts, that any parallels between the economics of international trade and the economics of machinery that were retained by Ricardo in the third edition of the *Principles* were intentional. Therefore, they merit careful scrutiny. I will accept as a premise that all such references, especially those in Chapter 7, are at some level consistent with Ricardo's revised position on machinery.

If Ricardo is convinced that the introduction of machinery could be detrimental to the working class, then we cannot rule out, *a priori*, the possibility that he had revised his position on the effect that free international trade could have on the economic condition of labor. Indeed, on a first reading, some of these references indicate that foreign trade, and the introduction of machinery, are to be seen as having an identical impact on the economy. Consider the following quotations:

If, therefore, by the extension of foreign trade, or by improvements in *machinery*, the food and necessaries of the labourer can be brought to market, at a reduced price, profits will rise.

(Ricardo 1951 [1821], 132, emphasis added)

If, by the introduction of cheap foreign goods, I can save 20 per cent. from my expenditure, the effect will be precisely the same as if *machinery* had lowered the expense of their production, but profits would not be raised.

(Ibid., 131–2, emphasis added)

If by foreign commerce, or the discovery of *machinery*, the commodities consumed by the labourer should become much cheaper, wages would fall; and this, as we have before observed, would raise the profits of the farmer, and therefore, all other profits.

(Ricardo 1951 [1815], 26n, emphasis added)

The effects [of free imports of corn] on the interests of this [working] class, would be nearly the same as the effects of improved *machinery* . . .

(Ibid., 35, emphasis added)

MACHINERY, FOREIGN TRADE, AND ACCUMULATION

Chapter 31 of the third edition of the *Principles* was an important event in the history of economic thought. McCulloch was correct to be concerned that it would provide the unorthodox views of Sismondi and Malthus with a new degree of credibility (McCulloch to Ricardo, June 5, 1821, in Ricardo 1952, 382). Indeed, we now know that it encouraged a number of important figures to develop radical interpretations of the economic system.[11] However, the machinery chapter also reveals the specific manner in which Ricardo was able to distinguish theoretically the effects of trade from the adjustment difficulties associated with innovation through machinery.

For Ricardo, the introduction of machinery leads to the following difficulty: it consumes part of the fund which is set aside for the hire of workmen, and simultaneously ties up those funds in the form of fixed capital (Blaug 1958, 67).[12] Ricardo does not perceive this to be a permanent situation. He believes that a capitalist who has the advantage of competing with machines will be able to save more out of his increased revenues. This leads to further accumulations of capital, and in this way the wage fund will eventually be expanded to hire some, or even all, of the labor which was left without employment (Ricardo 1951 [1821], 390). However, it follows from a decline in "gross produce," and from the logic of the wage fund, that in the short term the prognosis for labor is poor:

All I wish to prove, is, that the discovery and use of machinery may be attended with a diminution of gross produce; and whenever that is the case, it will be injurious to the labouring class, as some of their number will be thrown out of employment, and population will become redundant, compared with the funds which are to employ it.

(Ricardo 1951 [1821], 390)

We should be perfectly clear that when Ricardo discusses the problem of "machinery" he is concerned with the capitalist's direct expenditure on fixed capital. He carefully reiterates this point in a letter to McCulloch:

I have not said that if Almighty power would give us steam engines ready made, and capable of doing work for us without the assistance of human labour, that such a present would be injurious to any class – it would be far otherwise; but I have said that when a manufacturer is in possession of a circulating capital he can employ with it a greater number of men, and if it should suit his purposes to substitute a fixed capital of an equal value for this circulating capital, it will be inevitably followed by a necessity for dismissing a part of his workmen, for a fixed capital cannot employ all the labour which it is calculated to supersede. I confess that these truths appear to me to be as demonstrable as any of the truths of geometry, and I am only astonished that I should so long have failed to see them.

(Ricardo to McCulloch, June 18, 1821, in Ricardo 1952, 390)

Notice that in neither of these passages is Ricardo concerned with a change in technology *per se*. This can be seen through a close reading of the text; Ricardo generally reserves the words "art" and "skill" to discuss changes in technique. On other occasions he will use phrases such as "arts and machinery" (1951 [1821], 141) or "skill and machinery" (ibid., 142, 145) when he intends to convey an idea equivalent to our contemporary notion of "embodied technical change."

In Ricardo's system one type of change, machinery, was a replacement for labor in the sense that its purchase necessarily diminished the wage fund of the firm, and in consequence, the wage fund available to society as a whole. This interpretation is consistent with that offered by Joseph Schumpeter, who also argued that the key to understanding the machinery chapter was through a consideration of the effect of machinery on the size of the wage fund: "[Ricardo's machinery chapter] is an excellent illustration of the wage-fund doctrine, *considered as a method of analysis*. We shall ask: how does the introduction of a newly invented machine affect the size of the wage fund?" (Schumpeter 1954, 680).

The lengthy quotation above from the letter to McCulloch indicates that, by itself, an autonomous increase in "art or skill" does not have the effect of

74

lowering the wage fund. In a sense these are efficiency gains that emerge from better organization or an improved division of labor. It is the purchase of machinery or fixed capital, not technical improvement *per se*, that requires an actual decrease in the amount of "circulating capital" to be set aside for the hiring of labor. Only the purchase or construction of machinery requires that the firm congeal some of the fund set aside for the wages of labor into what Marx would later call "constant capital." The distinction between these two varieties of technical change is also the key to understanding the relation between Ricardo's respective positions on machinery and trade.

THE EFFECT OF TRADE ON THE REMUNERATION OF LABOR

Determining the effect of international trade on the employment of labor, wage levels, and the profit rate depends on two important factors. The first consideration is whether or not the goods traded are "wage-goods," in the sense of goods that would normally form the basket of goods that make up the "natural wage." The second consideration – this is crucial to the argument – is whether or not foreign trade actually diminishes, in any way, the wage fund out of which the remuneration of labor is derived.

If it is the case that foreign trade involves the import of nonwage consumption goods, goods that increase the variety of "luxury" goods available to a country, it follows that trade cheapens the price of such commodities in both countries without affecting either the wage or the profit rate:

> but if the commodities obtained at a cheaper rate, by the extension of foreign commerce, or by the improvement of machinery, be exclusively the commodities consumed by the rich, no alteration will take place in the rate of profits. The rate of wages would not be affected, although wine, velvets, silks, and other expensive commodities should fall 50 per cent., and consequently profits would continue unaltered . . . Foreign trade, then, though highly beneficial to a country, as it increases the amount and variety of the objects on which revenue may be expended, . . . has no tendency to raise the profits of stock unless the commodities imported be of that description on which the wages of labour are expended.
>
> (Ricardo 1951 [1821], 132–3)

In the above quotation, a change in the rate of profits requires that imports take the form of wage-goods. If there is a fall in the value of the basket of goods which make up the "natural wage" of the working class, it follows that the wage cost to the capitalist class will fall. This, in turn, will result in a rise in the profit rate. In this latter sense, international trade acts "like machinery" in its ability to increase the profit rate. However, in the scenario just described, the wage-fund remains intact; it follows that in such a case, profits rise without any negative repercussions for labor. For labor, this is the "best case" scenario. Trade, like machinery, increases the profit rate but, unlike machinery, it does not diminish the wage fund.

It follows that a correct understanding of Ricardo's *theoretical distinction* between trade and machinery can be grasped only by observing the effect of trade on the size of the "wage fund." Does it increase or diminish the quantity of the real purchasing power that is to be set aside in the form of a "circulating capital" for the purpose of hiring labor? If we keep in mind Ricardo's distinction between the purchase and/or construction of machinery and improvements in "art or skill," then a consistent answer emerges; trade in commodities is not detrimental to workers. When wage-goods are the object of international trade, the results are lower costs and increased profit rates through increased efficiency. Trade in commodities will have no effect on the size of the wage fund, which is the crucial variable from labor's point of view (Ricardo 1951 [1821], 130–1).[13] Likewise, should trade be exclusively in luxury goods, there is no effect on the size of the wage fund. As a result there is no change in either the wage or profit rate (Ricardo 1951 [1821], 132).

The rather complex points summarized in the previous paragraphs are captured in the following quotation from Ricardo:

> The remarks which have been made respecting foreign trade, apply equally to home trade. The rate of profits is never increased by a better distribution of labour, by the invention of machinery, by the establishment of roads and canals, or by any means of abridging labour either in the manufacture or in the conveyance of goods. These are causes which operate on price, and never fail to be highly beneficial to consumers; . . . On the other hand, every diminution in the wages of labour raises profits, but produces no effect on the price of commodities. One is advantageous to all classes, for all classes are consumers; the other is beneficial only to producers; they gain more, but everything remains at its former price.
>
> (Ricardo 1951 [1821], 133)

CONCLUSION

In light of the above analysis, it is tempting to believe that over the course of a transition period workers would be better off after the introduction of free trade since the purchasing power of the "natural wage" would go further than it otherwise would. Unfortunately, any such advantage would be of short duration. There is textual evidence – from one of the taxation chapters – which indicates that Ricardo thought that wages would adjust rapidly to changes in the price of "corn":

In regard then to a tax on raw produce, which is the point under discussion, it appears to me that no interval which could bear oppressively on the labourer, would elapse between the rise in the price of raw produce, and the rise in the wages of the labourer.

(Ibid., 166)

While Ricardo did not directly address the following scenario, on the premise of consistency we might infer that if a country spends some of its "gross revenue" on the import of machines, such revenues would no longer be available for the wage fund in the next period. In such a case, the problem that is thought to hold for the domestic purchase or construction of fixed capital is also relevant for the case of international trade. Once again, consistent answers can be obtained if we examine the effect of different policies and behaviors on the fund set aside for wages:

Like [an] increase in foreign trade, therefore, the process of mechanization was a matter of welfare . . . The reason why he thought that no (permanent) reduction in wages (total real wages in *our* sense of the word) would be induced by it, was that mechanization would not decrease the wage fund. But then he went on to confess that he had discovered reasons for believing that it would.

(Schumpeter 1954, 681)

In conclusion, I would submit that a consistent reading of the chapters on trade and machinery in the third edition of Ricardo's *Principles* can be achieved by reflecting on the various effects that trade in luxuries, trade in wage-goods, changes in "art and skill," and the construction of machinery can be thought to have on the size of the wage fund. On the basis of the evidence provided, to postulate the existence of a wage fund is simultaneously to provide a framework for a more consistent and coherent interpretation of Ricardo.

A most important, and potentially difficult, result follows from this argument. It is the conclusion that it is the wage fund doctrine that enables Ricardo to support consistently a regime of free international trade as being in the best interests of the capitalists and, as a result of enhanced accumulation, the working class. The reason is that when Ricardo makes direct comparisons between the economic effects that result from international trade and from the introduction of machinery, the wage-fund postulate maintains a crucial theoretical distinction between these two phenomena. By maintaining this distinction, he can remain optimistic with regard to the effects of international trade on labor even after he has revised his position on machinery.

In the final analysis, Ricardo's theoretical position, while consistent, is dependent upon a concept that is no longer thought to be a viable foundation for economic theorizing. From the perspective of modern debates, the

77

irony of Ricardo is that his innovative theoretical defense of *laissez-faire* may
be premised upon one of the constructs of classical political economy that
we are most reluctant to accept.

NOTES

1 The author would like to thank Spencer Pack, Terry Peach, Falguni Sheth, Gary
   Mongiovi, Mark Lutz, and Kevin McCarron for their careful and helpful comments. Earlier versions of this paper were presented to the University of New
   Hampshire Economics Seminar and the History of Economics Society.
2 Samuel Hollander (1971, 133–5) makes a persuasive argument to the effect that
   Ricardo's change of mind on the machinery issue happened over a relatively short
   period of time, specifically between January 25 and March 12, 1821.
3 "At the same time I must say (and I say it with that regret which I ever must feel in
   differing widely from one to whom I shall always be proud to look up to as my
   master) that in my humble opinion the Chapter on Machinery in this Edition is a
   very material deduction from the value of the work . . ." (McCulloch to Ricardo,
   June 5, 1821 in Ricardo 1952, 381–2).
4 Some recent interpretations of Ricardo, such as Hollander (1979, 331–4), have
   shed doubt on the previously accepted view that Ricardo adhered to a wage-fund
   doctrine. In an otherwise critical review, O'Brien (1981, 369) indicates that Hollander's position may have merit. While this paper does not *directly* address this
   issue, the argument indicates that a consistent reading of Ricardo's position on
   machinery and trade relies on the presupposition of a wage-fund doctrine. This
   being the case, one might conclude that this paper provides an *indirect* argument in
   support of the traditional interpretation.
5 Some recent interpretations grant a lesser role to the "corn laws" debate in the
   development of Ricardo's theoretical framework (Peach 1993, ch. 2). This is an
   important correction of the record. Nevertheless, policy issues, be they free trade,
   the currency question, or taxation, were never far from Ricardo's mind.
6 Since capital accumulation would eventually result in higher land rents, Ricardo was
   convinced that the policy of protection went against the "well understood," i.e.
   long-term, interests of the landlord class (Ricardo 1951 [1822], 238, 266).
7 There is a legitimate debate as to whether the classical economists, in particular
   Ricardo, felt that the rate of profit could fall fast enough to make the "stationary
   state" a tangible reality. In commenting on this issue, both Hollander (1979, 637–
   42) and Peach (1993, 94–6) reject the characterization of Ricardo as a "pessimist"
   with regard to future growth prospects.
8 For the record, Ricardo did not advocate a regime of completely free trade. On the
   contrary, he supported a duty on "corn" which would start at a relatively high rate,
   and then decline at a known and preset rate until such time as it reached a level
   which was equivalent to the incidental taxes which a landlord had to pay. Ricardo's
   proposal for a revised tariff was designed to create a "level playing field" between
   domestic and imported corn. See Ricardo (1951 [1822], Conclusion) for the
   specifics of his proposal.
9 "If I should ever change my opinion I will manfully avow it, and trust I shall be
   able to give reasons for the change as shall at least satisfy all candid men that I do
   so from a conviction of my error" (Ricardo to McCulloch, March 23, 1821, in
   Ricardo 1952, 356).
10 It is not quite accurate to argue that Ricardo *assumed* that capital would not flow
   overseas. On the contrary, the references just provided indicate that he thought

that it could, but that capitalists would not, in general, desire to do this if they could avoid it. He felt that with reasonable laws and moderate levels of taxation, which allowed capitalists a secure and competitive rate of profit, this eventuality would not occur. It is true that his model of comparative advantage assumes a trade in goods and not in capital. However, this generalization was based on the conditions stated above, not on an assumption that capital was immobile (Ricardo to McCulloch, in Ricardo 1952, 357–8). That the export of machinery was viewed as a reality, and something to be addressed at this time in English history, is clear from attempts made to prevent such movements (Jeremy 1977).

11 "In this chapter ['On Machinery'], Ricardo comes nearer than he does anywhere else to the profit analysis that Marx was to make his own. Nowhere else is their relation so clearly the relation of Professor Ricardo and tutee Marx – though, as may be the case sometimes, neither would have been completely pleased with the other's performance" (Schumpeter 1954, 682 n.104). See also Marx (1867: ch. xv; 1968: ch. xviii).

12 As I have already noted, some recent commentators have tried to play down the importance of the wage fund in both Ricardo and classical economics. Nevertheless, the resolution to the interpretative problem offered in the text draws upon the received interpretation which emphasizes the importance of the wage fund to the economics of Ricardo (Blaug 1958, 120–7; St Clair 1957, ch. 7). In his comment on an earlier draft of this paper, Spencer Pack (1995) stresses Ricardo's point that the effect of machinery was to lower the "gross produce" of society even as it increased the "net produce" of the capitalist (Ricardo 1951 [1821], 388–90). This is, of course, true. However, I would submit that it is exactly this "gross produce" that could be thought to make up the substance of the wage fund, "as the power of supporting a population, and employing labour, depends always on the gross produce of a nation, and not on its net produce, there will necessarily be a diminution in the demand for labour, population will become redundant, and the situation of the labouring classes will be that of distress and poverty" (ibid., 390). For this reason Pack's remarks are consistent with the explanation offered in the text. However, I do not wish to burden Professor Pack with an endorsement of the wage-fund concept. I alone remain responsible for offering an interpretation which retains that concept despite fair warning.

13 Spencer Pack points out that the trade chapter is predominantly concerned with trade in consumer goods (Pack 1995). Hence the discussion in that chapter, which draws parallels between trade and machinery, is specifically concerned with the effects that machinery has on the price of consumer goods. It follows that in Chapter 7 Ricardo did not address the relation between machinery and "gross revenue," which is the proper subject of Chapter 31. Professor Pack concurs with the primary conclusion of this paper, that the two chapters are consistent, by emphasizing that each of these chapters stressed different aspects of the machinery issue. Professor Pack's proposed resolution of this issue has the non-trivial merit of avoiding a potentially contentious debate over whether there is a "wage-fund" conception in Ricardo.

REFERENCES

Blaug, Mark (1958) *Ricardian Economics: A Historical Study*, Westport, CN: Greenwood Press.

Caravale, Giovanni A. (ed.) (1985) *The Legacy of Ricardo*, New York: Basil Blackwell.

Davis, John B. (1989) "Distribution in Ricardo's machinery chapter," *History of Political Economy* 21(3): 457–80.

Dobb, Maurice (1973) *Theories of Value and Distribution Since Adam Smith: Ideology and Economic Theory*, New York: Cambridge University Press.

Eltis, Walter (1985) "Ricardo on machinery and technological unemployment," in Giovanni A. Caravale (ed.), *The Legacy of Ricardo*, New York: Basil Blackwell, pp. 257–84.

Gomes, Leonard (1987) *Foreign Trade and the National Economy: Mercantilist and Classical Perspectives*, New York: St Martin's Press.

Hollander, Samuel (1971) "The development of Ricardo's position on machinery," *History of Political Economy* 3: 105–35.

Hollander, Samuel (1979) *The Economics of David Ricardo*, Toronto: University of Toronto Press.

Jeremy, D. J. (1977) "Damming the flood, British government efforts to check the outflow of technicians and machinery, 1780–1843," *Business History Review* (Spring): 1–34.

Marx, Karl (1867) *Capital*, vol. I, New York: International Publishers.

Marx, Karl (1968) *Theories of Surplus-Value*, vol. II, Moscow: Progress Publishers.

Meacci, Ferdinando (1985) "Ricardo's chapter on machinery and the theory of capital," in Giovanni A. Caravale, (ed.), *The Legacy of Ricardo*, New York: Basil Blackwell, pp. 285–302.

Mongiovi, Gary (1994) "Misinterpreting Ricardo: a review essay," *Journal of the History of Economic Thought*, 16(2): 248–69.

O'Brien, Denis P. (1981) "Ricardian economics and the economics of David Ricardo," *Oxford Economic Papers* New Series 33: 352–86.

Pack, Spencer (1995) "Comment on Prasch," remarks delivered to the History of Economics Society Meetings, Notre Dame, IN.

Peach, Terry (1993) *Interpreting Ricardo*, New York: Cambridge University Press.

Ricardo, David (1951 [1815]) *Essay on the Influence of a Low Price of Corn on the Profits of Stock*, in *The Works and Correspondence of David Ricardo*, ed. Piero Sraffa, vol. IV, Cambridge: Cambridge University Press.

Ricardo, David (1951 [1821]) *On the Principles of Political Economy and Taxation*, in *The Works and Correspondence of David Ricardo*, ed. Piero Sraffa, vol. I, Cambridge: Cambridge University Press.

Ricardo, David (1951 [1822]) *On the Protection of Agriculture*, in *The Works and Correspondence of David Ricardo*, ed. Piero Sraffa, vol. IV, Cambridge: Cambridge University Press.

Ricardo, David (1952) Letters, 1819–June 1821, in *The Works and Correspondence of David Ricardo*, ed. Piero Sraffa, vol. VIII, Cambridge: Cambridge University Press.

St Clair, Oswald (1957) *A Key to Ricardo*, London: Routledge & Kegan Paul.

Schumpeter, Joseph A. (1954) *History of Economic Analysis*, New York: Oxford University Press.

Sraffa, Piero (1951) "Introduction," in *The Works and Correspondence of David Ricardo*, ed. Piero Sraffa, vol. I, Cambridge: Cambridge University Press.

6

REFLECTIONS ON SCHUMPETER'S *HISTORY OF ECONOMIC ANALYSIS* IN LIGHT OF HIS UNIVERSAL SOCIAL SCIENCE

Yuichi Shionoya

THE TWO-STRUCTURE APPROACH

Joseph Alois Schumpeter, who maintained a great interest in the history of economics throughout his academic career, produced an extensive body of work in this field, covering the literature from the Greek period to contemporary times. His books on the subject include *Epochen der Dogmen- und Methodengeschichte* (1914), *Vergangenheit und Zukunft der Sozialwissenschaften* (1915), *Ten Great Economists* (1951), *History of Economic Analysis* (1954a), and *Dogmenhistorische und biographische Aufsätze* (1954b). *Ten Great Economists* and *Aufsätze* are collections of his separate articles edited after his death. *The History of Economic Analysis*, a revision and expansion of his 1914 study, was left unfinished at his death; it was edited and finally published through the efforts of his wife.

The history of science as science

The *History of Economic Analysis*, a magnum opus exceeding 1,200 pages, is a distinguished achievement among the studies of the history of economics. Outstanding features include its broad scope, the astonishing polymathy and unique judgment of its author, and his penetrating insight in constructing a scenario of scientific history. Although there exist fine historical studies in specific fields of economics and on individual economists, there is no precedent for attempting a doctrinal history that covers such a wide range of economic disciplines, includes not only the top-ranking authors but also many minor figures, and describes the history of economics against an intellectual and social background tracing back to the sources of Western thought. Nothing has taken its place; nothing has equaled it. Many will agree with Jacob Viner, who said:

YUICHI SHIONOYA

There is, as we shall see, much in this book which is redundant, irrelevant, cryptic, strongly biased, paradoxical, or otherwise unhelpful or
even harmful to understanding. When all this is set aside, there still
remains enough to constitute, by a wide margin, the most constructive,
the most original, the most learned, and the most brilliant contribution
to the history of the analytical phases of our discipline which has ever
been made.

(Viner 1954, 894–5)

However, to consider Schumpeter's work as unsurpassable would mean the
end of history, so to speak, and arrest the growth of study. The *History*
should be interpreted not as an artistic work but as a scientific work.
Because Schumpeter advocated the theoretical formulation of history or
the *histoire raisonnée*, it was incumbent on him to develop a theoretical framework in the study of history – be it the history of an economy or the
history of economics. History, of course, is subjective; no objective schema
or scenario for historical description is acceptable to everyone. However,
the rules of procedure by which to analyze the sometimes implicit framework of historians yielding subjective scenarios should be made explicit.
What is the basic idea that characterizes Schumpeter's approach to the
history of economics?

In the *History* a set of metatheories (the philosophy of science, the history
of science, and the sociology of science), a set of substantive theories
(economic statics, economic dynamics, and economic sociology), and a set
of analytic tools (theory, history, statistics, and institutions) are discussed
simultaneously to describe the history of economics and represent the
components of a theoretical framework for Schumpeter's historical study.

The following four major issues, which overlap to some extent, are the
focus of this paper. First, what are the method and framework of periodization in history? Second, how and when was economics established as an
autonomous science? Third, what was the relationship between external history and internal history, or between the philosophy of science and the
sociology of science in the context of economics? Fourth, how was the
genealogy traced for each theoretical system of economics (economic statics,
economic dynamics, and economic sociology)?

An evolutionary science of mind and society

In the first sentence of Chapter 1 of the *History*, Schumpeter wrote: "By
History of Economic Analysis I mean the history of the intellectual efforts
that men have made in order to understand economic phenomena or, which
comes to the same thing, the history of the analytic or scientific aspects
of economic thought" (1954a, 3). Most people who have read the book,
including Jacob Viner, have been puzzled by the gap between Schumpeter's

statement that the book is literally the history of economic analysis and what the *History* is actually about. They have complained that this work, which also delves into other history, policy, culture, and related disciplines, includes redundant and inconsistent material in disarray.[1] But this is a faulty understanding of Schumpeter's method for constructing a history of science, for the following reasons.

First, in undertaking a history of the developments in one area of social life Schumpeter did not mean to deny the importance of other areas. Rather, he believed that in order to write an accurate account of the changes in a particular field, one must consider the interrelationship between that field and other fields. The German Historical School believed in integrating the perspectives of development and unity in social life. According to this viewpoint, it was necessary for historians of economics to examine all other factors and to discern what was relevant.

Second and more specifically, Schumpeter intended to distinguish between economic thought and economic analysis. When human beings acquired some ideas about an economy, they did not separate economic analysis from economic thought. The further one goes back in time, the more often it will be found that the two were intermingled, and thus it is necessary to extract the analytic elements from the primitive ideas of an economy. Schumpeter (1954a, 10) wrote that

> the frontiers of the individual sciences or of most of them are incessantly shifting and . . . there is no point in trying to define them either by subject or by method. This particularly applies to economics, which is not a science in the sense in which acoustics is one, but is rather an agglomeration of ill-coordinated and overlapping fields of research in the same sense as is "medicine."

The mixing of economic thought and economic analysis cannot be avoided even today, because the economy is the ordinary business of ordinary people, and they are not barred from forming an understanding of it. Moreover, this remark of Schumpeter's cannot be disregarded:

> Let us recall our distinction between Economic Thought – the opinions on economic matters that prevail at any given time in any given society and belong to the province of economic history rather than to the province of the history of economics – and Economic Analysis – which is the result of scientific endeavor in our sense.
>
> (Ibid., 52)

Because, in his view, the tools of economic analysis consist of history, theory, statistics, and economic sociology, economic thought that provides information about the history and institutions of an economy is indispensable to a history of economic analysis.

Third, in a more fundamental sense, the diversity of the material in the

History of Economic Analysis is due to what I call the "two-structure approach" that Schumpeter properly developed for his volume. Schumpeter's total work includes the "system of theory" about economy and the "system of metatheory" about economics. His system of theory consists of three layers: economic statics, economic dynamics, and economic sociology. Analogically, his system of metatheory also has three layers: the philosophy of science, the history of science, and the sociology of science; the three metatheories are concerned with scientific activity from the perspective of statics, dynamics, and sociology, respectively. In economics, these metatheories relate to the inquiry into its static structure and rules of procedure (economic methodology), the inquiry into its dynamic developments (history of economics), and the inquiry into its activity in a social context (sociology of economics), respectively. The history of economics provides not only the context in which the three layers in the system or theory are historically examined, but also reveals the structure of the three layers in the system of metatheory in which economics is conditioned by economic methodology and the sociology of economics, so that the history of economics is explained internally and externally.

It is possible to interpret the two systems from a different viewpoint: as the system of theory for the two different social areas, that is, economy and thought, rather than as the system of theory for the economic area and the system of its metatheory. Thought and science are elements of culture, mind, and consciousness in a wider sense and represent the superstructure of society as defined by Karl Marx. Therefore, an inquiry into the relationships between the two systems has a perspective that is similar to the economic interpretation of history in Marx. Schumpeter's two-structure approach was fully developed in the *History of Economic Analysis*.

Referring to Giambattista Vico, the eighteenth-century Italian thinker, Schumpeter (1954a, 137) discussed the two-structure approach as follows:

> His New Science (*scienza nuova*) is best described by the phrase "an evolutionary science of mind and society." But this must not be interpreted to mean that the evolution of the human mind shapes the evolution of human society; nor, though this would be nearer the truth, that the historical evolution of societies shapes the evolution of the human mind; but that mind and society are two aspects of the same evolutionary process.

Nothing expresses the nature of Schumpeter's view of social science better than this passage. He identified the social sciences in the form of eighteenth-century moral philosophy with "the sciences of 'mind and society'" (ibid., 141). Thus it can be argued that the history of "an evolutionary science of mind and society" was the task of the *History*.

Regarding John Stuart Mill's *A System of Logic* (1843) as one of the great books of the nineteenth century, representing one of the leading components of its *Zeitgeist*, Schumpeter (1954a, 449–50) pointed out the family likeness that existed between Mill's *Logic* and his *Principles of Political Economy* (1848). According to Schumpeter, Mill was so modest that he did not claim to give the world a new theory of intellectual operations and of economic processes, but in fact he applied similar approaches to mind and society in order to coordinate existing elements of knowledge, to develop them, and to solve unsettled problems.

Figure 6.1 summarizes Schumpeter's two-structure approach to social

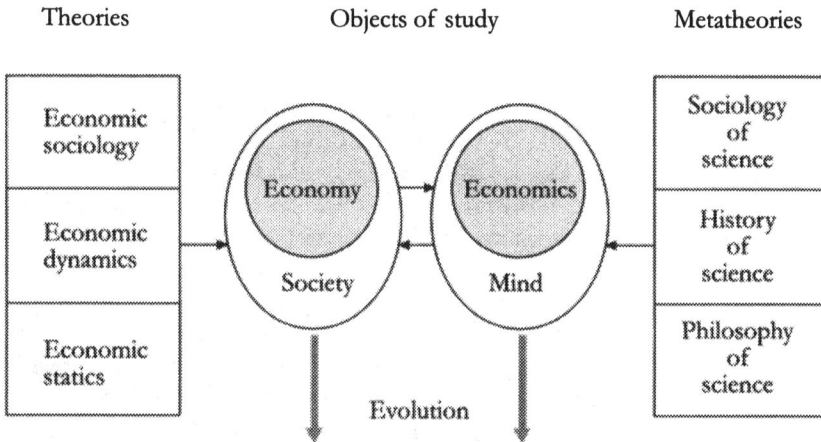

| Theories | Objects of study | Metatheories |

Figure 6.1 Schumpeter's two-structure approach

science, where theory and metatheory are concerned with society and mind, especially with economy and economics, respectively. Each structure consists of static analysis, dynamic analysis, and sociological analysis. Society and mind are in the process of evolution with bilateral relationships between them.

The two-structure approach represents a critique of other approaches that tended to interpret the evolution of mind and society unilaterally. On the one hand, Marx's economic interpretation of history explained human history by the modes of material production, and on the other hand, Hegel's idealistic philosophy of history and the "intellectualist evolutionism" (Schumpeter 1954a, 442) of Jean Antoine Condorcet, Auguste Comte, and Henry Thomas Buckle emphasized mind as the determinant of a society. Schumpeter lumped the two approaches together, calling it a "single hypothesis of the Comte–Buckle–Marx kind" (ibid., 811), and claimed that mind and society were interdependent and interactional.

THE CLASSICAL SITUATIONS AND THE FILIATION OF SCIENTIFIC IDEAS

On what methodology does the two-structure approach depend? Let us begin with a formal framework. Schumpeter (1954a, 51) introduced the concept of the "classical situation" as a device of periodization in history; he defined it as "the achievement of substantial agreement after a long period of struggle and controversy – the consolidation of the fresh and original work which went before". This quotation is from the editor of the *History*; although Schumpeter planned to discuss the concept generally, he did not do so. However, the intent of the concept is clear enough in his description of the three classical situations.

Interpretation of the three classical situations

Schumpeter (1954a, 7) defined the first classical situation as the establishment of economics as "tooled knowledge" in the latter half of the eighteenth century, when two sources of economics, that is, philosophy and politics, were joined in the *Wealth of Nations* (1776) of Adam Smith. This scenario will be examined more closely below; here the establishment of economics with Adam Smith is assumed. To be precise, the years around 1790 are regarded as the period of the first classical situation, allowing twenty years for the acceptance of Smith's work. The second classical situation refers to the years after Adam Smith when classical economics matured and was formulated by John Stuart Mill in his *Principles of Political Economy* (1848). The third classical situation was the identification of neoclassical economics in the *Principles of Economics* (1890) of Alfred Marshall and *Über Wert, Kapital, und Rente* (1893) of Knut Wicksell after the Marginal Revolution around 1870, allowing twenty years for their absorption.

Schumpeter's concept of the classical situation looks very much like Thomas Kuhn's concept of the establishment of normal science, which was made possible by the development of a paradigm. The formulation of a paradigm is achieved when, first, the conflict and competition among schools are over and a certain theory is supported by the dominant group of scholars, and second, such a theory has been equipped with clearly articulated problems and methods and indicates the direction of the entire research activity. After the fall of logical positivism and logical empiricism, however, various positions on the philosophy of science were proposed by Kuhn, Karl Popper, Imre Lakatos, and others. In view of the differences they perceived among those positions, it would be misleading to emphasize only the similarity between Schumpeter and Kuhn. In fact, it is possible to regard Schumpeter as similar to Lakatos on the problem of verification and falsification and on the relationship between statics and dynamics. Rather than comparing aspects of Schumpeter's approach fragmentally with others', it is more useful to define his own theory of scientific history from his description of a scenario in the history of economics. In this context of the history of science, it is important to recognize that he had views on the methodology of science and the sociology of science – specifically, on instrumentalism, schools, and vision – because these views must be applied to, and tested by, the actual process of scientific activity.

Werner Stark, a student of the history of economics and the sociology of knowledge, asked why the great syntheses of economics that Schumpeter expressed by the concept of the classical situation occurred in certain periods of time; a question, in Stark's opinion, that Schumpeter failed to answer. Stark argued that the classical situation in economics reflected all analogous crystallization and equilibrium in social and economic situations, and that the intervals between two classical situations were characterized not only by a disintegration of the theoretical reflection of reality but also by a disintegration of the reality itself. His argument was based on the idea that "these two concomitant developments are really only aspects of one total stream of happening" (Stark 1959, 58). This idea does not differ from Schumpeter's belief that "mind and society are two aspects of the same evolutionary process" quoted above, or from my notion of the two-structure approach. Yet Stark's further claim that a consolidation, crystallization, and equilibrium of thought reflect the parallel developments in reality seems farfetched and unacceptable. Schumpeter denied the unilateral causation from society to mind.

My general interpretation of Schumpeter's two-structure approach to mind and society is that because society is the object of thought and the field in which thought is created, society naturally influences thought, but thought has its own logic so that the relationships between mind and society are flexible. The exact nature of the relationships depends on specific cases and cannot be described in advance. Although the philosophy of science and the sociology of science are often developed in abstract terms, it is the task of the history of science to examine them in a practical context. My pragmatic interpretation is to relate the periodization of the three classical situations to that of the Kondratieff long cycles developed in Schumpeter's *Business Cycles* (1939).

In *Business Cycles* Schumpeter used the Kondratieff long cycles with a wave length of fifty years as the framework for the analysis of capitalist economic development, for two purposes: first, to analyze the ten-year Juglar cycles and the forty-month Kitchin cycles, and to describe economic and industrial history within a period of the Kondratieff cycle; and second, to characterize the nature of a Kondratieff wave length in terms of not only epochal technological innovation but also sociological features including civilization and the *Zeitgeist*. Thus, the first wave was called Industrial Revolution Kondratieff (characterized by cotton textile, iron, and steam power), the second wave Bourgeois Kondratieff (railroad), and the third wave Neo-mercantilist Kondratieff (electricity, chemicals, and the automobile).

In Schumpeter's view, Kondratieff long waves start from the neighborhood of economic equilibrium; according to the chronology by Kuznets (1940), which Schumpeter eventually approved, the first wave began in 1787, the second in 1843, and the third in 1898. These three dates almost coincide with the dates of the classical situations in the *History*. With these double heuristic frameworks Schumpeter tried to deal with developments in the economy and in economics. In this sense, the descriptions of economic history in *Business Cycles* and the history of economics in the *History of Economic Analysis* are parallel. The composition of history, however, does not follow the dating of the classical situations: Part II covers the period from Plato to the acceptance of Adam Smith's *Wealth of Nations* (around 1790); Part III, classical economics (1790–1870); Part IV, neoclassical economics (1870–1914 and after); and Part V, the present (to the 1940s). The division depends on the mechanism of scientific development.

Mechanism of scientific development: revolution and synthesis

Schumpeter planned to write a methodological introduction as Part 1 after completing the substantive portion of the *History*. Chapters 1 through 3 of Part I were finished; for Chapter 4, titled "The Sociology of Economics," section 1 ("Is the History of Economics a History of Ideologies?") was written; for two more sections ("The Motive Forces of Scientific Endeavor and the Mechanisms of Scientific Development" and "The Personnel of Science in General and of Economics in Particular"), Schumpeter left only fragmentary paragraphs. However, his sociology of science, as was more fully developed elsewhere, focused on vision (or ideology) and schools (or groups of scientists). Here I will examine how he applied his sociology of science and methodology of science to the study of the history of science in the *History* to explain his idea of the mechanism of scientific development. His concept of the "classical situation" is part of that mechanism; another part is provided by his concept of the "filiation of scientific ideas." By combining the two, I will set forth an interpretation of Schumpeter's leading idea in the *History*, which until now has remained rather ambiguous, as compared with his evaluation of individual figures in which scholars have shown a keen interest.

A classical situation is a period that represents the establishment of uniform ideas about the method and problems of economics, a time during which advances that have been made over a number of decades are consolidated and coordinated. Doctrines are formulated and standardized by influential textbooks, and a comprehensive school, such as the classical or neoclassical schools, in economics is established for the discipline as a whole. The appearance of a classical situation is a remarkable phenomenon of the sociology of science. After this the scientific development enters a phase of gradual growth, an age of normal science, as Thomas Kuhn put it, during which one can speak of the progress of science according to the standard of scientific methodology.

Prior to consolidation and coordination, new ideas must be presented, leading to struggles and controversies among competing schools as they pursue legitimacy. Also, in the process after consolidation, new ideas will soon appear. To command the stream of ideas in this new age of disturbance, scientists need a conscious and an unconscious strategy. Even a prominent scientist might diverge from the right course of scientific development in the long run; or conversely, even if one hit on a good idea, it might not be accepted at the time. Therefore, the history of science must engage not only in the follow-up of the mainstream but also in the critical evaluation of why other potentialities failed in light of the sociology of science as well as the methodology of science.

Concerning the success of a revolution, the rise in fame, or the neglect of valuable contributions, Schumpeter (1954a, 46, 480) observed:

> Owing to the resistance that an existing scientific structure offers, major changes in outlook and methods, at first retarded, then come about by way of revolution rather than of transformation and elements of the old structure that might be permanently valuable or at least have not yet had time to yield their full harvest of result are likely to be lost in the process.
>
> . . .
>
> [H]istorical performances are rarely like erratic blocks in a plain. They are more like peaks that rise from clusters of smaller eminences. In other words, a science develops by small accretions that create a common fund of ideas from which, by chance as well as by merit, emerge the works that enter the hall of fame. Therefore we must add at least a few of those writers who, though they failed to achieve historic fame, yet did important work and exerted an influence upon developments in analysis that are anonymous but not negligible.

To explain the emergence of new ideas Schumpeter's thesis of vision is applicable. Because scientific acts consist of the formation of vision and its theoretical formulation, a revolution can take place on either side. According to Schumpeter, "it is much more difficult for the human mind to forge the most elementary conceptual schemes than it is to elaborate the most complicated superstructures when those elements are well in hand" (ibid., 602). But unless vision is provided, economics has no object of recognition and elaboration. The history of economics is partly a history of the attempts to formulate a vision by means of theoretical structures: "[T]o a great part, advance in theoretical analysis precisely consists in elaborating implications of older thought that had not been seen or not clearly seen before" (ibid., 674). The combination of vision and theory over time produces continuity in thought, and this is what Schumpeter called the filiation of scientific thought. In many places in the history of economics he actually found the lines of filiation, such as that of equilibrium theory from Richard Cantillon through Jacques Turgot and Jean-Baptiste Say to Léon Walras. As this example indicates, the Marginal Revolution had some predecessors and, from the stream of ideas, progress in analytic techniques can be perceived; the filiation of scientific ideas, along with development within a paradigm established during a classical situation, shapes another concept of progress in science.

It is clear from the following extract that Schumpeter regarded revolution and synthesis as the two moments in scientific development:

> so far as pure theory is concerned, Walras is in my opinion the greatest of all economists. His system of equilibrium, uniting, as it does, the quality of "revolutionary" creativeness with the quality of classical synthesis, is the only work by an economist that will stand comparison with the achievements of theoretical physics.
>
> (Ibid., 827)

If by the emergence of a classical situation, as its definition signifies, synthesis establishes a universal basis of a science, revolution makes scientific thought continuous in human history through the discovery of the filiation of cognate ideas. The thesis that revolution implies continuity with the past appears to be a paradox that would please Schumpeter. The ordinary concept of revolution is one-sided in emphasizing the critical aspects of revolutionary versus mainstream thought; a science could make significant (rather than piecemeal) progress if a novel idea could resort to past thought that had been neglected.

Joseph Spengler, in discussing the endogenous and exogenous influences on the development of economics, presented the noteworthy view that the relative importance of influences depends on how the scope of economics is defined (Spengler 1968). If economics is perceived as a kit of tools, exogenous factors exert little influence on its development. If, however, economics is conceived more broadly to also include ideological, philosophical, and preanalytic elements, it becomes sensitive to exogenous influences. This view accords with Schumpeter's; he thought that the role of preanalytic vision is important for the analysis of long-term changes in an economy and that exogenous influences including ideology have a larger role to play in this type of research. Moreover, an association with past thoughts through visionmaking sometimes produces revolutionary leaps, whereas the progress of analytic techniques and the elaboration of theoretical structures depends on the internal development of science.

Vision as well as theoretical tools, however, cannot permit foreseeable development. Schumpeter (1954a, 10) observed that "science as a whole has never attained a logically consistent architecture; it is a tropical forest, not a building erected according to blueprint." Nevertheless, his philosophical idea that a science would take a reasonable course *ex post* might partly presume the idea of natural law in history and partly reflect the biologism of Ernst Mach and Henri Poincaré.[2] Although, like evolution in an economy, evolution in thought cannot be explained *ex ante*, it is argued that, in the analogy with biological evolution, thought changes so as to adapt to facts; otherwise a theory cannot survive. Intellectual history is a history of the survival of the fittest, and theories must vie with each other in a competition to fit the facts.

Only survivors, however, are not necessarily superior. Schumpeter rejected the view that important concepts, methods, and conclusions were all embodied in the current theories, and argued that only a recollection and conversation with the past would ensure the filiation of scientific ideas. In the *Science of Mechanics* (1933 [1883]), Mach warned that the prevailing theories were not inevitable and might not have taken over important past ideas.[3]

THE SCENARIO OF THE ESTABLISHMENT OF ECONOMICS

Two sources of economics

In *Epochen der Dogmen- und Methodengeschichte*, Schumpeter developed a scenario that economics, as it was established as a science at the end of the eighteenth century, had two different sources in Europe: the speculation of philosophical *Weltanschauung* and the debate of current topics (1954c, 9–10). The first source was the thoughts about society by philosophers, beginning with Aristotle, progressing through medieval theology, and crystallizing in eighteenth-century "moral philosophy." The second source was the "vulgar economics" discussed by merchants and officers who were engaged in ordinary economic practice; it was called mercantilism and cameralism. The *History of Economic Analysis* adopted the same scenario. Investigating the sources of a science includes answering the question of how a science was established thereafter as an autonomous science, the first question that the history of a science always encounters. Schumpeter acknowledged the separation of these two sources as an expository device, implying that his history of economics was based on the instrumentalist formulation of history.

For the sake of convenience, the two sources can be called philosophy and policy. According to Schumpeter, "Social problems interest the scholarly mind primarily from a philosophical and political standpoint; scientifically they do not at first appear very interesting or even to be 'problems' at all" (1954a, 53), because economic life is merely an ordinary experience in which everyone participates.

The first stream of thought, he argued, began in Greece and the Roman Empire, then skipped five hundred years from the sixth to the tenth century

(Schumpeter called this period "the great gap"), and finally ran into medieval scholasticism, the natural law, and moral philosophy. Schumpeter admitted that this stream of thought was dominated by the moral, legal, and normative perspective, but paid scrupulous attention to the analytic viewpoint, which might be involved and stimulated: "There is no point in throwing out the analytic baby with the philosophic bath-water" (ibid., 111). The analytic elements he wanted to uncover in history were always those of economics and sociology.[4]

Let us examine a few examples of resolving a mixture of analytic and philosophical elements. Schumpeter called Aristotle's *Nicomachean Ethics* and *Politics* the first known systematic presentation of a unitary social science. Aristotle's economic sociology consisted of a discussion of institutions such as private property, slavery, communism, and the family. Schumpeter took notice of Aristotle's embryonic pure economics that was based on wants and their satisfaction, and regarded his analyses of values, exchange, and money as the starting point of later economics. Although it had been held that Aristotle was so preoccupied with the philosophical and ethical problems of justice in exchange that he was diverted from the analytic issues of actual pricing, Schumpeter interpreted the normal competitive prices in Aristotle as standards of commutative justice. Similarly, he regarded the concept of just price in the work of St Thomas Aquinas as belonging to pure economics, and identified his sociology with a study of the social function of private property focusing on the concept of public good.

In this stream, Schumpeter observed, the most important element was the thought of natural law, which had a fundamental significance as the origin of all of the social sciences. According to him, a science originated where a body of interdependent phenomena was recognized; this recognition was a prerequisite to analyzing apparently commonplace phenomena. Social science discovered itself in the concept of natural law. *Natural* meant the nature of things or naturally right things. Based on this conception, he wrote, "Just as we may look upon the physical universe ... as a logically consistent whole that is modeled upon an orderly plan – so we may look upon society as a cosmos that is possessed of inherent logical consistency" (1954a, 114).

On the other hand, philosophers of the seventeenth and eighteenth centuries tried to find natural law through a psychological inquiry into universal human nature. In this way, the scholastic concept of public good was formulated into the utilitarian doctrine of the greatest happiness of the greatest number. Schumpeter saw utilitarianism as the last system of the natural law. Utilitarianism had widely influenced the social sciences, among them economics, on the basis of the formulation of human motives in terms of egoism and the pursuit of pleasure. Moral philosophy, including utilitarianism, had emerged as a comprehensive theory of society that covered broad areas of the social sciences.

92

Two points that Schumpeter discussed in the *History* with regard to natural law – the postulate of individual rationality and the discovery of the order in social phenomena – he had more sharply emphasized as the formative ideas of science in a previous book, *Epochen der Dogmen- und Methodengeschichte*:

> We shall, therefore, understand that on the one side thinkers arrived at an individualist point of view, which saw in the world of motives within the individual the key to an understanding of social problems, while on the other side they maintained that there was an immutable and universally valid order which alone corresponded to Reason.
>
> (Schumpeter 1954c, 18)

Schumpeter interpreted this earlier recognition as strictly scientific in the modern sense.

The second stream leading to economics encompassed the debates of contemporary economic policy. With the fall of the feudal society and the rise of monarchy after the fourteenth and fifteenth centuries, the authority of the Roman Catholic Church and thus the international cultural world of the Middle Ages gradually declined. In contrast, the nation states appeared on the stage, and they were concerned about economic policy. Their goals were to raise government revenue internally and to increase trade surplus externally. Schumpeter labeled the authors of economic literature during sixteenth- and seventeenth-century mercantilism and cameralism in Europe, before Adam Smith's *Wealth of Nations*, "Consultant Administrators" and "Pamphleteers" (1954a, 159).

One of the major policy debates was about the program for the development of industry and commerce, and the main results were discourses on trade and money. Although they aimed directly at solving practical issues, the logic inherent in the economic process was gradually uncovered. Another major debate was on public finance.

The discovery of economic circulation and the integration of economics

Schumpeter, having depicted the history of economic thought by reference to philosophical thought and practical policy issues as the sources of economics, faced the task of judging whether economics was established as a science somewhere in the latter half of the eighteenth century. His two studies on the history of economics provided different conclusions. This might mean a change of mind, but, more importantly, it gave rise to a theoretical problem about periodization in history. In *Epochen der Dogmen- und Methodengeschichte* Schumpeter had emphasized the "discovery of economic circulation" by the Physiocrats. They not only belonged to the stream of thought of natural law, but also supported a policy favoring agriculture; therefore, they represented the confluence of the two mainstreams:

93

Before the Physiocrats appeared on the scene only local symptoms on the economic body, as it were, had been perceived, while they enabled us to conceive this body physiologically and anatomically as an organism with a uniform life process and uniform conditions of life, and it was they who presented to us the first analysis of this life process.

(Schumpeter 1954c, 44)

Primitive and elementary as the *Tableau économique* was, Schumpeter attributed the establishment of economics to François Quesnay, who acquired through this framework a recognition of the interdependence of economic phenomena.[5]

In the *History of Economic Analysis*, in contrast, the two streams were joined at Smith's *Wealth of Nations*. Although Schumpeter here too emphasized the importance of the work of the Physiocrats, he did not treat them as epoch-makers; the two streams from the Greek period, being still not confluent at the Physiocrats, ran further to Adam Smith.[6]

In both books Schumpeter thought that after Quesnay a synthesis of existing elements of economics was still needed. The Physiocrats, a true school, had appeared and disappeared like a shooting star. In *Epochen*, Schumpeter regarded Turgot and Smith as qualified to undertake the synthesis. Smith actually performed the task, but Schumpeter's (1954c, 65) evaluation was that "he [Smith] was a man of systematic work and balanced presentation, not of great new ideas, but a man who above all carefully investigates the given data, criticizes them coolly and sensibly, and coordinates the judgment arrived at with others which have already been established." In the *History* the two streams were united at the *Wealth of Nations*, but Schumpeter (1954a, 184, 185), unlike most scholars, did not regard Smith as the founder of economics:

No matter what he actually learned or failed to learn from predecessors, the fact is that the *Wealth of Nations* does not contain a single analytic idea, principle, or method that was entirely new in 1776.

. . .

But though the *Wealth of Nations* contained no really novel ideas and though it cannot rank with Newton's *Principia* or Darwin's *Origin* as an intellectual achievement, it is a great performance all the same and fully deserved its success. The nature of the one and the causes of the other are not hard to see. The time had come for precisely that kind of coordination. And this task A. Smith performed extremely well. He was fitted for it by nature: no one but a methodical professor could have accomplished it.

Schumpeter marked the epoch by Smith's synthesis of economics and called it the first classical situation.

These contrasting views about the birth of economics as a science do not mean that either one is the right version by itself. The question is which one more appropriately explains the historical reality. Without a doubt Quesnay was epochal to Schumpeter, who attached the highest importance to the recognition of general equilibrium in an economy. In this view, however, it is difficult to interpret the process from Quesnay to Smith as a synthetic development because Smith did not follow Quesnay's whole system. As Schumpeter admitted, the analytic work of Quesnay was not comprehended by his contemporary and later economists; because it included a curious thing like the *tableau*, the scrupulous Smith did not link Quesnay's ideas with his system:[7] "Karl Marx was the only first-rank economist to give Quesnay his due" (Schumpeter 1954a, 232). As long as Marx was influential enough to form a paradigm and a school, Quesnay was for the first time brought into the process of the filiation of scientific ideas.

It can be argued that although the discovery of economic circulation by the Physiocrats was epochmaking in terms of the criterion of the philosophy of science, it did not have a great influence in actually shaping a paradigm in economics.[8] In contrast, Smith's framework of economics was far from being ideal from the standpoint of the philosophy of science, but owing to its external success, engendered considerable power in professional circles from the outlook of the sociology of science. What is important from the latter perspective was that, in view of Schumpeter's third definition of science (1954a: 7) – that science is carried out by groups of professional scientists – Adam Smith was not a bureaucrat, a politician, a merchant, let alone a doctor, but a typical university professor: "From about 1790 on, Smith became the teacher not of the beginner or the public but of the professionals, especially the professors" (ibid., 193–4). Schumpeter found Smith's larger success in his influence on professionals rather than in the number of books sold. In other words, Quesnay was epochal in terms of internal history but Smith was so in terms of external history. In the internal history describing the filiation of scientific ideas, Quesnay was later linked with Walras, who was to establish the Magna Carta of economic theory, in addition to Marx. Unlike the *Epochen*, a small book that did not encompass the sociology of science, the *History*, with a broader scope, could introduce the sociology of science as another coordinate axis for describing the history of economics.[9]

Theoretical exercises in the sociology of science

The *History* reveals very interesting thought in the sociology of science. In that volume Schumpeter attempted to compare the ability of three contemporaries to perform the integration of economics, which was the demand of the age: Jacques Turgot, Adam Smith, and Cesare Beccaria. According to him, Turgot was undoubtedly the most brilliant of the three. Turgot's *Reflexions sur la formation et la distribution des richesses*, though no more than an elaborate analytic table of contents for the book that he planned to write, was distinctly superior to the skeleton of Smith's *Wealth of Nations*; if their outlines were compared, nobody would have admired Smith's (Schumpeter 1954a, 248). In comparing Smith and Beccaria too, Schumpeter remarked, Beccaria's *Elementi di economia pubblica*, though only lecture notes, was superior to Smith's lectures at the University of Glasgow. Schumpeter reflected that if Beccaria had spent his time expanding the notes instead of working for the Milanese administration, for as many years as Smith had, the outcome would have been comparable to the *Wealth of Nations*. Smith's success was attributed to the fact that, as a university professor, he could invest enough time in writing (ibid., 180–1).

This conjecture may sound unreasonable to Smith's adherents. But what Schumpeter did in the *History* was to present a theoretical analysis of the factors responsible for the success of the *Wealth of Nations* by making counterfactual assumptions. He found that Smith's work was "the product of patience, of meticulous care, of self-discipline," and that its success was due to "its mature wisdom, its luxuriant illustrations, its effective advocacy of policies" and, in addition to intellectual performance, to "elaboration, application, and illustration" (ibid., 248). Schumpeter's evaluation, which is based on the imagination and analytic inference, is rare in the study of the history of economics.

Schumpeter made similar comparisons for Heinrich von Thünen (and Antoine Cournot) versus David Ricardo in the period of the classical school and for Léon Walras versus Alfred Marshall in the period of the neoclassical school. In every comparison his judgment was against the British.

THE GENEALOGY OF STATICS, DYNAMICS, AND ECONOMIC SOCIOLOGY

After Adam Smith, economists reached a consensus about the fundamentals of economics such as the subject matter, method, and goals of economics. This permitted the integration of analytic efforts. Thus with Smith the classical situation, in terms of the synthesis of economics, was established and the development of classical economics (1790–1870) began. What did the economics of this period mean to Schumpeter, who thought that economics as an autonomous science was first realized by Walras?

Relative immaturity

Responding to this question, Schumpeter (1954a, 463) characterized this period as one of "relative immaturity." Indeed, the solidification of a certain framework of economics by Adam Smith meant that "relative maturity" was achieved. By relative immaturity Schumpeter meant that important advances were recognized not immediately but only later, so that the progress of economics was obstructed. The Smithian synthesis overlooked and sterilized some development possibilities contained in the work of predecessors. Moreover, the prevalence of Ricardian economics made economic research stray from the pursuit of a general equilibrium theory. Thus the discoverers of the marginal utility theory, such as Antoine Cournot, Jules Dupuit, Hermann Gossen, and William Lloyd, did not attract much attention; instead, the labor theory of value gained currency. The forerunners of the demand-and-supply theory of exchange values, such as James Lauderdale, Jean-Baptiste Say, and Robert Malthus, were ignored. Heinrich von Thünen, the great neglected economist who discovered the idea of the marginal productivity theory and applied differential calculus to maximization (economizing), the central problem of economics, was the second scholar (next to Cournot) to express the general interdependence of economic magnitudes by an equation system. John Rae, who anticipated the Austrian capital theory, was also overlooked.

Following the comparative evaluation of Turgot (and Beccaria) versus Smith, Schumpeter (1954a, 465) compared Thünen with Ricardo. He said that, if judged exclusively by his purely theoretical abilities, Thünen was superior to Ricardo and to all economists of the time except Cournot. According to him, Ricardo's major influence stemmed from his findings on the current policy issues. Rejecting Schumpeter's emphasis on Cournot, Lionel Robbins asked: Which would have caused the greater impoverishment of economics if their contribution had been withdrawn, Cournot or Ricardo? (Robbins 1955, 5). This is a mediocre rebuttal, because Schumpeter did not try to compare the actual achievements and influences of the two economists, but to separate the causes of their performances into factors by counterfactual assumptions.

In fact, Ricardo formed a school, whereas, in Schumpeter's view, the Ricardian system was distorted by a policy-oriented viewpoint and digressed from the development of economics. Schumpeter regarded the work of John Stuart Mill as the core of the classical political economy and of Smith–Mill–Marshall as the mainstream representing the British line of economic statics. In France, the line of Cantillon–Quesnay–Turgot–Say–Cournot–Walras grasped the economic equilibrium (ibid., 492).

In the age of classical economics, the apparent dynamic elements found in Smith, Ricardo, and Mill were not concerned with changes emerging from the economic process but with responses to changes in exogenous data; their vision of a future economy was no more than the discussion of the stationary state that the economy would achieve. Schumpeter (1954a, 571) complained about the poverty of vision in the British Classical School:

The most interesting thing to observe is the complete lack of imagination which that vision reveals. Those writers lived at the threshold of the most spectacular economic developments ever witnessed. Vast possibilities matured into realities under their very eyes. Nevertheless, they saw nothing but cramped economies, struggling with ever decreasing success for their daily bread.

He compared it with the grand vision of Karl Marx.

The only development in dynamic economics during this period was that of Marx; Schumpeter called it "the only genuinely evolutionary that the period produced" (ibid., 441). The idea, forged by economic sociology, that the capitalist order is a phenomenon in a historical phase and will be transformed into another by virtue of its own inherent logic belonged to Marx alone (ibid., 544). In the second German edition of *Theorie der wirtschaftlichen Entwicklung*, the description of stationary flow in Chapter 1 is followed by an appendix that provides a summary of the history of economics in order to demonstrate the static nature of the previous theories. This appendix is not translated in the English version. Here, too, Schumpeter (1926, 84) wrote that "the only great attempt to tackle development problems is that of Marx," because apart from the historical vision in the economic interpretation of history, Marx set forth the economics of the inherent evolution of the economic process.

After the Marginal Revolution

The Marginal Revolution by William Stanley Jevons, Carl Menger, and Léon Walras achieved the establishment of the general equilibrium system and was linked with the latent line beginning with Richard Cantillon. Schumpeter (1954a, 918) wrote:

> It was only in the period under discussion that the conception of an economic cosmos that consists of a system of interdependent quantities was fully worked out with all its problems, if not quite satisfactorily solved, at least clearly arrayed and with the idea of a general equilibrium between these quantities clearly established in the center of pure theory.

According to Schumpeter, the most important among the three was Walras; the revolutionariness of the Marginal Revolution was not marginal utility or marginal analysis but the recognition of general equilibrium.

After neoclassical economics had been developed as static theory, Schumpeter must have been confident that his theory of economic development was a real contribution to dynamic theory. His theory was the filiation of scientific ideas that linked only with Marx in the entire history of economics. But he did not claim it explicitly in his study of the history of economics. In the *History of Economic Analysis* Schumpeter tried to discover dynamic theory in the development of economics after the First and Second World Wars, but he did not find a theory of endogenous economic evolution that was related to Marx's vision. Despite the influence of Keynesian economics, Schumpeter referred to it as aberrations leading to what he called the "Ricardian vice."

Economic sociology and a universal social science

I have paid attention to the fact that Schumpeter traced the descent of economic sociology as well as economics in the *History of Economic Analysis*. Until economics gained scientific autonomy, economic thinking had been inseparable from the overall view of society and often was combined with sociological thinking. Schumpeter (1954a, 58) called this overall view a "unitary Social Science" and applied the concept to Aristotle, utilitarianism (ibid., 429), and Marx (ibid., 441); similarly, he called the thought of the scholastic writers and of the philosophers of natural law a "universal social science" (ibid., 141). Although he was fascinated by a grand approach, he was critical of a monolithic view that explained social phenomena by a single factor. Thus he rejected a "single hypothesis of the Comte–Buckle–Marx kind" that attempted to attribute historical evolution to simple factors (ibid., 811).

Schumpeter was particularly interested in the structure of the unitary social science of Marx and examined it closely to find out whether Marx's synthesis rested on the same concept of social classes in both economics and sociology. He admitted that such a synthesis without a doubt enhanced the analytic vitality:

> The ghostly concepts of economic theory begin to breathe. The blood-less theorem descends into *agmen, pulverem et clamorem*; without losing its logical quality, it is no longer a mere proposition about the logical properties of a system of abstractions; it is the stroke of a brush that is painting the wild jumble of social life. Such analysis conveys not only richer meaning of what all economic analysis describes but it embraces a much broader field – it draws every kind of class action into its picture, whether or not this class action conforms to the ordinary rules of business procedure.
>
> (Schumpeter 1950, 45–6)

Schumpeter, nevertheless, pointed out that the unity of the social sciences in Marx also suffered from defects. Viewing the economic category "labor" and the social class "proletariat" as identical might conceal the diversity of wage earners. In such a monolithic synthesis a theory would be directed to a single purpose and liable to lose its usefulness: "A valuable economic theorem may by its sociological metamorphosis pick up error instead of richer meaning and vice versa. Thus synthesis in general and synthesis on Marxian lines in particular might easily issue in both worse economics and worse sociology" (ibid., 46). Therefore, Schumpeter proposed to break down Marx's system into economics and economic sociology. The model of economic sociology, in Schumpeter's view, was that of the German Historical School, and he determined that his work in economic sociology would belong to this line of thought.

Another relative immaturity

With the trend towards the specialization of sciences in the first half of the twentieth century, the synthetic and comprehensive orientation of economic sociology lost its appeal. As time went on, the work of economic sociology was in decline. As for economic dynamics, some aspects of the analytic technique gradually began to make progress in the field of macroeconomics, but no theory was related to Marx's vision. From Schumpeter's evaluation of the immaturity of dynamic economics and economic sociology, a false interpretation may even follow that the *History of Economic Analysis* was an absolutist history headed for the static general equilibrium theory. But, in fact, his investigation included not only static theory but also dynamic theory and economic sociology. His principle of eliminating his own work from the history of economics might obscure the fact that he traced the lines of dynamic economics and economic sociology from the Greek period to the present. He would have viewed the post-First World War period as another era of relative immaturity.

CONCLUSIONS

The aim of this paper has been to identify Schumpeter's theoretical framework in the *History of Economic Analysis* and to review a number of fundamental issues in the history of economics by using his framework. Let me summarize what has been accomplished.

First, what is noteworthy about Schumpeter's conception of science is his view that scientific activities are also social activities and thus the object of a universal social science; therefore the history of science constitutes a part of the history of society as a whole. This explains why he was so interested in the history of economics. Schumpeter's idea of universal social science, I contended, can be represented by the "two-structure approach to mind and society," with his analysis of economic development pairing with his analysis of the development of economics. The *History* posited as the object of study what he meant by a universal social science and described its evolution. The parallelism between the periodization of business cycles in terms of Kondratieff waves and that of the development of economics in terms of sequential "classical situations" shows the conceptual framework of his two-structure approach applied to the history, although it was not fully exploited.

Second, Schumpeter's history of science, while focusing on scientific tools, describes the interplay between the evolution of the relationships between society and scientists addressed by the sociology of science, on the one hand, and the development of problems and methods addressed by the methodology of science, on the other. Two key terms in the *History of Economic Analysis*, the "filiation of scientific ideas" and the "classical situation" are specifically devised to deal with the development of economic theories embedded in the sociological and methodological inquiries of science. In my interpretation, Schumpeter's idea of the mechanism of scientific development that consists of revolution and synthesis is uncovered by combining his two instrumental concepts, the "filiation of scientific ideas" and the "classical situation."

Third, when one applies the sociology of science and the philosophy of science to the history of science, as Schumpeter did, there emerges a conflict between the criteria of revolution and synthesis, which is illustrated by an evaluation of François Quesnay and Adam Smith, who compete to be the founder of economics. While Quesnay was epochal in terms of the philosophy of science or the internal history, Smith was so in terms of the sociology of science or the external history. It was shown that, in Schumpeter's view, the greatness of Quesnay was to be proved not so much by his link with a synthesizer, Smith, as by his anticipation of the revolutionaries Marx and Walras.

Fourth, contrary to what is generally believed, Schumpeter's *History* is not a description of the developments in economics in the narrow sense, which converged in the establishment of the general equilibrium theory. I paid attention to his concept of the "relative immaturity," the opposite of the "relative maturity" that is associated with the "classical situation." Economic dynamics and economic sociology, both pioneered by Marx and the German Historical School, remained to be elaborated and matured before a consensus could be reached in these fields by the effort of revolutionists, including Schumpeter himself.

NOTES

1 Lionel Robbins (1955, 4–5) remarked that there were two defects in the *History of Economic Analysis* (although they were not so serious as to detract importantly from its total achievement): undue length or discursiveness and overemphasis of certain scholars.

2 Poincaré (1929 [1905], 208) wrote: "The advance of science is not comparable to the changes of a city, where old edifices are pitilessly torn down to give place to new, but to the continuous evolution of zoologic types which develop ceaselessly and end by becoming unrecognizable to the common sight, but where an expert eye finds always traces of the prior work of the centuries past. One must not think then that the old-fashioned theories have been sterile and vain."

3 Mach (1960 [1883], 316) wrote: "We shall recognize also that not only a knowledge of the ideas that have been accepted and cultivated by subsequent teachers is necessary for the historical understanding of a science, but also that the rejected and transient thoughts of the inquirers, nay even apparently erroneous notions, may be very important and very instructive. The historical investigation of the development of a science is most needful, lest the principles treasured up in it become a system of half-understood prescripts, or worse, a system of prejudices. Historical investigation not only promotes the understanding of that which now is, but also brings new possibility before us, by showing that which exists to be in great measure conventional and accidental."

4 For example, the following remarks are found in many places in the *History of Economic Analysis*: "Later on, especially in the sixteenth century, sociological and economic topics were treated within the system of scholastic jurisprudence" (Schumpeter 1954a, 83); "Let us return to the classic period [of scholasticism], the thirteenth century, in order to search for elements of sociological and economic analysis" (ibid., 90); "All the facts presented above about eighteenth-century thought go to show that the natural-law approach to sociology and economics held its own to a considerable extent" (ibid., 141); "We simply recognize him [Marx] as a sociological and economic analyst whose propositions (theories) have the same methodological meaning and standing and have to be interpreted according to the same criteria as have the propositions of every other sociological and economic analyst" (ibid., 385). Clearly off the mark is the interpretation that in the *History* Schumpeter pursued the genealogy of economic theory exclusively culminating in the formulation of general equilibrium by Walras.

5 The great figures among the Physiocrats were Quesnay, Cantillon, and Turgot. Schumpeter formulated a theory on the sociology of their scientific discovery and success. According to him (1954a, 222), "Cantillon was the first to make this circular flow concrete and explicit, to give us a bird's-eye view of economic life. In other words, he was the first to draw a *tableau économique.*" Thus he attributed the discovery of economic circulation not only to Quesnay but also to Cantillon. Regarding the *tableau*, Schumpeter emphasized that "most important, the Cantillon–Quesnay *tableau* was the first method ever devised in order to convey an explicit conception of the nature of economic equilibrium" (ibid., 242). In this connection he mentioned three criteria for attributing inventions to individuals: first, the scientific need for some tool; second, the idea of how to construct one; and third, the actual construction of the tool. Based on the view that the original perception of another man's work belongs to discovery, Schumpeter (ibid., 240) admitted that an essential part of the *tableau* was perceived through an analogy with the circulation of the blood in the human body discovered by William Harvey and credited to Quesnay's independence from Cantillon.

6 Despite this scenario, the place of Smith in the *History* seems strange. In Part II, which deals with the development of economic analysis from the beginning to around 1790 when *Wealth of Nations* was accepted, Smith is located in Chapter 3, section 4(e), before the description of the Physiocrats and mercantilism. As the editor of the *History* noted (Schumpeter 1954a, 181), Schumpeter removed the long account of Smith, including the Reader's Guide to the *Wealth of Nations*, from the manuscript. In restoring it, the editor did not insert it in the appropriate place. I think it should have been located at the end of Part II, which would then conclude with the establishment of the first classical situation by Smith.

7 Although Schumpeter stated so in the *History* (1954a, 232), he had written in *Epochen* (1954c, 66) as follows: "In 1764 he [Smith] went with a fairly complete system to France where he established contact with the Physiocrats. In the serene years in Kirkcaldy he added those points in their system which we have described as essential to his own so that he burst its frame with the result that symmetry suffered seriously." In *Epochen*, since he marked an epoch by Quesnay, he might have had to regard Smith as succeeding Quesnay, although Schumpeter here meant that Smith was concerned with Quesnay's idea of productive and nonproductive labor, not with Quesnay's notion of the *tableau*.

8 By the criterion of the philosophy of science I mean that the general equilibrium theory is considered by Schumpeter as the complete economic model in the sense that it satisfies the requirements of the economy of thought, phenomenalism, and instrumentalism.

102

9 Robbins said that to discuss the whole history from Plato and Aristotle to Adam Smith as one unit, as Schumpeter did in the *History*, has two disadvantages: it tends to underestimate the achievements of Smith and Quesnay, and it tends to create a break between Smith and the classical school (Robbins 1955, 6). According to Robbins, the arrangement of *Epochen*, which dealt with the discovery of Quesnay and Smith's economic system as a distinct period, excluding the earlier philosophers, consultant administrators, and pamphleteers, was superior. I disagree. In my view, as a result of that arrangement, *Epochen* failed to show the synthesis of developments from Quesnay to Smith.

REFERENCES

Kuhn, Thomas S. (1962) *The Structure of Scientific Revolutions*, 2nd edn, Chicago: University of Chicago Press, 1970.

Kuznets, Simon (1940) "Schumpeter's business cycles," *American Economic Review* 30(2): 257–71; reprinted in S. Kuznets, *Economic Change: Selected Essays in Business Cycles, National Income, and Economic Growth*, New York: W. W. Norton, 1953.

Mach, Ernst ([1833] 1933) *Die Mechanik in ihrer Entwicklung: Historisch-kritisch dargestellt*, 9th edn, Wiesbaden: Verlag F. A. Brockhaus *(The Science of Mechanics: A Critical and Historical Account of its Development*, trans. T. J. McCormack, Lasalle, IL: Open Court Publishing Co., 1960.)

Marshall, Alfred (1890) *Principles of Economics: An Introductory Volume*, 9th edn, London: Macmillan, 1961.

Mill, John Stuart (1843) *A System of Logic*, 2 vols, London: John W. Parker.

Mill, John Stuart (1848) *Principles of Political Economy, with Some of Their Applications to Social Philosophy*, 2 vols, London: John W. Parker.

Poincaré, Henri (1905) *La Valeur de la Science*, Paris: Ernest Flammarion. (*The Foundations of Science*, trans. G. B. Halsted, New York: Science Press, 1929.)

Robbins, Lionel (1955) "Schumpeter's *History of Economic Analysis*," *Quarterly Journal of Economics* 69(1): 1–22.

Schumpeter, Joseph Alois (1914) *Epochen der Dogmen- und Methodengeschichte*, Tübingen: J. C. B. Mohr. (*Economic Doctrine and Method: An Historical Sketch*, trans. R. Aris, London: George Allen & Unwin, 1954.)

Schumpeter, Joseph Alois (1915) *Vergangenheit und Zukunft der Sozialwissenschaften*, Leipzig: Duncker & Humblot.

Schumpeter, Joseph Alois (1926) *Theorie der wirtschaftlichen Entwicklung: Eine Untersuchung über Unternehmergewinn, Kapital, Kredit, Zins und den Konjunkturzyklus*, 2nd rev. edn, Leipzig: Duncker & Humblot. (*The Theory of Economic Development: An Inquiry into Profits, Capital, Credit, Interest, and the Business Cycle*, trans. Redvers Opie, Cambridge, MA: Harvard University Press, 1934.)

Schumpeter, Joseph Alois (1939) *Business Cycles: A Theoretical, Historical and Statistical Analysis of the Capitalist Process*, 2 vols, New York: McGraw-Hill.

Schumpeter, Joseph Alois (1950) *Capitalism, Socialism and Democracy*, 3rd edn, New York: Harper.

Schumpeter, Joseph Alois (1951) *Ten Great Economists, from Marx to Keynes*, New York: Oxford University Press.

Schumpeter, Joseph Alois (1954a) *History of Economic Analysis*, New York: Oxford University Press.

Schumpeter, Joseph Alois (1954b) *Dogmenhistorische und biographische Aufsätze*, ed. E. Schneider and A. Spiethoff, Tübingen: J. C. B. Mohr.

Schumpeter, Joseph Alois (1954c) *Economic Doctrine and Method: An Historical Sketch*, trans. R. Aris, London: George Allen & Unwin.

Spengler, Joseph J. (1968) "Exogenous and endogenous influences in the formation of post-1870 economic thought: a sociology of knowledge approach," in Robert V. Eagly (ed.), *Events, Ideology and Economic Theory*, Detroit: Wayne State University Press, pp. 159–90.

Stark, Werner (1959) "The 'classical situation' in political economy," *Kyklos* 12: 57–65.

Viner, Jacob (1954) "Schumpeter's *History of Economic Analysis*: a review article," *American Economic Review* 44(5): 894–910.

Wicksell, Knut (1893) *Über Wert, Kapital, und Rente*, Jena: G. Fisher. (*Value, Capital and Rent*, trans. S. H. Frowen, London: Allen & Unwin, 1954.)

JOHN MAYNARD KEYNES ON SOCIO-ECONOMIC CLASSES IN TWENTIETH-CENTURY CAPITALISM

John E. Elliott and Hans E. Jensen

This paper examines the views of John Maynard Keynes on socio-economic classes and their relations to his theory of involuntary unemployment. Although Keynes did not provide a rigorous or systematic theory of socio-economic classes in the manner of, say, Karl Marx, his understanding and interpretation of class relations in twentieth-century capitalism was integral to what Schumpeter (1954, 195) aptly calls the pre-analytic "vision" which undergirded his economic analysis. Because Keynes' theoretical conceptualizations were substantially motivated by his policy positions, his underlying views on the changing institutional and class structure of modern economic society are more important and have greater implications for his economic theory than might well otherwise be the case.

· In the introductory section of this paper, we explicate Keynes' conception of the shift from old-style, small-scale, proprietary economy to big-business, corporate, oligopoly capitalism, and its consequences for class structures and thereby economic behavior. In succeeding sections, we examine in turn each component in Keynes' tripartite classification of socio-economic classes into finance capitalists, industrial capitalists or entrepreneurs, and workers. In each instance, we identify the implications for Keynes' economic theory, notably his analysis of the causes and cures for involuntary unemployment, of Keynes' classificatory schema of twentieth-century socio-economic class relations.

John Maynard Keynes viewed the class structure of twentieth-century capitalist society as the offspring of technological developments that had wrought a fateful impact upon the institutions of that society. In 1930, he described these technological revolutions:

> From the sixteenth century, with a cumulative crescendo after the eighteenth, the great age of science and technical inventions began, which since the beginning of the nineteenth century has been in full

flood – coal, steam, electricity, petrol, steel, rubber, cotton, the chemical industries, automatic machinery and the methods of mass production, wireless, printing . . . and thousands of other things . . . too famous and familiar to catalogue.

(*CW* **9**, 324[1])

"What is the result?" Keynes asked (ibid., 424). As far as institutional arrangements are concerned, he had provided the beginning of an answer to this question some three years earlier:

The old picture, the old schematism as to the actual nature of the economic world we live in is hopelessly out of date; the picture of numerous small capitalists, each staking his fortune on his judgement, and the most judicious surviving, bears increasingly little relation to the facts . . . Businesses are increasingly . . . run in their daily management by salaried persons who, perhaps, are risking little or nothing of their own fortunes . . . How remote that is from the old picture of owners staking their fortunes on their judgement, and the most judicious surviving.

(*CW* **19**(2), 641–2)

Professional managers constitute a new class that has been split off from the old class of owner–capitalists. The remainder of the latter group is composed of financial "investors." Thus, as Keynes saw it, "by the beginning of the twentieth [century]," the "propertied classes" had been divided into "two groups – the 'business men' and the 'investors' – with partly divergent interests" (*CW* **4**, 5). The former, Keynes labeled "entrepreneurs," and he praised them as "the active and constructive element in the whole capitalist society." The latter, who constitute "the richer section of the community," he christened "rentiers"[2] because they are "functionless [financial] investor[s]"[3] (*CW* **7**, 92; **2**, 149; **7**, 262, 92, 376, 154).

In short, technological change has vastly expanded the absolute and relative size of businesses and radically altered their organizational form, from proprietary and small capitalist firms to large corporate behemoths. Keynes does not criticize these institutional consequences of technological progress in terms of adverse effects upon the productive efficiency of business. Indeed, in *The General Theory of Employment, Interest and Money* (hereafter *GT*), he states that

if we have dealt otherwise with the problem of thrift, there is no objection to be raised against the modern classical theory as to the degree of consilience between private and public advantage in conditions of perfect and imperfect competition respectively.

(*CW* **7**, 379)

Because of the new dominance of big corporations, however, two dichotomies have occurred in capitalist institutions. First, a dichotomy between "finance" and "industry," and thus between financial capitalists and industrial capitalists or entrepreneurs.[4] In his *Treatise on Money* (*CW* **5** (1), 217), Keynes defines "finance" as "the business of holding and exchanging existing titles to wealth, . . . including Stock Exchange and Money Market transactions, speculation and the process of conveying current savings into the hands of entrepreneurs." He defines "industry" as "the business of maintaining the normal process of current output, distribution and exchange and paying the factors of production their incomes for the various duties they perform from the first beginning of production to the final satisfaction of the consumer."

Keynes' second dichotomy, adumbrated in the *GT*, is between "speculation" and "enterprise." By speculation, Keynes means "the activity of forecasting the psychology of the [stock] market . . ." Enterprise refers to the "the activity of forecasting the prospective yield of assets over their whole life . . ." Although "it is by no means always the case that speculation predominates over enterprise," the "risk" of its doing so increases as "the organization of investment markets improves." Certainly, the influence of stock exchange speculation is "enormous" in financially advanced capitalist societies such as the United States. And the "national weakness" of being "unduly interested in what average opinion believes average opinion to be . . . finds its nemesis in the [New York] stock markets" (*CW* **7**, 158–9).

In the *GT*, these bifurcations appear as underlying causative factors in each of three major components of his argumentarium: the demand for and supply of money, and thereby the rate of interest; the expected rate of profit and thereby the volume of investment; and the propensity to consume. First, the transactions and precautionary demands for money, for example, are based primarily upon the needs of industry, whereas the speculative demand for money and the money supply of banks and other financial institutions reflect the activities of speculators and finance capitalists. The development of advanced financial markets raises the total volume of funds available for investment. But it serves as a two-edged sword, by also increasing the role of speculation. Hence, uncertainty and its potentially destabilizing consequences have increased under the impact of the institutions and new class structure of twentieth-century corporate capitalism.

Second, in Chapter 12 of the *GT*, Keynes discusses the role of "business psychology" in determining the "state of long-term expectations." The argument is rooted in his distinction between industry and finance:

> In former times, when enterprises were mainly owned by those who undertook them or by their friends and associates, investment depended on a sufficient supply of individuals of sanguine temperament and constructive impulses who embarked on business as a way of life, not really relying on a precise calculation of prospective profit . . .

Decisions to invest in private businesses of the old-fashioned type
were ... decisions largely irrevocable, not only for the community as a
whole, but also for the individual.

(CW 7, 150–1)

By contrast, with the "separation between ownership and management"
which characterizes the twentieth-century capitalist corporation, and the
emergence of organized markets for corporate securities, a "new factor of
great importance has entered in, which sometimes facilitates investment but
sometimes adds greatly to the instability of the system." In the "absence of
security markets," there is no purpose in "frequently attempting to revalue
an investment to which we are committed." But stock markets revalue
investments "daily," and thereby provide a "frequent opportunity for an
individual (though not the community as a whole) to revise his commitments." These daily revaluations "exert a decisive influence on the rate of
current investment." On the one hand, purchase of a new enterprise will be
forgone if "a similar existing enterprise can be purchased at lower cost." On
the other, a speculator has an inducement to start a new project at an
"extravagant sum," if it can be "floated off" on the stock market at "an
immediate profit." Consequently, some types of investment are determined
by the "average expectation" of stock market speculators, "as revealed in the
price of shares, rather than by the genuine expectations of the professional
entrepreneur" (ibid.):

> Speculators may do no harm as bubbles on a steady stream of enter-
> prise. But the position is serious when enterprise becomes the bubble
> on a whirlpool of speculation. When the capital development of a
> country becomes the by-product of the activities of a casino, the job is
> likely to be ill-done.

(ibid., 159)

Third, overall, and for the working class in particular, the propensity to
consume, Keynes states, is a "fairly stable function."[5] But for financiers and
speculators, this may not be true. "The consumption of the wealth-owning
class may be extremely susceptible to unforeseen changes in the money-value
of its wealth. This should be classified amongst the major factors capable of
causing short-period changes in the propensity to consume." Similarly, in
general, the impact of small, short-run changes in interest rates upon spending out of income "is secondary and relatively unimportant." The "most
important influence" of changes in interest rates on the propensity to consume results from their effects upon "the appreciation or depreciation in the
price of securities and other assets. For if a man is enjoying a windfall
increment in the value of his capital, it is natural that his motives toward
current spending should be strengthened, even though in terms of income
his capital is worth no more than before; and weakened if he is suffering

108

capital losses." For example, a "severe decline in the value of Stock Exchange equities" "naturally exerts a very depressing influence" upon "the class who take an active interest in their Stock Exchange investments, especially if they are employing borrowed funds." Finance capitalists "are, perhaps, even more influenced in their readiness to spend by rises and falls in the value of their investments than by the state of their income." Thus, with a "'stock-minded' public" such as in the United States, "a rising stock market may be an almost essential condition of a satisfactory propensity to consume" (ibid., 92–4, 96, 319).

In addition to bringing about the separation of "the management of property from its ownership," developing technology threw more and more people into "a rapidly increasing" class of propertyless workers who earned their livelihood by selling their labor power to the entrepreneurs. Keynes called workers the "earning class" because he wished to stress two things. First of all, in contradistinction to the "unearned income" of the "rentier," the income of the worker is a truly earned one in the sense that it is a payment for efforts put forth. Second, the welfare of the working class depends essentially on decisions made by financiers and managers, decisions that have resulted in "a chronic condition" of massive "'involuntary' unemployment" (*CW* **4**, 4; **19** (1), 128; **19** (2), 846; **7**, 249, 6).

Consequently, Keynes conceived of society in terms of "a triple classification ... into the investing class, the business class, and the earning class." Although he admitted that these "classes overlap, and [that] the same individual may earn, deal, and invest, ... in the present organization of society such a division corresponds to a social cleavage and an actual divergence of interest" (*CW* **4**, 4; **29**, 77, 99–100; **7**, 150–1, 153).

The members of the three classes live in households. Hence every economic actor plays a dual role: as a procurer of income and as an income-dispensing consumer. In each of these two activities, Keynes interpreted the individual's behavior in terms of a "nature-*cum*-nurture theory of behavior" that he inherited mostly from Alfred Marshall (Jensen 1983, 77). Accordingly, Keynes depicted each actor's instinctive desire for "utility" and innate aversion to "disutility" as having been molded operationally by the particular subculture in which the individual lives because the "power to become habituated to his surroundings is a marked characteristic of mankind" (*CW* **7**, 128; **2**, 1).

On occasion (for example, *CW* **9**, 297), Keynes identified the intellectual elite (the "educated bourgeoisie") as a class. Not being "directly involved" in the processes of production or finance, and being neither pro- nor anti-working class but "non-working class," the intelligentsia was, for Keynes, an aristocracy "outside or above class. It criticized bourgeois society from the point of view of the good life, but was anti-socialist too." To combat the scourge of unemployment, it propounded "organization, which it called [liberal] socialism, but in individual life, it wanted more freedom" (Skidelsky

1992, 233–4). Its attitude toward the rentier was that of critique; toward entrepreneurs and managers, that of admiration (when properly led by the "educated bourgeoisie"); toward the workers that of sympathy but condescension; and toward working-class organizations, such as the Labour Party, that of occasional common cause but frequent rejection on grounds of perceived labor sectionalism and class-based politics.

THE RENTIERS

According to Keynes, it is because of their gradual separation from the active management of business enterprises that the rentiers' basic craving for satisfaction has become concertized in a desire to obtain financial gains, not through production, but through the speculative demand for or placement of liquid funds. In other words, being the product of an historically evolved "psychological attitude to liquidity," the "speculative motive" of the rentiers amounts to an institutionally conditioned manifestation of their basic appetite for utility (*CW* **7**, 247, 170).

For all practical purposes, such conditioning is a product of individual and collective experiences among the rentiers – experiences that convince them that the demand for or placement of liquid funds is undertaken under conditions of "risk, uncertainty, and ignorance" (*CW* **9**, 291). This fact makes it almost impossible for the individual rentier to estimate the future returns on current financial investments. Thus, knowing that his "individual judgment is worthless," the rentier "endeavour[s] to fall back on the judgment of the rest of the world which is perhaps better formed." That is, the individual rentier "endeavour[s] to conform with the behaviour of the majority or the average" of the community of rentiers. "The psychology of a society of individuals each of whom is endeavouring to copy the others leads" to what Keynes termed a "*conventional* judgment," or for short, a "*convention*" (*CW* **14**, 114; **7**, 152). Being based "on so flimsy a foundation," such a convention of a group of "ignorant individuals" is "subject to sudden and violent changes" whenever there is a "sudden fluctuation of opinion due to factors which do not really make much difference to the prospective yield" of financial instruments (*CW* **7**, 154; **14**, 114).

Suddenly emerging new "fears and hopes will, without warning, take charge of human conduct. The force of disillusion may suddenly impose a new conventional basis of valuation. All these pretty, polite techniques, made for a well-panelled board room and a nicely regulated market, are liable to collapse." Consequently, the financial "market will be subject to waves of optimistic and pessimistic sentiment, which are unreasoning and yet in a sense legitimate where no solid basis exists for a reasonable calculation" (*CW* **14**, 114–15; **7**, 154). But why is it that "competition between expert professionals, possessing judgment and knowledge beyond that of the average private [financial] investor" does not "correct the vagaries of the ignorant individual left to himself" (*CW* 7, 154)? Because, said Keynes:

> the energies and skill of the professional [financial] investor and specu-lator are mainly occupied otherwise. For most of these persons are, in fact, largely concerned, not with making superior long-term forecasts of the probable yield of an investment over its whole life, but with foreseeing changes in the conventional basis of valuation a short time ahead of the general public. They are concerned, not with what an investment is really worth to a man who buys it "for keeps", but with what the market will value it at, under the influence of mass psy-chology, three months or a year hence ... Thus the professional [financial] investor is forced to concern himself with the anticipation of impending changes, in the news or in the atmosphere, of the kind by which experience shows that the mass psychology of the market is most influenced.
>
> (CW 7, 154–5)

But in addition to and "apart from the instability due to speculation, there is the instability [in the financial market] due to the [fact that most] ... decisions ... [are] taken as a result of animal spirits – of a spontaneous urge to action rather than inaction, and not as the outcome of a weighted average of quantitative benefits multiplied by quantitative probabilities." Consequently, "if the[ir] animal spirits are dimmed and the[ir] spontaneous optimism falters," the rentiers' convention-fed "panic fears" are reinforced and they refuse to make funds available to entrepreneurs at a rate of interest that is attractive to the latter. In other words, the rentiers "prefer the control of liquid cash to parting with it in exchange for a debt on the terms indicated by the market rate of interest" (*CW* 7, 161, 162; **14**, 115; 7, 205–6).

In an effort to make it perfectly clear why the rentiers' liquidity preference may become unusually high, if not "virtually absolute in the sense that almost everyone [among them] prefers cash to holding a debt which yields so low a rate of interest" (*CW* 7, 207), Keynes recast this proposition in the form of a rhetorical question and an answer thereto. His question was: "Why should anyone outside a lunatic asylum wish to use money as a store of wealth?" (*CW* **14**, 115–16). Fancying himself in the position of the rentiers, he provided the following answer:

> Because, partly on reasonable and partly on instinctive grounds, our desire to hold money as a store of wealth is a barometer of the degree of our distrust of our own calculations and conventions concerning the future. Even though this feeling about money is itself conventional and instinctive, it operates, so to speak, at a deeper level of our motiv-ations. It takes charge at the moment when the higher, more precarious conventions have weakened. The possession of actual money lulls our

111

disquietude; and the premium which we require to make us part with money is the measure of our disquietude.

(Ibid., 116)

According to Keynes, the rentiers' disquietude may become so great that the rate of interest at which they would part with liquidity might be "so much above zero" that it could exceed the rate of future profits that the (by now) pessimistic entrepreneurs expect to earn on new investments, a rate that Keynes labeled the "marginal efficiency of capital." And the central bank may be impotent: any increase in the money supply that it brings about in an attempt to force down the rate of interest may tend instead to cause a "mass movement into cash" on the part of the rentiers. The relatively high rate of interest, in conjunction with the low marginal efficiency of capital, would then bar the entrepreneurs from calling "to the aid of their enterprises" the wealth of the rentiers (*CW* 7, 218, 135, 172; **4**, 5). The former class therefore could be forced to curtail its investments and reduce its workforce drastically. Consequently, the entire economy could become stuck "in a chronic condition of sub-normal activity" and high unemployment "without any marked tendency either towards recovery or towards complete collapse." Thus it was Keynes' opinion that depression is not just the normal trough of a normal business cycle. It is a condition that, in his "opinion, [is] inevitably associated – with present-day capitalistic individualism" (*CW* 7, 249, 381).

Keynes confessed, therefore, that he "dislike[d]" the capitalist system and that he was "beginning to despise it" (Keynes 1933, 761). And, as intimated above, he blamed the rentiers to a great extent for the economic disaster that had befallen the system in the form of the Great Depression. Because of their excessive propensity to be liquid, "rentier-capitalists" refused to accommodate the financial needs of entrepreneurs. More broadly, Keynes attributed the "psychological attitude to liquidity" to an unwholesome "love of money as a possession," a love that he characterized as "a somewhat disgusting morbidity, one of those semi-criminal, semi-pathological propensities which one hands over with a shudder to the specialists in mental disease." In any event, Keynes concluded "that the duty of ordering the current volume of investment cannot safely be left in [the] private hands" of the rentiers (*CW* **29**, 99; **7**, 247; **9**, 329; **7**, 320).

Thus, one ingredient in Keynes' critique of the financial rentier class is its constraint upon investment and thereby aggregate demand and employment. If money had (a) a small elasticity of production, that is, could be "readily produced" by employing greater amounts of labor to produce more of it in response to an increase in its price, or (b) a high elasticity of substitution, that is, if other commodities could be substituted easily for money as its price rose, then the rentiers would not be able to hold money hostage to the real investment needs of entrepreneurs. But because the opposite is true (that is, because money exhibits low elasticities of production and substitution), the rate of interest tends to be high and downwardly sticky. The interest rate on money thus "rules the roost" because "it is the greatest of these rates that the marginal efficiency of a capital-asset must attain if it is to be newly produced" (*CW* 7, 223, 230). Consequently, the financial rentiers, who control the speculative demand for and (through the banking system, the endogenously created) supply of money, and thereby profoundly affect interest rates, are in a strategic position to dominate and to take advantage of entrepreneurs and workers. In short, the demand for money is not a demand to buy goods or to employ labor (Darity 1995, 27; Darity and Horn 1993). Indeed, by interposing a larger liquidity premium between money and goods/labor, an increase in the demand for money carries as its corollary a decrease in the demand for goods and labor.

A second element in Keynes' critique of finance capital (and defense of industrial capital) was his preference, in the event of the necessity of a choice between them, for inflation over deflation. Although Keynes "objected to both inflation and deflation," he "viewed moderate inflation as the lesser evil" (Dillard 1948, 303), partly because "it is worse, in an impoverished world, to provoke unemployment than to disappoint the *rentier*" (*CW* 4, 36). Inflation, by decreasing the real burden of debt, redistributes wealth from creditors to debtors and thereby from rentiers to entrepreneurs. Historically:

> depreciated money assisted the new men and emancipated them from the dead hand; benefited new wealth at the expense of the old, and armed enterprise against accumulation ... It has been a loosening influence against the rigid distribution of old-won wealth ... By this means each generation can disinherit in part its predecessors' heirs.
>
> (*CW* 4, 9)

By contrast, Keynes excoriated deflation, as he adumbrated in his mid-1920s critique of Winston Churchill's policy of a return to the international gold standard at pre-First World War parity, because it: brought redistributive windfall gains to the rentiers; depressed the "standard of life" of the working class through wage cuts and increased unemployment; and, by raising the real burden of debt, imposed the "dead hand ... [of] the past" on the creation of new wealth, retarded entrepreneurial investment, and caused industrial distress (*CW* 9, 211; 4, 9). Indeed, as Keynes subsequently argued in the *GT*, "the depressing influence on entrepreneurs of their greater burden of [private] debt" from a deflationary regime may at least "partly offset" any benefits from wage cuts. Moreover, if wage- and price-level reductions go too far, "heavily indebted" entrepreneurs "may soon reach the point of insolvency, – with severely adverse effects on investment." In any event, the increase in the real burden of the public debt and of taxation caused by price-level reductions "is likely to prove very adverse to business confidence" (*GT* 1936, 264; Minsky 1975; Elliott 1992). Because rentiers, bankers, and financial capitalists benefit from deflation at the expense of entrepreneurs and workers, their position is basically antagonistic, in Keynes' view, to that of the rest of society.

A third component in Keynes' indictment of finance capital is that it is essentially functionless. As Keynes put it in Chapter 24 of the *GT*:

> interest today rewards no genuine sacrifice, any more than does the rent of land [see note 2]. The owner of capital can obtain interest because capital is scarce, just as the owner of land can obtain rent because land is scarce.
>
> (*CW* 7, 376)

Traditionally, a high rate of interest was justified (as, for example, in Mill 1965 [1848]), Keynes states, by an alleged "necessity of providing a sufficient inducement to save." But this assumes a fully employed economy in which a rise in investment requires a diminution in consumption. If this proposition were analytically and empirically valid, the "growth of capital" would depend "upon the strength of the motive toward individual saving" and thus, "for a large proportion of this growth" we would be "dependent on the savings of the rich out of their superfluity." Additionally, were the presupposition of full employment correct, and investment and thereby full employment were dependent upon the high propensities to save of wealthy rentiers, a fundamental conflict would exist between prosperity and distributive justice, because the "arbitrary and inequitable distribution of wealth and income," together with the "failure to provide for full employment," is one of the two "outstanding faults of the economic society in which we live" (*CW* 7, 372–3, 375).

Happily, however, as long as unemployment exists, capital growth depends "not at all on a low propensity to consume but is, on the contrary, held back by it." Only under full employment is a high propensity to save, by constraining consumption, "conducive to the growth of capital." Until full employment prevails, it is investment which (by raising national income) determines saving, rather than the reverse, and investment "is promoted by a low rate of interest" and a high propensity to consume. Consequently, it is not necessary to bribe the rentiers or to acquiesce to their inequitable ownership of wealth or dysfunctional receipt of interest income. Instead, large-scale increments in the money supply, to foster reductions in interest rates, and redistributive fiscal policy "likely to raise the propensity to consume may prove positively favourable to the growth of capital," and thereby to simultaneous achievement of both full employment and distributive justice (*CW* 7, 372, 373, 375).

In view of these considerations, there was only one solution to the economic problem of depression and unemployment: radical excision of "the rentier aspect of capitalism" from the body economic. The "events which . . . [Keynes was] advocating" with this objective in mind involved the substitution of the state for the rentiers as a provider of investable funds for the entrepreneurs. Thus he recommended that entrepreneurs be supplied with low-cost funds to be obtained from "communal saving[s] through the agency of the State." The state's activities involved in raising these funds and dispensing them to the entrepreneurs, Keynes called "a somewhat comprehensive socialization of investment," which, he said, "will prove the only means of securing an approximation to full employment" (*CW* 7, 376, 378).[6]

Keynes optimistically believed that the successful implementation of government policies, namely, redistributive measures to raise the propensity to consume,[7] robustly expansionary monetary policies to lower interest rates, and the socialization of investment to expand and stabilize public and private investment, would not only enable the attainment of full employment and egalitarian social justice, but would radically modify twentieth-century capitalism's class relations. Through these means, he states, it should be possible to expand the stock of capital to such an extent as to bring expected profit rates down to a "very low figure"; indeed, "approximately to zero in a single generation." If so, returns from investment goods would "just cover their labour-costs of production plus an allowance for risk and the costs of skill and supervision." This "would mean the euthanasia of the rentier, and, consequently, the euthanasia of the cumulative oppressive power of the capitalist to exploit the scarcity-value of capital" (*CW* 7, 220, 375–6).

Keynes thus sees the "rentier aspect of capitalism as a transitional phase which will disappear when it has done its work." This, he declares, is a "most sensible way of gradually getting rid of many of the objectionable features of capitalism." The "gradual disappearance of a rate of return on accumulated wealth" would engender "enormous social changes." Opportunities for "enterprise," "skill," and risk-taking by financiers and entrepreneurs would continue to exist. But accumulated capital would lose its "oppressive power," the "functionless investor would no longer receive a bonus," and systems of taxation could be designed so that financiers "(who are certainly so fond of their craft that their labour could be obtained much cheaper than at present), [could] be harnessed to the service of the community on reasonable terms of reward" (*CW* 7, 221, 376–7).

THE ENTREPRENEURS

Whereas Keynes viewed the rentiers as the villains of the capitalist system, the entrepreneurs, led by the "educated bourgeoisie" (*CW* 9, 297), were, in his opinion, the potential saviors of the economy and society as a whole. To repeat what was stated above, he hailed the "entrepreneur class of capitalists ... [as] the active and constructive element in the whole capitalist society" (*CW* 2, 149). Thus he agreed with H.G. Wells, author of *The World of William Clissold*, that the "forces which are 'to change the laws, customs, rules, and institutions'" dwell among "the great modern business men" as well as in the "bourgeois and the intelligentsia." These groups "carry the seed of all human advancement." But agreeing again with Wells, Keynes stressed that we "must recruit our revolutionaries . . . from . . . amongst the scientists and the great modern businessmen" (*CW* 9, 318, 319, 258, 319).

It seems, therefore, that Keynes divided the entrepreneurs into two groups: the great businessmen on the one hand, and the run-of-the-mill entrepreneurs on the other. Significantly, the former group had shed most of the traditional bourgeois ideology that still clung to the latter. How did this bifurcation of the entrepreneurial class come about?

Superentrepreneurs

According to Keynes, it occurred in an historical process in the course of which a superentrepreneurial function was shaped in a particular institutional mold, namely in that of the *large* "joint stock institutions" (*CW* 9, 289). Keynes put it in this way:

> T[he] trend of joint stock institutions, when they have reached a certain age and size, [is] to approximate to the status of public corporations rather than that of individualistic private enterprise. One of the most interesting and unnoticed developments of recent decades has been the tendency of big enterprise to socialize itself. A point arrives in the growth of the big institution – particularly a big railway or big public utility enterprise, but also a big bank or a big insurance company – at which the owners of the capital, i.e. the shareholders, are almost entirely dissociated from the management, with the result that the direct personal interest of the latter of making of great profit becomes quite secondary. When this stage is reached, the general stability and reputation of the institution are more considered by the management than the maximum of profit for the shareholders.
>
> (*CW* 9, 289)

Keynes viewed this as "a natural line of evolution. The battle of Socialism against unlimited profit is being won in detail hour by hour" in a process of institutional evolution, rather than in revolution (ibid., 290).

Of course, it is the institution of superentrepreneurship that has been socialized. The significance of this phenomenon is that the corporate super-entrepreneurs have, by virtue of their very socialization, become institutionally adequate for entering into partnership with the government for the purpose of effecting a permanent socialization of investment.

It can be argued that the partnership between "the *nuclear state*" of the constitutional government, on the one hand, and the class of enlightened corporate superentrepreneurs, on the other, constituted in Keynes' mind an "*extended state*" that was to engineer, and make permanent, the socialization of investment. "*Planning*" by the institutions of the extended state "was the instrument that Keynes offered as *the* method" for the achievement of this objective (Jensen 1991, 302, 304):

> Let us mean by planning, or national economy [he said in 1932], the problem of the *general* organization of resources as distinct from the *particular* problems of production and distribution which are the province of the individual business technician and engineer. Now the business technician and the engineer … have already carried their improvement to a point at which, if we could take full advantage of them, we should have gone far toward solving the problem of poverty altogether.
>
> (*CW* 21, 87)

Planning by the extended state was the method by which society could, and should, take full advantage of the skills and abilities of the business managers and their engineers. In 1939, Keynes reiterated his conviction that "so much more central planning than we have at present" was needed, "if we are to enjoy prosperity and profits." For the institutionalization of such a "scheme of collective planning," he recommended the establishment of a "National Investment Board" to oversee the allocation of investment and the location of industry (*CW* 21, 492; 20, 475; 21, 591). In all of this, the superentrepreneurs would play a dominant role. In so doing, they would assist in setting the stage on which the ordinary, or run-of-the-mill, entrepreneurs were to perform their acts.

Ordinary entrepreneurs

The much more numerous ordinary entrepreneurs, who manage the "individualistic private enterprise[s]" and the smaller corporations, are still imbued with the bourgeois desire to garner a "maximum [rate] of profit." This rate "depends on the *prospective* yield of capital, and not merely on its current yield" (*CW* 9, 289; 7, 141). That is so because current outlays on capital goods will only "produce results, or potential results, at a comparatively distant, and sometimes at an *indefinitely* distant, date." But the future is "uncertain" in the sense that, for example, "the price of copper and the rate of interest twenty years hence" are uncertain. "About these matters there is no scientific basis on which to form any calculable probability whatever. We simply do not know" (*CW* 14, 113, 114). For this reason, the "facts of the existing situation enter, in a sense disproportionately, into the [ordinary entrepreneurs'] formation of … long-term expectations." In other words, they "take the existing situation and … project it into the future" (*CW* 7, 148).

In the early 1930s, this situation was dismal. Because of large and (at least during the 1920s) growing "*inequality* of the distribution of wealth" and "incomes" (ibid., 372), mass purchasing power had not kept pace with the economy's aggregate capacity to produce final goods and services.[8] One fateful consequence of this was that unsold goods piled up at an accelerating rate in the inventories of the majority of ordinary entrepreneurs. Hence their revenues plummeted. But, as just stated, "facts of the existing situation enter[ed]" into the entrepreneurs' "long-term expectations." Consequently, their marginal efficiencies of capital dropped below the rates of interest at which the rentiers would provide funds. Furthermore, said Keynes, because the "accumulation of capital . . . [is] already larger" than warranted by aggregate demand, the volume of investment necessary to bring about full employment could cause "a growth of capital up to the point where it ceases to be scarce." Thus, as noted earlier, if sufficient investments were made, the marginal efficiency of capital could be brought down "approximately to zero." Such an expansion of investment, however, would not occur in a setting in which the liquidity preference of the rentiers "prevents the rate of interest from being negative." On the contrary, financiers "set a limit much above zero to the practicable decline in the rate of interest" (*CW* 7, 149, 31, 376, 220, 218).

Keynes, in the *GT*, was therefore "sceptical of the success of a merely monetary policy directed towards influencing the rate of interest," especially for the purpose of pulling a market capitalist economy out of a deep depression. An expansionary monetary policy, although a "great aid to recovery and, probably, a necessary condition of it," is likely to be insufficient for this purpose. The combination of a "fickle" and collapsed marginal efficiency of capital and high and downwardly sticky interest rates can create a depression which "can scarcely be corrected, so as to secure a satisfactory rate of investment, by any practicable reduction in the rate of interest." Moreover, the central banks in societies such as Great Britain and the United States were on the verge of losing "effective control over the rate of interest" because of the high, if not "virtually absolute," rentiers' "liquidity-preference." That is to say, financiers often preferred "cash to holding a debt" which would yield only that very low rate of interest which the monetary authority strove to establish (*CW* 7, 164, 207, 316, 319, 378).

It is precisely because it is "unlikely" that a purely monetary policy designed to reduce interest rates "will be sufficient *by itself*" to achieve an "optimum rate of investment" that a vigorous and radically expansionary fiscal program is also needed. Concretely, the state, partly because of the anti-social behavior of functionless rentiers and partly because of cyclically unstable and secularly low expected profit rates, must take "an ever greater responsibility for directly organizing investment." Consequently, as suggested above, "a somewhat comprehensive socialization of investment will prove the only means of securing an approximation to full employment" (*CW* 7, 164, 378; emphasis added).

At the same time, Keynes was also somewhat skeptical of a purely fiscal policy, even of the efficacy of debt-financed public works by themselves, without the accompanying stimulus of monetary expansion and lower interest rates. In his discussion of the potential multiplier effects of increased "public works" based on "loan expenditures" (*CW* **7**, 128, 179)[9] Keynes cites two reasons why expanded public expenditures need to be accompanied by expansionary monetary policy:

(i) The method of financing the policy and the increased working cash, required by the increased employment and the associated rise of prices, may have the effect of increasing the rate of interest and so retarding investment in other directions, unless the monetary authority takes steps to the contrary; whilst, at the same time, the increased cost of capital goods will reduce their marginal efficiency to the private investor, and this will require an actual *fall* in the rate of interest to offset it.

(ii) With the confused psychology which often prevails, the Government programme may, through the effect on "confidence", increase liquidity preference or diminish the marginal efficiency of capital, which, again, may retard other investment unless measures [including, presumably, an expanded money supply] are taken to offset it.

Thus, temporary loan-financed public works, without an accompanying expansion in the money supply, would at best have a (relatively) small and possibly only temporary effect. On the one hand, a larger money supply is needed to elicit lower interest rates (or at least to minimize their increase) as public and private investment expand. On the other, an expanded money supply is necessary to channel funds to entrepreneurs to stimulate private investment to rise along with increased public investment. Otherwise, temporary loan-financed public works would have only a short-term expansionary effect on income and employment. In this event, public-works spending would be in the nature of pump-priming, but the pump would go dry again after all the public works were completed because there would be no self-sustaining spread effect from the public to the private sector. Hence the multiplier could shift into reverse gear.

In Keynes' opinion, ordinary entrepreneurship, in alliance with the state, was the only private institution that could shift the multiplier into a high-speed forward gear.[10] In the first place, the ordinary entrepreneurial firms are efficient. The entrepreneurs' "self-interest . . . determine[s] what in particular is produced, in what proportion the factors of production will be combined to produce it, and how the value of the final product will be distributed among them." In other words, Keynes saw "no reason to suppose that the existing system seriously misemploys the factors of production which are in use." It is in "determining the volume, not the direction, of actual employment that the existing system has broken down." And it has broken down, not because of any anti-social act on the part of the entrepreneurs, but because the rentiers became frustrated in their efforts to exploit the vanishing "scarcity-value of capital" (*CW* **7**, 379, 376). Hence they brought almost

119

to a complete standstill the transmission belt that in the nineteenth century used to carry their funds to entrepreneurs.

Second, if the extended state were successful in providing ordinary entrepreneurs with sufficient funds at a cost that would permit them to exploit their efficiency up to the point where it generated an acceptable spread between the rate of interest and the marginal efficiency of capital, the entrepreneurs could be relied upon to provide that steady stream of autonomous spending that temporary public spending could not deliver. In other words, when the latent energies and capabilities of entrepreneurs are awakened by means of the socialization of investment, they, and society at large, will be able to free themselves from the "cumulative oppressive power" of the rentiers (CW 7, 376). Once this is an accomplished fact, Keynes was convinced that the economy would enter a full-employment path leading to "its destination of economic bliss"; a blissful state in which the "economic problem . . . of want and poverty and the economic struggle between classes and nations" would finally be solved (CW 9, 331, xviii).

Thus Keynes was convinced that, with the aid of the extended state, ordinary entrepreneurs were the only class that would be able to lift the economy out of the depression, thereby preventing it from entering the danger zone of the "authoritarian state systems" that are capable of solving the "problem of unemployment at the expense of efficiency and freedom." Hence he hailed the common entrepreneurs as the heroes of the economy and the saviors of "individualism" and "freedom" because the socialization of investment would empower them to be instrumental in bringing about an economic and political "democracy" that would be both "wise and sensible" (CW 7, 380, 381; 22, 155).

THE WORKERS

Among the three major classes, it was the working class that suffered most from poverty in the depression decade of the 1930s. In Keynes' opinion, this "abject poverty," which "consume[d] the possibilities of life" and made "crumbles" of "civilization," had been caused by the perverse "working of the motives" of the rentiers and entrepreneurs, especially the former. Their motives worked perversely because, whereas they "should lead to decisions and acts of will, [that are] necessary to put in movement the resources and technical means we already have," these motives led to acts that have precisely the opposite effect, namely that of stopping the flow and employment of many of the available resources and technical means (CW 21, 189; 9, 335).

Thus it was largely workers that Keynes had in mind when he referred to the "paradox of poverty in the midst of plenty," including, but not confined to, the "paradox . . . to be found in 250,000 building operatives out of work in Great Britain [in the early 1930s], when more houses are our greatest material need" (CW 22, 108; 7, 30; 9, 336).

There is no doubt, therefore, that Keynes' sympathy and "feelings ... [were] with the workers," as he put it in a different context (*CW* **19**(2), 532).[11] His feelings were based on the conviction that the institutions of capitalism had placed workers in an inferior social and economic position. The society of the age "which came to an end in August 1914" was "so framed," he said, "as to throw a great part of the increased income into the control of the class least likely to consume it," namely the property-owning class. The working class, on the other hand, received such a small part of the national income that its members were forced "to forgo ... the comforts of life" (*CW* **2**, 6, 11, 13). "It was precisely the *inequality* of the distribution of wealth," according to Keynes, "which made possible those vast accumulations of fixed wealth and of capital improvements which distinguished that age [up to the First World War] from all others" (*CW* **2**, 10). Why did the workers acquiesce? Because

> the labouring classes accepted from ignorance or powerlessness, or were compelled, persuaded, or cajoled by custom, convention, authority, and the well-established order of society into accepting, a situation in which they could call their own very little of the cake that they and nature and the capitalists were cooperating to produce.
>
> (*CW* **2**, 11–12)

During the nineteenth century, Keynes states in the *GT*, "employers were strong enough to prevent the wage-unit from rising much faster than the efficiency of production." Wages and working-class consumption were also constrained by the fact that employment was "substantially below full employment" (although "not so intolerably below it as to provoke revolutionary changes") (*CW* **7**, 308). The propensity to consume of the capitalist class, notably the rentiers, was also constrained by habit and culture. Saving by the wealthy was both "duty" and "virtue," and economic growth through capital accumulation was "the object of true religion." The "main justification of the capitalist system," with its attendant great disparities in wealth, lay in the presupposition that the capitalist class had a duty to act *de facto* as the guardian of civilized progress, much of the fruits of which was "never to be consumed" (*CW* **2**, 10, 11). In principle, capitalists' benefits from economic growth were expected to take substantially the form of the enjoyment of the power provided by unequal accumulated wealth as opposed to luxurious consumption.

Thus, the patterns of saving and consumption and the social class relations of nineteenth-century capitalism rested on highly unstable conventions and a special cultural milieu subject to potential disintegration. "It was not natural," Keynes observes in *The Economic Consequences of the Peace* (*CW* **2**), "for a population, of whom so few enjoyed the comforts of life, to accumulate so hugely." The First World War "disclosed the possibility of consumption to all and the vanity of abstinence to many." The "bluff" or deception upon which prewar social class relations rested was thereby revealed. The working class, he states, "may be no longer willing to forgo so largely, and the capitalist classes, no longer confident of the future, may seek to enjoy more fully their liberties of consumption so long as they last, and thus precipitate the hour of their confiscation" (*CW* **2**, 13).

Although the First World War had thus "disclosed the possibility of consumption to all" (ibid.), unemployment in the 1920s deprived large numbers of workers of that possibility. Keynes observed in 1929, for example, that "one tenth or more of the working population of this country have been unemployed for eight years – a fact unprecedented in our history. The number of insured persons counted . . . as out of work has never been less than one million since . . . 1923. Today (April 1929) 1,140,000 work-people are unemployed." Unemployment increased dramatically in the early 1930s. It was this malaise that prompted Keynes to write *The General Theory* of 1936 in order to show that it might "be possible by a right analysis of the problem to cure the disease" (*CW* **9**, 92; **7**, 381). Thus, when he was in the process of completing his *magnum opus*, Keynes wrote to George Bernard Shaw that he, Keynes, "believe[d] [him]self to be writing a book on economic theory which will largely revolutionize . . . the way the world thinks about economic problems." And he concluded: "When my new theory has been duly assimilated and mixed with politics and feelings and passions, I can't predict what the final upshot will be in its effects on action and affairs. But there will be a great change" (*CW* **28**, 42).

A major character trait that Keynes admired was "an unselfish and enthusiastic spirit, which loves the ordinary man." Not shying away from admitting that he was imbued with the same spirit, Keynes labeled himself a "humanitarian" who worked for "an advance towards economic equality greater than any which we have had in recent times" (*CW* **9**, 211, 428, 368). Hence he described himself as a "leveller": "I want to mould a society in which most of the existing inequalities and causes of inequality are removed," he said (Keynes, in Skidelsky 1992, 233). And then he asked rhetorically in a much-quoted statement:

> Ought I, then, to join the Labour Party? Superficially that is . . . attract-ive. But looked at closer, there are great difficulties. To begin with, it is a class party, and the class is not my class. If I am going to pursue sectional interests at all, I shall pursue my own. When it comes to the class struggles as such, my local and personal patriotisms, like those of every one else, except certain unpleasant zealous ones, are attached to my own surroundings. I can be influenced by what seems to me to be justice and good sense; but the *class* war will find me on the side of the educated *bourgeoisie*.
>
> (*CW* **9**, 297)

As Robert Skidelsky (1992, 234) has pointed out, one of Keynes' criti-cisms of the Labour Party was directed toward its "anti-elitism." Moreover,

Keynes argued that "doctrinaire State Socialism . . . is in fact, little better than a dusty survival of a plan to meet the problems of fifty years ago, based on a misunderstanding of what someone said a hundred years ago." On the other hand, Keynes did not criticize socialism "because it seeks to engage men's altruistic impulses in the service of society, or because it departs from *laissez-faire*, or because it takes away from a man's natural liberty to make a million, or because it has courage for bold experiments." "All these things I applaud," he said (*CW* 9, 290–1).

And Keynes was convinced that all these things, and more, could only be achieved if an elite of educated superentrepreneurs and intellectuals were put in charge of the organs of the extended state. Especially, unemployment could, and would, be abolished through the elite's socialization of investment. It was this small elite of "revolutionaries," as he called them (*CW* 9, 319), that Keynes had in mind when he included himself in the *educated* bourgeoisie. Once it is realized that it was these kinds of bourgeois "revolutionaries" with whom he identified himself, the following declaration of his is not in conflict with his above-quoted confession that the class war would find him on the side of the bourgeoisie:

> I am sure that I am less conservative in my inclinations than the average Labour voter; I fancy that I have played in my mind with the possibilities of greater social changes than come within the present philosophies of, let us say, Mr. Sidney Webb, Mr. Thomas, or Mr. Wheatley. The republic of my imagination lies on the extreme left of celestial space.
>
> (*CW* 9, 308–9)

As Keynes put it in 1937, this republic informed him that

> [t]he natural evolution should be towards a decent level of consumption for every one; and, when it is high enough, towards the occupation of our energies in the non-economic interests of our lives. Thus we need to be slowly reconstructing our social system with these ends in view.
>
> (*CW* 21, 393)

CONCLUSIONS

This last observation leads to several final conclusions pertaining to Keynes' position on social classes. First, although he did not sympathize with the Labour Party, it was those who voted for the party's candidates whom Keynes identified as the chief beneficiaries of such a development.[12] Second, in view of what has been said above, one must agree with Sir Austin Robinson's characterization of Keynes "as the perfect 'do-gooder', identifying the things that the world most needs to have done and using all his brains and persuasion to get them done" (Robinson 1975, 21–2). Third, Keynes believed that in some respects, the implications of his theories (in the *GT*, but also elsewhere) were "moderately conservative" and, because of his eschewal of government ownership of the means of production, were opposed to what he called "State Socialism" (*CW* 7, 377, 378). At the same time, in some ways, notably in his vision of the transcendence of the rentier phase of capitalism, his commitment to a "somewhat comprehensive socialization of investment," and his strong egalitarian bent, Keynes' position on capitalism's long-run prospects was closer to social democracy than to old-style, *laissez-faire* capitalism. Indeed, in at least one prominent recent interpretation (O'Donnell 1989, 293), Keynes' "ultimate goal" is characterized as "a decidedly non-capitalist utopia, a form of society with greater similarities to communist or left-wing utopias than to ideal societies built on capitalist or free market norms."

Finally, in a twentieth-century analogue to David Ricardo (Milgate and Stimson 1991), Keynes presupposed that a mutually agreeable and workable political alliance could be forged among the working class, the entrepreneurial component of the capitalist class, and the managerial and bureaucratic elite in business and government, led, as noted earlier, by a "class" or stratum of "educated bourgeoisie." "Despite their significant conflicts and differences," each would "find it advantageous to support" the excision of the rentiers, the surviving "institutions of a [socially reformed] capitalist market economy and the associated policies of a government devoted to fostering material prosperity and economic growth" (Elliott 1994, 517).[13]

At the close of the *GT*, Keynes asks whether his particular variant of "individualism," "purged of its defects and its abuses," can indeed serve as the "best safeguard of personal liberty," and thus save a middle way between liberal capitalism and socialism from the "destruction of existing economic forms in their entirety" through the advance of communism and dictatorship no less than from the scourge of unemployment. Keynes' moderately optimistic answer hinges strategically on the belief that the "ideas of economists and political philosophers ... are more powerful than is commonly understood." Not only do the ideas of the intelligentsia have sufficient "roots in the motives which govern the evolution of political society." Over time, they even outweigh "vested interests," the "power" of which is "vastly exaggerated compared with the gradual encroachment of ideas ... [S]oon or late, it is ideas, not vested interests, which are dangerous for good or evil." "Indeed the world is ruled by little else" (*CW* 7, 380, 383–4). It was this conviction which permitted Keynes to suppose that he, and his "class" of like-minded intellectuals and public servants, could actually function as "savior" (Skidelsky 1992) of the possibility of liberal individualist civilization.

124

NOTES

1 Unless otherwise indicated, references to Keynes' works are to *The Collected Writings of John Maynard Keynes* (Keynes 1971–89), abbreviated *CW*, followed by volume and page numbers. Some volumes are published in two parts. For example, volume 19 is split into Part 1 and Part 2. Hence when a reference is made to Part 1, the part number is entered after the volume number thus (*CW* **19** (1)).

2 Keynes viewed the interest paid to financiers as a rent-like "bonus" (*CW* **7**, 376) akin to David Ricardo's concept of "rent of land . . . [as] that compensation, which is paid to the owner of land for the use of its original and indestructible powers" (Ricardo 1951 [1821], 68–9). Rent is, therefore, an unearned income in that it is not a payment for any effort, or sacrifice, on the part of the landlord.

3 Keynes viewed the rentiers as unproductive because he did not accord them the status of a factor of production. He "sympathise[d], therefore, with the pre-classical doctrine that everything is *produced* by *labour*, aided by . . . technique, by natural resources which are free or cost a rent according to their scarcity or abundance, and by the results of past labour, embodied in assets, which also command a price according to their scarcity or abundance. It is preferable to regard labour, including, of course, the personal services of the entrepreneur and his assistants, as the sole factor of production" (*CW* **7**, 213–14).

4 John Stuart Mill was one of the first economists to point out that the capitalist class had been bifurcated into owners who do not control private enterprises and managers who control but do not own these enterprises. In Mill's words, the "administration of a joint stock association is . . . administration by hired servants." Although they are "supposed to superintend the management," the members of the "board of directors" do not do so because they "have no pecuniary interest in the good working of the concern" because "the shares they individually hold . . . are always a very small part of the capital of the association, and . . . but a small part of the fortunes of the directors themselves." Moreover, they divide "their time with many other occupations." Consequently, the business is "the principal concern of no one except those who are hired to carry it out" (Mill 1965 [1848], 137). Alfred Marshall accepted Mill's proposition in statements that amount to a paraphrasing of Mill's original statement. Thus Marshall observed that when "a private firm is thrown into joint stock form . . . the ownership of capital is effectively divorced from its control: so that those, who are in control, have not nearly the same pecuniary interest in its economic and efficient working as they would have, if they owned the business themselves" (Marshall 1919, 317). "To the Managers and their assistants is left a great part of the work of engineering the business, and the whole of the work of superintending it: but they are not required to bring any capital into it." Thus, "in all these matters the great body of the shareholders of a joint-stock company are . . . almost powerless" (Marshall 1961, 302, 303). The *locus classicus* of the distinction between "industry" and "finance" in the context of separation between ownership and managerial control is, of course, Thorstein Veblen (1942 [1919], 304). Although Keynes does not make as much out of the distinction as Veblen did, it is certainly germane to characterizing his work, especially in light of his discussion (in *GT*, ch. 12) on the impact of the modern corporation.

5 Keynes' view of the working-class propensity to consume as relatively stable is reinforced by his correspondence with James E. Meade in 1943. In a letter to Keynes on April 19 (*CW* **27**, 317–18), Meade states that because of difficulties in controlling investment, public measures "to prevent violent fluctuations in national income" may need to include "a tax policy which stimulates (or restricts), say, personal expenditure." In his reply to Meade, on April 25 (*CW* **27**, 319–20), Keynes demurs. First, he doubted whether "short-term variations in consumption

125

are in fact practicable" because "people have established standards of life. Nothing will upset them more than to be subject to pressure constantly to vary them up and down." Thus, a tax cut for "an indefinitely short period might have very limited effects in stimulating consumption." There is "a huge time lag," for example, in the response of consumption to changes in income taxes, and "short-run changes are most inconvenient." Second, "it is not nearly so easy politically and to the common man to put across the encouragement of consumption in bad times as it is to induce the encouragement of capital expenditure" because investment would, "partially, if not, wholly, pay for itself."

6 Keynes never specified the precise meaning of "socialization of investment" (see Jensen 1984, 1991, 1994). It did *not* mean social ownership of the means of production, which Keynes characterized as unnecessary rather than inefficacious, partly because of the *de facto* socialization of large, quasi-public enterprises, such as the London port and dock authorities. Nor did it mean (simply) "Keynesian" postwar counter-cyclical monetary and fiscal policy or that Keynes maintained one position concerning investment policy before, in, and after the *GT*. Broadly speaking, "socialization of investment" presupposes the stabilization of private investment at a high level through a vigorously expansionary monetary policy and downward manipulation of long-term interest rates. However, as noted in the text of this paper (p. 118), Keynes was skeptical concerning the efficacy of a "merely monetary policy" toward influencing the rate of interest and thereby investment and employment. It "seems unlikely," he stated in the *GT*, that the "influence of banking policy on the rate of interest will be sufficient by itself to determine an optimum rate of investment." Therefore, the "duty of ordering the volume of investment cannot safely be left in private hands." Keynes expected "to see the State, which is in a position to calculate the marginal efficiency of capital goods on long views and on the basis of the general social advantage, taking an ever greater responsibility for directly organizing investment." Thus, the socialization of investment would supplement private investment by public-works projects and control the level (and to some extent direction) of investment by quasi-public corporations (*CW* 7, 164, 320, 378). The net result of these measures, hopefully, would be the establishment of a new convention character-ized by the expectation of full employment rather than unemployment (see Bateman 1994).

7 In the *GT*, Keynes supplemented the socialization of investment (and the "eutha-nasia of the rentier") with social control over the propensity to consume. "Whilst aiming at a socially controlled rate of investment with a view to a progressive decline in the marginal efficiency of capital, I should support at the same time all sorts of policies for increasing the propensity to consume. For it is unlikely full employment can be maintained, whatever we may do about investment, with the existing propensity to consume." Only "experience can show how far the common will, embodied in the policy of the State, ought to be directed to increasing and supplementing the inducement to invest; and how far it is safe to stimulate the average propensity to consume, without forgoing our aim of depriving capital of its scarcity-value within one or two generations" (*CW* 7, 325, 377).

8 As Keynes explained it, the maldistribution of income had engendered a rise in the "savings propensities" of the "wealthier members" of society, largely the rentiers, at the same time as it caused a "falling off . . . [of] the propensity to consume" on the part of the multitude of wage earners. The result was a reduction of the "*collective* propensity*" to consume for the "community as a whole." Hence, said Keynes, "I have called repeated attention to this factor [the maldistribution of incomes] in my book," that is, the *GT* (*CW* 7, 31, 173; **14**, 271).

9 Peter Clarke (1988, 305) has stated that there is "nothing" in the *GT* "on fiscal methods and demand management, nor on deficit budgeting." Keynes' brief discussion of the multiplier effects of public works cited in the text and his ensuing discussion (*CW* 7, 128–9n) of "loan expenditures" render this claim a bit overstated, although essentially on target. Keynes clearly regarded loan-financed public works as superior to public spending financed by taxation, but inferior to an expansionary fiscal policy accompanied by a robustly expansionary monetary policy.

10 The moral of this story is that, for Keynes, (a) government investment in public infrastructures cannot viably be merely temporary (that is, purely counter-cyclical), but must be maintained "permanently" in order to keep income and employment permanently close to full-employment levels. However, (b) the magnitude of public works (and other kinds of public expenditure) required to accomplish sustained full employment varies inversely with the extent to which private investment is stimulated by a bold expansion in the money supply and low interest rates, that is, in terms of socio-economic class relations, the degree to which the "euthanasia of the rentier" is actually achieved. Thus, neither expansionary monetary nor expansionary fiscal policy, by itself, is sufficient to supersede the two "outstanding faults" of contemporary society, that is, involuntary unemployment and the social injustice of its "arbitrary and inequitable" wealth and income distribution (*CW* 7, 372).

11 The context in which Keynes made this observation was the General Strike of 1926. When the coal miners refused to accept a cut in wages, they were locked out by the owners in the spring of 1926, whereupon the "Trades Union Council . . . supported them with a General Strike" that collapsed after nine days. Keynes could not, however, "be stirred so as to feel the T.U.C. as deliberate enemies of the community, who must be crushed before they are spoken with" (*CW* 19 (2), 530, 532).

12 Keynes' critique of rentiers and financial capitalism and defense of industrial capitalism did not make him an advocate of working-class interests *per se*. For example, he did not propound the social democratic strategy of a high wage economy, and (in Keynes 1930, 110–24) warned that wage rate increases, by raising costs, could well have adverse effects on Great Britain's balance of payments. On the other hand, his sharp critique of the inefficacy of wage cuts as a remedy for depression and mass unemployment, his advocacy of fiscal measures to foster upward shifts in the propensity to consume and significant reductions in wealth and income inequality, and his radical strategies for full employment, if implemented, could yield substantial material benefits for workers, including the likelihood of higher wages.

13 The implications of such a political alliance for the functioning of democracy and the state, as well as the evolution of Keynes' thought on public policy, will be examined in a separate paper.

REFERENCES

Bateman, Robert W. (1994) "Rethinking the Keynesian revolution," in John B. Davis (ed.), *The State of Interpretation of Keynes*, Boston, MA: Kluwer.

Clarke, Peter (1988) *The Keynesian Revolution in the Making, 1924–1936.* Oxford: Clarendon Press.

Darity, William Jr (1995) "Keynes' political philosophy: the Gesell connection," *Eastern Economic Journal* 21 (1): 27–41.

Darity, William Jr and Horn, Bobie L. (1993) "Rational expectations and Keynes' *General Theory,*" *Research in the History of Economic Thought and Methodology* 11: 17–47.
Dillard, Dudley (1948) *The Economics of John Maynard Keynes,* New York: Prentice-Hall.
Elliott, John E. (1992) "John Maynard Keynes on the inefficacy of wage cuts as anti-depressionary strategy," in Warren J. Samuels (ed.), *Annual Research in the History of Economic Thought and Methodology,* vol. 10, Greenwich: JAI Press.
Elliott, John E. (1994) Review of *Ricardian Politics,* by Murray Milgate and Shannon C. Stimson, *History of Political Economy* 26 (Fall): 515–18.
Jensen, Hans E. (1983) "J.M. Keynes as a Marshallian," *Journal of Economic Issues* 17 (March): 67–94.
Jensen, Hans E. (1984) "Some aspects of the social economics of John Maynard Keynes," *International Journal of Social Economics* 11(3/4): 72–91.
Jensen, Hans E. (1991) "J.M. Keynes's theory of the state as a path to his social economics of reform in *The General Theory,*" *Review of Social Economy* 49 (Fall): 292–316.
Jensen, Hans E. (1994) "Aspects of J.M. Keynes's vision and conceptualized reality," in John B. Davis (ed.), *The State of Interpretation of Keynes,* Norwell, MA: Kluwer.
Keynes, John Maynard (1930) "The question of high wages," *Political Quarterly* 1(1), 110–24.
Keynes, John Maynard (1933) "National self-sufficiency," *Yale Review* 22 (June): 755–69.
Keynes, John Maynard (1936), *The General Theory of Employment, Interest and Money,* London: Macmillan. (See also *Collected Writings,* vol. 7.)
Keynes, John Maynard (1971–89) *The Collected Writings of John Maynard Keynes,* London: Macmillan. The cited volumes are:
2 (1971) *The Economic Consequences of the Peace.*
4 (1971) *A Tract on Monetary Reform.*
5 (1971) *A Treatise on Money,* vol. 1: *The Pure Theory of Money.*
7 (1973) *The General Theory of Employment, Interest and Money.* (See also Keynes 1936.)
9 (1972) *Essays in Persuasion.*
14 (1973) *The General Theory and After. Part II: Defence and Development,* ed. Donald Moggridge.
19 Part 1 (1981) *Activities, 1922–1929: The Return to Gold and Industrial Policy,* ed. Donald Moggridge.
19 Part 2 (1981) *Activities 1922–1929: The Return to Gold and Industrial Policy,* ed. Donald Moggridge.
20 (1981) *Activities, 1921–1931: Rethinking Employment and Unemployment Politics,* ed. Donald Moggridge.
21 (1982) *Activities, 1931–1939: World Crises and Policies in Britain and America,* ed. Donald Moggridge.
22 (1978) *Activities, 1939–1945: Internal War Finance,* ed. Donald Moggridge.
27 (1973) *Activities, 1940–1946: Shaping the Post-war World: Employment and Commodities,* ed. Donald Moggridge.
28 (1982) *Social, Political and Literary Writings,* ed. Donald Moggridge.
29 (1979) *The General Theory and After: A Supplement,* ed. Donald Moggridge.
Marshall, Alfred (1919) *Industry and Trade,* London: Macmillan.
Marshall, Alfred (1961) *Principles of Economics,* vol. 1: *Text,* 9th (variorum) edn with annotations by C.W. Guillebaud, London: Macmillan.
Milgate, Murray and Stimson, Shannon C. (1991) *Ricardian Politics,* Princeton, NJ: Princeton University Press.
Mill, John Stuart (1965 [1848]) *Principles of Political Economy,* Books I–II, ed. J. M.

Robson. Vol. 2 of the *Collected Works of John Stuart Mill,* Toronto: University of Toronto Press.

Minsky, Hyman P. (1975) *John Maynard Keynes,* New York: Columbia University Press.

O'Donnell, R. M. (1989) *Keynes: Philosophy, Economics and Politics,* New York: St Martin's Press.

Ricardo, David (1951 [1821]) *On the Principles of Political Economy and Taxation,* ed. Piero Sraffa with the collaboration of M. H. Dobb. Vol. 1 of *The Works and Correspondence of David Ricardo,* Cambridge: Cambridge University Press.

Robinson, Sir Austin (1975) "A personal view," in Milo Keynes (ed.), *Essays on John Maynard Keynes,* Cambridge: Cambridge University Press, 9–23.

Schumpeter, Joseph A. (1951) *Ten Great Economists from Marx to Keynes,* New York: Oxford University Press.

Schumpeter, Joseph A. (1954) *History of Economic Analysis,* New York: Oxford University Press.

Skidelsky, Robert (1992) *The Economist as Saviour.* Vol. 2 of *John Maynard Keynes,* London: Macmillan.

Veblen, Thorstein (1942 [1919]) *The Place of Science in Modern Civilization, and other Essays,* New York: Viking Press.

8

HICKS AND LINDAHL ON MONETARY INSTABILITY

Elasticity of price expectations versus elasticity of interest expectations

Domenica Tropeano[1]

INTRODUCTION

The aim of this paper is to compare Hicks' and Lindahl's views on stability in economies with inside money. This comparison is fruitful since they share a different approach to the problem from that which prevailed in economic debates in the postwar period. In Keynesian macromodels with money the existence and stability of equilibrium was either simply assumed or demonstrated by relying on some real balance effect mechanism following Patinkin's work (*Money, Interest and Prices*).

The issue re-emerged in the 1980s in Walrasian market-clearing models (see Grandmont 1983; Hahn 1988) and in Keynesian macromodels with money and expectations, where money was modelled as inside money. These themes, which were fashionable in the 1920s and 1930s, have since come to the forefront of economic debate once again. The current debate has largely recognized Hicks' early contribution, particularly *Value and Capital* (1946), whereas Lindahl's ideas have been largely ignored. In what follows I wish to show that Hicks' main tool in dealing with the stability issue in a dynamic economy with money, namely, the notion of elasticity of price expectations, had already been developed by Lindahl in 1929, perhaps following Wicksell. It is highly probable that the Wicksellian cumulative process was behind this notion of both authors.[2]

Hicks' treatment of stability in the first part of *Value and Capital* has been widely studied by general equilibrium theorists. The issue of the relation between his theory of stability and the criteria later developed by Samuelson and by Arrow and Debreu has been examined in several works (see, for a brief summary, Collard 1993, 335, and for a detailed theoretical analysis, Hands 1994). The third part of *Value and Capital*, which deals with the temporary equilibrium of the whole system and with the link between temporary equilibria, has not received the same attention. Collard (1993, 337) argues that the device Hicks invented to deal with this problem, the elasticity of price expectations, was a little too mechanical. Hahn (1988) argues instead that this notion entails the revision of price expectations in the light of observed prices of previous weeks and is similar in this regard to the notion of learning in market-clearing models with no intrinsic uncertainty, where prices can be considered parametric. He builds a simple model to show that elasticity matters for stability when expectations on prices are not parametric but the action of one agent leads to a change in price that affects the agent. He deals with the output decision of a firm which forms conjectures on future receipts and therefore future prices. This implies a departure from Hicks' original assumption of a perfectly competitive economy. There is, however, another important change with respect to the third part of *Value and Capital*. The elasticity in Hahn's model matters because it affects entrepreneurs' decisions on future outputs whereas in *Value and Capital* it was important because of the possibility of intertemporal substitution in consumption in accordance with the competitive assumption. Lindahl uses instead the elasticity notion in the same framework that Hahn describes, deals with the entrepreneurs' decision during a cumulative process, but explicitly departs from Wicksell's story by allowing capital accumulation in an uncertain environment.[3] In his analysis prices are not taken as given by the firm but, on the contrary, expected prices affect capital decisions. Intertemporal substitution in consumption is not considered a source of possible instability whereas another mechanism previously mentioned by Hicks in the first part of *Value and Capital* is taken into consideration. Higher prices may raise consumption instead of lowering it because they cause a redistribution of income in favour of capitalists, who are supposed to have a higher propensity to consume with respect to other classes.

Moreover, in the first part of his *Studies*, written in 1939, he explicitly interprets Hicks' notion of elasticity as a learning process, and stresses that the theory of expectations formation underlying it is not necessarily an adaptive expectations mechanism.

Elasticity is defined as the ratio between the expected change in price with respect to the base point and the current price with respect to the same base point. Hicks himself wrote that elasticity was likely to increase with the length of the period. Divergences between expected and realized prices could be neglected in the short run but their sum over a long period would matter.

Lindahl used the same tools in a way that is more similar to Hahn (1988), allowing price expectations and their revisions through time to affect entrepreneurs' decisions both on short-run output and desired capital. The contribution that distinguishes him from both Hicks (1946) and Hahn (1988) is his introduction of capital accumulation and the analysis of income effects. The purpose of this paper is to show how these different settings of the problem led to different conclusions concerning the likely sources of instability in a monetary economy and to different opinions on the possible remedies.

While an economy with flexible prices is the starting point for both economists, Hicks retains this assumption throughout the book, whereas Lindahl derives the motion of quantities from the failure of the price mechanism to clear the market due to the lack of homogeneity between agents and to problems of information.

HICKS' VIEW ON MONETARY INSTABILITY IN *VALUE AND CAPITAL*

The starting point of *Value and Capital* is a search for the existence and stability of equilibrium in a flexprice model.

The research begins by considering disturbances in a single market neglecting expectations. In a single market both existence and stability will be ensured if the excess demand curve is negatively sloped. This condition will be satisfied if there is some degree of substitution among goods and if income effects do not matter in the aggregate. Income effects behave in this way if agents are identical as the theory of general equilibrium assumes they are (see Hicks 1946, 66). Even if agents were different the final outcome would not change if the substitution effect and the income effect went in the same direction.

The most important part of the book is that which deals with the temporary equilibrium of the whole system (see Hicks 1946, chs 20–23).

Hicks laid the foundations for these later chapters by studying in earlier chapters (chs 15–19) the effects of different elasticities of price expectations on the planned supply of output by entrepreneurs and on planned consumption. In Chapter 16 he studies the effects of different assumptions on price expectations, *ceteris paribus*, holding the interest rate constant; in Chapter 17 he studies what happens if price expectations are unchanged but current or expected interest rates change. The same procedure is used in Chapter 18 when dealing with the consumption plan.

The definition of elasticity of expectations which Hicks works with is: The elasticity of a particular person's expectations of the price of commodity X as the ratio of the proportional rise in expected future prices of X to the proportional rise in its current price (see Hicks 1946, 205). This is not a mechanical rule, as the author himself explains; when the elasticity is greater than unity we can imagine that people will recognize a trend by looking at changes in current prices and extrapolating; a process of learning would happen in this case. The value of the elasticity will be negative if they make the opposite kind of guess, interpreting the change as the culminating point of a fluctuation (Hicks 1946, 205). In this case, we can imagine that they know the equilibrium value of the variable price and foresee that any value above or below this level will be only temporary since forces inside the system will re-establish equilibrium. A comparison with the literature on speculative markets could be attempted. The first case would be similar to destabilizing expectations; the second to stabilizing ones.

As I will argue later, the same idea about expectations is contained in Lindahl's works before the publication of *Value and Capital* (see Lindahl 1939, Part I). The main difference is that, unlike Hicks, he does not rule out the possibility that "a change in the current price of X may affect to a different extent the prices of X expected to rule at different future dates" and, above all, that "it may affect the expected future prices of other commodities and factors" (Hicks 1949, 205).

The case with unit elasticity is the limit between stability and instability. If a change in one price occurs, the result will be a sort of imperfect stability (ibid., 254). If the elasticity is greater than one, the likely result will be total instability since no opportunity for intertemporal substitution is available (ibid., 255).[4]

What Lindahl tries to do through his very confused example, which takes the cumulative process as the standard case, in the second part of the *Studies* and in the Swedish book "The Means of Monetary Policy" (1930), Hicks does in Chapters 23 and 24 of *Value and Capital*, which deal respectively with the *accumulation of capital* and *the trade cycle*. In Chapter 23, he analyzes the differences in the speed of adjustment of output and income to expected changes in prices and interest rates and the effects of these prices on the development of the price level. This is not related, however, to the previous discussion of the microeconomic behavior of entrepreneurs and the elasticity of price expectations (Hicks 1946, 203–26).

In particular, he does not consider the interaction of prices and quantities, which he intended to study later by using the stock-flow approach (see Hamouda 1990). This would also have been possible within the temporary equilibrium approach by taking into account the results at the end of the period, however long it was, and by linking planned output to the integral of price increase over the period and to the expected change in the interest rate in the next period.

LINDAHL ON MONETARY INSTABILITY

The effect of price expectations on planned supply: the cumulative process

Both Hicks and Lindahl take Wicksell's cumulative process as the starting point for their descriptions of the emergence of instability in monetary economies.

However, Lindahl's reading of the process differs from that of Hicks, since he takes into account the effects of the lowering of the monetary rate of interest on the capital structure according to the Austrian capital theory, and on the new savings via the change in the distribution of income that the change in the rate of interest causes. These changes are reinforced during the process by the changes in prices. If the period of production is rigid and the economy is stationary, a lower rate does not cause a cumulative process. This is a criticism of what Wicksell himself asserted in *Interest and Prices*.

Lindahl's criticism of the cumulative-process version of *Interest and Prices* is related to the view that the cumulative process will continue in each period because the monetary demand for output will always exceed the supply since the increase in price gives rise to entrepreneurial gains that are consumed in the next period (see Lindahl 1939, 166–7). In this example it is assumed that the price expected for the next period will be equal to the price observed one period ahead. The elasticity should therefore be one in this case. Thus the process, being cumulative, would not depend on this value but only on the expenditure lag regarding gains. The author instead approvingly quotes a passage in *Lectures* (II, 194) where the cumulative character of the process is linked to the price expectations by entrepreneurs (see Lindahl 1939, 169n). However, in both versions (in *Interest and Prices* and in *Lectures*) the stationary-state assumption is retained so that a change in interest rate cannot change either the capital structure (through the effect on the length of the production process) or savings (via the change in income distribution that it causes) since new savings are supposed to be zero. Thus a lag in production rather than in expenditure, price expectations that affect entrepreneurs' plans, and income effects of changes in interest rates and prices are all factors that cause a cumulative process.

Hicks retains instead Wicksell's theory, according to which a cumulative process (without implying changes in capital decisions or in quantities offered) will be set in motion by a lowering of the interest rate if people expect the new higher prices to persist or to continue. As we have seen, Hicks applies the same scheme to the demand for consumption goods in order to explain why the value of the elasticity of price expectations was so important for stability. The other possible source of instability, namely income effects, had been ruled out by the assumption that individuals are homogeneous.

In the first part of *Value and Capital* it is clearly stated that prices clear the market each Monday morning, although the process that leads to this outcome is not clearly sketched (see Collard 1993). Prices are determined by supply and demand each Monday morning although they may be different from those prevailing the previous Monday. In any case, prices fulfill the task of clearing the market. Hahn (1988) argues that this happens because of the assumption of perfect stability and low elasticity. A corresponding strong assumption of this type cannot be found in Lindahl. Under perfect foresight it is assumed that everyone knows the equilibrium prices. In this case no price adjustment mechanism is necessary. Every agent in the economy supplies exactly what is being demanded. Equilibrium is attained without any type of price mechanism. In reality, prices do change but their changes do not act in a stabilizing way as described in general equilibrium theory and in *Value and Capital*. A price rise does not solve problems of excess demand but may exacerbate them. Demand and supply may rise again and the process may go on *ad infinitum*, being thus really cumulative, or may stop at a certain point. This result is due to the particular structure of the economy that Lindahl considers. He does not deal with anonymous representative agents but with agents performing different functions and having different economic behaviors. The device that ensured short-period equilibrium in Hicks is not considered here. The price mechanism does not fulfill the coordination function that general equilibrium theorists assign to it. Thus price changes, instead of solving disequilibrium problems, may give rise to further changes in quantities which then become endogenous from period to period. At the end of a period entrepreneurs may accumulate or decumulate inventories but sooner or later they will decide to change the quantities offered.

The structure of the economy

The agents in Lindahl's economy are workers, entrepreneurs, and capitalists. Entrepreneurs are not the owners of capital but are somewhat like managers. Capitalists are the owners of capital but they do not take investment decisions. They can be considered as shareholders although no stock market exists. Moreover, whereas entrepreneurs are supposed to have a high propensity to save and invest, capitalists are supposed to have a low propensity to save and a high propensity to consume. Since consumption does not depend on income but on the present value of wealth, and since wealth includes capital, a rise in capital values caused by a rise in the prices of consumption goods will raise this value and therefore consumption. Demand may increase instantaneously, even before these expected gains accrue as dividends to the capitalists-shareholders because they can obtain credit from banks. This would correspond to what Hicks later defined as an overdraft economy. The problem arises, however, that the goods required are not available at the same moment in the market since production takes time and the structure of production is now changing towards the production of more capital goods. The reason why both consumption and investment plans are revised upwards is that the expected increase in the price level boosts capital values and consumption while at the same time the expectation of increased profits and the change in the distribution of income cause entrepreneurs' savings and their investment to increase.

Price expectations, dynamics and history

The elasticity of price expectations is essential for Lindahl also to establish whether or not a cumulative process will converge. The structure of the economy considered is different in so far as prices are not supposed to clear the market unless perfect foresight is assumed. Both aggregate demand and aggregate supply seem to depend positively on prices. In this context both prices and quantities are allowed to vary. Though not explicitly distinguishing between short-term and long-term expectations, Lindahl often describes entrepreneurs' behavior as motivated by considerations on the past behavior of prices. The case in which continuous increases in current prices for some period give rise to a revision in investment plans would result in an unstable upward movement of both price and quantities.

Lindahl uses examples where the elasticity is less than one and the expectations of relative price changes are correct (expectations on relative prices are fulfilled) as the benchmark case for stability. This happens if a cumulative process starts, following a lowering of the interest rate. The price of capital goods will rise relative to that of consumer goods but entrepreneurs will foresee that this change in the price relation will soon be reversed if nothing else changes (savings, wages, etc.).[5] In the opposite case, if continuous changes in the general price level in the same direction were anticipated, the cumulative process would go on *ad infinitum*.[6] Imperfect stability outcomes, with unitary elasticity of expectations, are also considered, though only in marginal observations and footnotes. These footnotes have been used to argue that Lindahl was a precursor of Keynes' theory of underemployment equilibrium. Since he deals with two sectors, this result would not depend only on the elasticity of expectations but on the input–output link between sectors and on the wage regimes there prevailing.

In this idea of the elasticity of price expectations is contained a theory of learning. The connection between the length of the period and the sensitivity of the expectation parameter was discussed in *Value and Capital* (Hicks 1946, 272):

> We must never forget that our "week" is arbitrary in length; this is of great importance in the formation of expectations. The elasticity of expectations depends upon the relative weight which is given to experience of the past and experience of the present; now if the "present" is taken to cover a longer period of time, "present experience" will necessarily weigh more heavily, and (even in the same psychological condition) expectations will tend to become more elastic . . . People do not usually expect to be able to foresee the actual prices ruling on any particular day with complete accuracy, so that an appreciable variation from what they had thought the most probable price may fail to disturb their expectations at all. But if the average price realized over a longer period fails to agree with what had been expected, it is likely to disturb the further expectations of the most stolid. Thus it is reasonable to assume that sensitivity will increase with the length of the "week".

A formalization of the theory of expectations that distinguishes between

136

short-term and long-term expectations in relation to Keynes' theory can be found in Dutt (1991–2). Dutt endogenizes the parameter linking short-term to long-term expectations as a function of observed past prices. This would lead to path dependency in some cases. Lindahl, in my opinion, by describing the formation of entrepreneurs' expectations, is dealing with the same problem. An important conclusion of Dutt's model is that if a stable equilibrium exists, history matters. Lindahl seems to think more of the unstable case than of the stable one.[7]

Lindahl's treatment of expectations would be similar to the Keynesian case with short-term expectations that may be disappointed and shifting long-term expectations. Keynes, however, does not endogenize long-term expectations as Lindahl does by including, among the variables that affect them, learning of past prices and announced price-stabilization policy by the central bank. Moreover Lindahl does not believe in a short-period equilibrium on which policy prescriptions may be based. His policy prescriptions refer to medium-term stabilization objectives rather than to a fine-tuning type of intervention.

THE POSSIBLE STABILIZERS:
HICKS VERSUS LINDAHL

I have argued so far that, although both economists labeled the source of possible instability, namely the elasticity of price expectations, in the same way, the economic meaning attached to this expression was quite different. Hicks was thinking of the absence of intertemporal substitution in consumption plans[8] whereas Lindahl was thinking of a very high value of the relation between long-term and short-term expected price levels and thus of the revision of investment plans by entrepreneurs.

Therefore, the proposed solution to the problem may be expected to be, and in fact is, different. The ideal candidate for this task is, according to Hicks, wage rigidity, whereas for Lindahl it could be high elasticity of interest expectations.

Why has wage rigidity been preferred to other possible stabilizers? Wage rigidity fulfills the task of stabilizing the economy since, unlike the fixing of other prices, it ensures that the aggregate demand for goods will fall. Fixing a price in an otherwise competitive market implies that total sales realized will be less than they would have been. The price, however, is higher than in the competitive case. A rise in the general price level, the rigid price being constant, affects both the buyers' price and the sellers' price. This will have repercussions that may either lower or raise the general price level again. In particular the sellers' price will be higher. If it is the price of a factor of production, such as labor, the problem does not arise since its shadow price is equal to zero (see Hicks 1946, 267–9).

By contrast, the interest rate as a stabilizer is not so effective. First, it is not clear to what extent the rise in the short rate can be transmitted to the long rate. Second, even if this were possible, only plans for future periods would be affected. Moreover, big fluctuations in interest rates do not correspond to everyday experience.

Lindahl thinks instead that people can use short-term rates and announced changes in future short-term rates to calculate the future level of the long-term rate[9] and believes further that the plans that must be affected are by definition long-term plans since they are mainly investment projects.[10] He thinks that people's guesses about future long-term loans may be based on the information that is available in the current period, and if they trust the central bank they will use the information provided by this institution to revise their plans. Investment plans are mainly determined by technological factors and forecasts of future receipts based on extrapolation of past trends in prices. But these forecasts may also be changed within the longer period if the agents involved pick up some information that is worth including in their calculations.[11] If they trust the central bank and if this institution has the power to control the variable interest rate, then Lindahl's reasoning applies. Thus a change in the short-term rate will cause a revision of the expected long-term rate. The institutional environment with which Lindahl was working was different from the one Hicks had in mind. The supply of money was endogenous and the central bank, by fixing the discount rate, could determine the conditions on which credit was given. Moreover, since financial markets in Sweden were not highly developed, this type of money-supply management could not cause particular problems. Lindahl may also have been influenced by the way in which Swedish firms financed their investment expenditure: mainly by bank loans and by the sale of bonds on the market. These loan contracts were usually long-term.[12] The British financial market was instead much more developed and the Stock Exchange played a more important role in the financing of firms' projects.

As in portfolio models, the interest rate in *Value and Capital* was determined on the market for money mainly by the volatility of the demand for money relative to other available assets.[13] It was therefore inconceivable that an interest rate change, however big, could be believed to last for long periods. Demand for money was mainly a function of investment financing needs, since it was assumed that people did not hold any money balances[14] and that financial markets were so weakly developed that the financing of operations on these markets was empirically not a significant item in the demand for money.

According to this view, only anticipated monetary policy matters. This is just the contrary of what the rational-expectations school argues. The point is worth a comment since both Lindahl and Hicks are dealing with forward-looking, although not always self-fulfilling, expectations.[15]

Moreover, investment was mainly intended as investment in new projects rather than as the expansion of capacity with a given technology. New investment would thus require more time in order to yield returns than would the simple replacement of old equipment. Therefore the sensitivity of this type of investment to interest rates may have been considered greater (see, on this, Hicks 1989, 117–18).

Both Lindahl and Hicks agree on the inefficacy of the interest rate tool in depressions, though the reasons are slightly different. Hicks argues that the interest rate cannot fall as much as would be required because of the liquidity trap, whereas Lindahl thinks that the forecast of future negative receipts based on the extrapolation of falling prices may more than counterbalance the weight of the interest rate fall in entrepreneurs' calculations. Moreover, debt deflation will worsen firms' finances. As Hicks himself stated, the elasticity of expectations will increase with the length of the period. Lindahl, in contrast to Keynes and in a singular concordance with Keynesian growth theorists like Harrod, was more concerned with the exhilarationist case than with the stagnationist one (see Taylor 1991). He thought that due to optimistic expectations about capital values and free supply of credit the boom could at the end explode and that the main constraint on growth was the supply of labor. The attempt to overcome this problem would have caused big transfers of labor from one sector to another with repercussions on relative prices.

CONCLUSIONS

Lindahl and Hicks, using similar analytical tools, reached the same conclusion on the likely monetary instability of a general equilibrium system. In particular, the notion of elasticity of expectations was essential to draw this conclusion. The economic reasons behind this point were different, though their view concerning the formation of expectations was similar. Hicks had in mind one single period of variable length but of short duration. Expectations were related to this period and, as he himself wrote, their elasticity was supposed to increase with the length of the period. Lindahl was dealing, although not explicitly, with at least two periods of different lengths: the market period and the period with unchanged long-term expectations. Hicks was not so worried about what happened at the end of the period, and only in one of the last chapters did he consider the issue of capital accumulation. In this context a high value of the elasticity of price expectations is dangerous in so far as it makes the best stabilizing device that a "dynamic"[16] system has, the intertemporal substitution effect, disappear. Since the substitution effect was expected to prevail over the income effect, and since, therefore, a static system is always stable, a high value of this elasticity could be the only problem to be solved. Lindahl instead stressed the role of income effects due to the differences in the behavior of groups of agents, entrepreneurs, capitalists, and workers and the possibility that the value of the elasticity will be quite high. Since he did not deal separately with these two issues, both destabilizing effects are described in his sequences. Although present here and there in *Value and Capital,* capital is not considered in an economy with three commodities: goods, money, and securities. The possible solution is considered to be wage rigidity since the main cause of trouble is consumers' behavior.

For Lindahl, the main source of instability is instead investment behavior; being investment linked to price expectations, forward-looking expectations concerning inflation stabilization policy by the central bank would mitigate over- and underinvestment problems. Therefore the difference in the remedies proposed stems from their different views on the causes of instability.

The difference in opinion about how interest rates work may be traced to the difference in the institutional environments they used as reference points.

NOTES

1 Financial support from the CNR Working Group on the Relevance of Hypotheses in Economics, directed by Professor G. Tattara, University of Venice, is gratefully acknowledged.

2 This idea is stated in Hahn (1988). Recently it has been argued that Hicks could have been inspired by Hayek while inventing the notion of elasticity of price expectations (see Fuss 1995, 355 fn 9).

3 The big difference is that Hahn's model does not allow for capital accumulation.

4 Hicks (1949, 255) writes: "If elasticities of expectations are generally greater than unity, so that people interpret a change in prices, not merely as an indication that the new prices will go on, but as an indication that they will go on changing in the same direction, then a rise in all prices by so much per cent. (with constant rate of interest) will make demands generally greater than supplies, so that the rise in prices will continue. A system with elasticities of expectations greater than unity, and a constant rate of interest, is definitely unstable."

5 This opinion contrasts with Hayek's interpretation of the cumulative process. Hayek writes that the fall in the rate of interest will make relative prices change. The entrepreneurs will therefore change their production plans. This behavior will be mistaken, since relative prices will change again later in the opposite direction (reverse movement). See on this Loasby (1995).

6 See Lindahl (1930, 46, and 1939, 181). See also Lindahl (1930, 47): "The reasoning undertaken until now is based on the assumption that entrepreneurs in their profitability calculations anticipate only changes in relative prices but no continuous change in the general price level. If we reject this assumption and make the more realistic assumption that the public, after a certain time that the price rise continues, thinks as likely that it will go on, the result will be different." (The translation from the original Swedish is mine.) This sentence has been deleted in the English translation although the same concept is less clearly expressed in the preceding sentences.

7 A simplified aggregate model, where, however, the reasoning is based on a given exogenous value of the expectation parameter, can be found in Tropeano and Gallegati, forthcoming in a selection of conference papers edited by A. Jolink and P. Fontaine.

8 The instability of a general equilibrium system with money is also stated in a recent work by Grandmont (1983). In this work, money supply is endogenous so that

spending plans are not constrained by the current money supply. The same could apply to Lindahl, who considered both consumption and investment plans as financed through credit. Paradoxically Lindahl calls "forced" saving the impossibility of realizing consumption plans based on a revised estimate of capital values due to a credit restriction by banks.

9 Lindahl (1939, 187–8) writes: "In the first place it should be noted that the long-term rate – if we disregard expectations due to the risk factor and other frictions – is, in principle, governed by anticipated short-term rates for future periods. It is manifestly possible for the Monetary Authority to make an announcement concerning its future policy, and by this means to influence the beliefs of the public concerning the future level of interest rates, and thereby the bond rate." On this point, see Tropeano (1989).

10 It is worth mentioning in passing that Lindahl's treatment of the term structure of interest rates is very similar to Hicks (1946, ch. 11).

11 Plans can be revised even though they are not falsified. This especially holds true for plans made under uncertainty. Optimization under uncertainty and incomplete information yields suboptimal results. Even if they are not making losses, entrepreneurs may discover new opportunities to improve their profitability pattern. This theme has been dealt with in Myrdal (1927).

12 The Swedish banking system was more akin to the German one, with strong relations between banks and firms, than to the English one. On this, see Sjögren (1991).

13 The monetary part of *Value and Capital* is derived from Hicks' (1935) article on monetary theory.

14 An exception in this respect among the economists who belong to the Swedish School is D. Hammarskjöld.

15 The reason why only anticipated money matters is that only if it is anticipated can it affect investment plans. A similar view can be found in Neary and Stiglitz (1983).

16 Hicks warns that in his book "dynamic" means a temporary equilibrium system rather than a truly dynamic system.

REFERENCES

Collard, D.A. (1993) "High Hicks, deep Hicks, and equilibrium," *History of Political Economy* 25(2): 331–50.

Dutt, A.K. (1991–2) "Expectations and equilibrium: implications for Keynes, the neo-Ricardian Keynesians, and the Post Keynesians," *Journal of Post Keynesian Economics* 14(2): 205–24.

Fuss, N.J. (1995) "More on Hayek's transformation," *History of Political Economy* 27(2): 349.

Grandmont, J.M. (1983) *Money and Value*, Cambridge: Cambridge University Press.

Hahn, F. (1988) *Hicksian Themes on Stability*, Economic Theory Discussion Paper no. 136, Department of Applied Economics, University of Cambridge.

Hammarskjöld, D. (1933) *Konjunkturspridningen* [The transmission of economic fluctuations] Stockholm: Norstedt.

Hamouda, O.F. (1990) "Hicks's changing views on economic dynamics," in D.E. Moggridge (ed.), *Perspectives in the History of Economic Thought*, vol. 4, Aldershot, Hants.: Edward Elgar, 162–76.

Hands, D. Wade (1994) "Restabilizing dynamics: construction and constraint in the history of Walrasian stability theory," *Economics and Philosophy* 10(2): 243–83.

Hicks, J.R. (1935) "A suggestion for simplifying the theory of money," *Economica New*

Series no. 5; also reprinted in *Critical Essays in Monetary Theory*, Oxford: Clarendon Press, 1967, 61–82.

Hicks, J.R. (1946) *Value and Capital*, Oxford: Oxford University Press. (First edition 1939.)

Hicks, J.R. (1956) "Methods of dynamic analysis," in *25 Economic Essays* (Festschrift for Erik Lindahl), Stockholm: Ekonomisk Tidschrift.

Hicks, J.R. (1965) *Capital and Growth*, Oxford: Clarendon Press.

Hicks, J.R. (1973) *Capital and Time*, Oxford: Clarendon Press.

Hicks, J.R. (1989) *A Market Theory of Money*, Oxford: Oxford University Press.

Hicks, J.R. (1991) "The Swedish influence on value and capital," in L. Jonung (ed.), *The Stockholm School of Economics Revisited*, Cambridge: Cambridge University Press, 369–77.

Lindahl, E. (1929) "Prisbildningsproblemet från kapitalteoretiskt synspunkt" [The problem of capital in the theory of price], *Ekonomisk Tidskrift*; partially translated in Lindahl (1939, Part III).

Lindahl, E. (1930) *Penningpolitikens medel* [The means of monetary policy], Malmö: Gleerup; partially translated in Lindahl (1939, Part II).

Lindahl, E. (1939) *Studies in the Theory of Money and Capital*, London: Allen & Unwin.

Loasby, B.J. (1995) "Co-ordination failure in economic theory," paper presented at the European Conference on the History of Economic Thought, Rotterdam, February 8–11; forthcoming in a selection of conference papers edited by A. Jolink and P. Fontaine, to be published by Routledge.

Lundberg, E. (1937) *Studies in the Theory of Economic Expansion*, London: R.S. King.

Myrdal, G. (1927) *Prisbildningsproblemet och föränderligheten* [Pricing and Change], Uppsala: Almquist & Wicksell Förlag.

Neary, P. and Stiglitz, J. (1983) "Towards a reconstruction of Keynesian economics: expectations and constrained equilibria," *Quarterly Journal of Economics* 98: 403–29.

Patinkin, J. (1965) *Money, Interest and Prices*, New York: Harper and Row.

Sjögren, H. (1991) "Long-term contracts in the Swedish bank-orientated financial system in the inter-war period," *Business History* no. 3: 119–37.

Taylor, L. (1991) *Income Distribution, Inflation and Growth*, Cambridge, MA: MIT Press.

Tropeano, D. (1989) "La struttura dei mercati finanziari e il modus operandi della politica monetaria: Lindahl versus Ohlin" [The structure of financial markets and the working of monetary policy: Lindahl versus Ohlin], *Moneta e Credito*, March: 89–102.

Tropeano, D. and Gallegati, M. (1995) "Lindahl on disequilibrium growth: price expectations, wage regimes and the distribution of income," paper presented at the European Conference on the History of Economics, Rotterdam, February 8–11, forthcoming in a selection of conference papers edited by A. Jolink and P. Fontaine, to be published by Routledge.

Wicksell, K. (1936 [1898]) *Interest and Prices*, London: Macmillan.

Wicksell, K. (1934 [1905]) *Lectures on Political Economy*, London: Routledge.

9

(DIS)TRUSTING THE TALE
Werner Sombart and the narrative of economics

Jonathon Mote[1]

(DIS)TRUSTING THE TALE

The complaint that contemporary economic theory is bereft of historical and empirical forces has been a common one recently. Given the perennial drive towards greater levels of abstraction, it is becoming increasingly recognized that a reintroduction of these forces is imperative for the continued vitality of economics as an edifying discipline. Yet the search for ways to more fully incorporate these forces into the discipline's methodology has so far been incomplete. Often dismissed from serious consideration are perspectives that were usurped by the rise of neoclassical theory, but which may hold potential for incorporating the complex, and often ambiguous, events of the past. For example, the Institutional and German Historical Schools represent two schools of economic thought which could provide some insights into how one might proceed in this effort, yet they have received little attention from mainstream contemporary theorists. But this neglect is far from benign. In fact, the two schools suffer from a pervasive interpretation within the discipline's historical narrative as being incomplete or misleading.[2]

What is the nature of the disciplinary historical narrative which serves to exclude the two schools of thought from the discipline? The narrative underlying the book *Economics without Time: A Science Blind to the Forces of Historical Change* by Graeme D. Snooks (1993) provides a convenient example. The narrative constructed by Snooks quickly eliminates the two schools from further investigation after a cursory and incomplete examination of their contributions. In the case of Institutionalism, the school is not even differentiated in method from the more deductively oriented techniques of econometrics. In fact, the Institutionalists are credited with maintaining a closer link between economics and history, and their considerable body of work, as well as their distinctively inductive approach, is homogenized as simply an earlier period in the development of economic history. The reader is forced

143

to conclude that the school was simply a precursor of the excessively deduct-ive work of the cliometricians. Such a conclusion drastically overlooks the differences, both notable and subtle, between the two schools. While the Institutionalists are, at the very least, regarded as contributing members to the discipline of economics, the German Historical School is rejected out of hand. Without a proper examination, Snooks (1993, 27) states that "it [the German Historical School] failed in its attempt to overthrow deductive eco-nomics because it did not produce an alternative structure of inductive thought." In this manner, Snooks perpetuates what Horst Betz (1988, 409) characterizes as the orthodox tradition of "reinforcing the stylized view of it [the German Historical School] as being non-theoretical, occupied with detailed historical studies in the vain hope of creating a new, inductively-based economics."

The narrative provided by Snooks supports his argument and conclusion by eliminating the two schools from consideration, and in the process effectively circumvents a closer inspection by the reader of their contribu-tions. Yet Snooks' narrative treatment of the two schools is not an idio-syncratic one. Rather, it is just one manifestation of the conclusion drawn by the discipline's "official" narrative. Of the two schools, however, the elimination of the German Historical School from the intellectual heritage of the discipline is particularly pronounced. Indeed, the school and its contributions are rarely mentioned within the discipline of economics. Such a situation is striking because many of America's first professional econo-mists were educated in Germany; the economic ideas, methods, and policies which arose in Germany were vigorously discussed in the United States in the mid- to late 1800s. Indeed, the American Economic Association was originally proposed to resemble the *Verein für Sozialpolitik* (Union for Social Policy), the venerable German academic and professional association (Coats, in Barber 1988, 352). Nonetheless, many of these German-trained American economists undertook an effort to "de-Germanize" the discipline in order to move away explicitly from their German teachings and forge a distinctively "American" economics.[3] As a result, relatively few works by members of the German Historical School have been translated into English. Those contributions that have been translated – such as those by Werner Sombart, Max Weber, and Gustav Schmoller – have undergone an almost constant barrage of criticism from the mainstream of the econom-ics discipline and are often relegated to existence in other "noneconomic" disciplines, such as sociology or regional science. Any positive inclusion of the German Historical School that has occurred within the intellectual heri-tage of the discipline has had to rely on a small group of commentators sympathetic to the school, such as Talcott Parsons, Leo Rogin, and Joseph Dorfman.

The effort by American economists to purge the discipline of its German aspects coincided with the growing predominance, also led largely by Anglo-

American economists, of deductive, neoclassical theory within the discipline. Arising from this milieu, the resulting disciplinary narrative has exerted a lasting influence due to its adoption and use by many of the newly emerging leaders. Ironically, it is perhaps Joseph Schumpeter and his monumental *History of Economic Analysis* that has played a decisive role in this regard. While Schumpeter is often considered a later member of the historical school, he was often quite emphatic about distancing himself, at least in public pronouncement, from their methods. His conclusion on the school's methodology is that it consisted merely of "generalizations from historical monographs" and that the "science of the discipline lay in a mastery of historical technique" (Schumpeter 1954, 807). Given Schumpeter's stature in the discipline of economics in the postwar period, most notably as president of the American Economics Association in the 1950s, such a statement served to provide the disciplinary authority for effectively closing the door for a generation of scholars to pursue further explorations of the school's contributions. Indeed, one can point to Schumpeter's text as a decisive influence in the discipline's move to define the historical school in terms of a superseded economic epoch (Betz 1988, 429). For example, within Blaug's *Economic Theory in Retrospect* (1985), the successor text to Schumpeter's as the most widely read in the history of economic thought, the school is mentioned only in vague, passing references.[4]

Yet, because the German Historical School had a profound influence on the early origins of economics, the discipline's narrative conclusion remains a puzzling one. In speaking of the use of narratives, Martin Kreiswirth (1992, 650) has warned that "narratives ... are human constructs that operate by certain conventions, in certain times, places, contexts, and whose claims need to be investigated ... especially at a historical moment when they have been given ... so much theoretical and institutional prominence." It would seem prudent, therefore, to investigate the judgement rendered on the German Historical School and ascertain its legitimacy. Unfortunately, an encompassing survey of the entire school is beyond the scope of this paper. It will attempt to provide a summary of the contributions of one member of the German Historical School as an initial exercise in this reinvestigation. For this endeavor, the work of Werner Sombart has been chosen for this dubious distinction as someone who has suffered acutely at the hands of the discipline's historical narrative.

In his career, Sombart achieved a large amount of recognition within and beyond the boundaries of Germany, most notably with the voluminous study of modern capitalism entitled *Der Moderne Kapitalismus*. Yet, as Horst Betz (1971, 1) points out, "Sombart is an almost forgotten figure in English-speaking academic circles." In part, the outcome is a result of the early disciplinary politics mentioned above; but another, more insidious type of narrative censure has also left its imprint on Sombart. The examinations of Paul de Man and Martin Heidegger[5] have highlighted the use of personal beliefs or actions by disciplinary authorities in determining the legitimacy of intellectual contributions, particularly if such figures threaten the status quo of the discipline. With regard to Sombart, such a practice is epitomized by Mark Blaug's (1986, 236) statement that "Werner Sombart started his career as a Marxist in the 1890s and ended it as a Nazi sympathizer in the 1930s," which discards Sombart's contributions on the basis of alleged personal and political beliefs. However, upon comparing the receptions afforded Sombart and Schumpeter, it is interesting to note that this treatment is far from even-handed. While both expressed somewhat controversial views on such topics as Semitism, Marxism and Nazism, the discipline has chosen to disregard the views of Schumpeter in their assessment of his contributions (Semmel 1992, 3–16). Such disparity highlights one method by which past contributors can be selectively eliminated from the narrative of the discipline. In this manner, Blaug's allusions to Sombart's self-recognized continuation of Marx's project and his questionable "conversion" to National Socialism act as a narrative cudgel to thwart any attempts at further study of Sombart's contributions in economics.

The following analysis of Sombart will eschew any discussion of specific contributions to economic theory or personal politics. Because the orthodox economics narrative excludes Sombart and other members of the school on the perception that they failed to provide a viable alternative to the rising influence of deductive method and theory, this paper will examine in more detail Sombart's project to define an alternative methodology. The scope of the analysis is further narrowed in that it will delineate Sombart's ideas through an examination of two of three articles which have been translated and are readily accessible to English-speaking readers. In the first article, entitled "Economic theory and economic history" (Sombart 1929), Sombart mediates between those who would emphasize either history or theory to the exclusion of the other. In this endeavor, he attempts to define more fully their relationship and also to articulate his own economic methodology. Sombart broadens his perspective in the second article, entitled "Sociology: what it is and what it ought to be" (Sombart 1949), and, after providing an overview of the main types of sociology, establishes an outline for a more appropriate science of society, noö-sociology. While the articles are only an attempt by Sombart to summarize his methodology, they provide a more than adequate overview. Indeed, Sombart himself believed the latter article to be one of his best (ibid., 182).[6]

SOMBART'S INTELLECTUAL MILIEU

Similar to that of other members of the German Historical School, Sombart's methodology is a distinct product of the neo-Kantian movement which took hold of the German academic community in the middle and later years of the nineteenth and early twentieth centuries. Throughout this period, there existed an ongoing and shifting dialogue surrounding which

146

elements of Kant's philosophical system were to be emphasized (Willey 1978, 21). As one of the editors for the *Archiv für Sozialwissenschaft and Sozial-politik*, the leading journal of German social science, Sombart was situated at the center of the neo-Kantian debate. One of the central issues, particularly as it related to the methodology of the social sciences, was the attempt to provide a solution to the problem posed by Kant's separation of the natural and moral realms. Because the objects of the latter – morals and values – presuppose an essentially free subject, it was felt by many that this realm necessitates a different way of studying than the methodology used for the natural world, which attributes a determinism to its objects. Because it was based on Kant's belief that the possibility of true understanding can only arise from material that is constructed by humans, the *verstehen* methodology was viewed by many of Sombart's contemporaries as the way to "put on a firm footing the independence and scientific status of the *Geisteswissenchaften*, or human sciences" (Schnadelbach 1988, 109). While unique in its final structure, Sombart followed many of his contemporaries in propounding a *verstehen* methodology. As Floyd House (1970, 55) has remarked, "however great the importance may be of the theoretic foundations laid down for *die verstehende Soziologie* by Dilthey, Windelband, Rickert and others who might be mentioned, it is to . . . Werner Sombart that we are chiefly indebted for the elaboration of the possibilities of application of the viewpoint and method."

Wilhelm Dilthey provided the initial basis for the attempt to provide a separate methodology for the human sciences based on the foundation of lived experience, expression, and understanding (Mitzman 1987, 188). While Sombart adopted the *verstehen* concept articulated by Dilthey at least superficially, he rejected the attempt to formulate laws on the basis of a comprehensive, uniform psychological connection. The "psychologism" propounded by Dilthey was not an option for Sombart because of its inability to be observed (Sombart 1949, 183). In rejecting the possibility of psychological laws, Sombart adopted a distinction similar to Ferdinand Tonnies' volitional forms of "the will to be" and "the will to choose" (Mitzman 1987, 185). This distinction found its manifestation in Sombart's dichotomy between mind and psyche, to be discussed more fully below (pp. 149–50). As we will see, similar to Sombart's concept of mind, the will to choose causes individual actions that are both observable and unique to humans, and the amalgam of these actions Tonnies terms *Gesellschaft*, or society.

Despite these affinities, it is the figure of George Simmel who looms predominantly in Sombart's attempt to systematize the *verstehen* methodology for economics. While Sombart utilizes a variation of Tonnies' concept of society, he follows Simmel in rejecting Tonnies' positivist notion that society alone constitutes an objective system (Swingewood 1984, 134). Much like Simmel's concept of "social forms," Sombart focused on human inter-actions or "associations," as opposed to individual actions, as the basis for society. Because associations/social forms constitute a social context for

147

human interactions, these structures encompass social phenomena within an objective realm, what Sombart terms "culture." As will be discussed below (pp. 151–3), the articulation of the concept of culture as the tangible manifestation of this observable realm is the decisive move which distinguishes Sombart's project of establishing the human sciences as a science with its own special domain and methodology. However, in contrast to Simmel's predilection for making social forms fixed and static, Sombart retained a strong commitment to a direct and evolutionary epistemological linkage to human society – either past or present (Sombart 1949, 187).

HISTORY AND THEORY

Sombart explicitly defined his methodology in opposition to the rising use of deductive theory in economics. The adoption of neoclassical theory, along with promotion of the natural science methodology by many within the discipline, had given economics an excessively theoretical character. The rise of the use of neoclassical theory had the effect of reducing the events of the past to discrete, objective facts for use solely as an empirical foundation to fit economists' deductive theories. Sombart identified the two dominant schools of economic thought – classical and neoclassical – and criticized them for failing to provide a useful, socially relevant body of economic theory. Specifically, the two schools were criticized for building elaborate systems, utilizing analogies and models drawn from the natural sciences and for seeking "economic principles which have universal and uniform applicability under every variety of conditions" (Sombart 1929, 8). Sombart went further, and stated that economists "take no account of historical forces" and "deal with economic phenomena as though they were substances like those which physical scientists study" (ibid.). In short, "the economic theorists moved in an unreal, abstract world" and "failed to reap the abundant harvest offered by the manifold variety of actual life" (ibid.).

In response to these incipient methodologies, Sombart sought to broaden the concept of history and elevate its stature in relation to theory. In the pronouncement that "*all society is mind and all mind is society*" (Sombart 1949, 189), he made it clear that history should not be grasped simply as an atomistic aggregation of isolated facts and events, but as a psychological and experiential totality. Sombart's concept of "mind" is an explicit rejection of the view of human nature offered by the proponents of deductive theory, a concept he labels the human "psyche." For Sombart, rather, human "mind" is a more appropriate conception and refers to that aspect of human nature which is *acquired* and manifested through human relationships, as opposed to a "psyche" which is given and shaped by nature. In this manner, the empirical past now becomes "society" by virtue of the fact that it arises from relationships among humans, rather than by the mere operation of natural law. Sombart employed the concept of society – past or present – to embody the totality of the complex web of human relationships. As such, it is not a "natural" reality like that studied by the natural sciences, but is a social reality.

However, while history *qua* society does consist of an empirical field similar to the natural science-based economics, Sombart stated that it is of primary importance for the historian to concern himself "not with isolated facts but with connected systems" (Sombart 1929, 2). Displaying a historicism reminiscent of the Romantic school, history consists of a series of connected systems, or wholes, and only as a part or in relation to a whole do the events of the past acquire any meaning. However, in speaking of "wholes," Sombart did not refer to a universal or totalizing conception of history, which he deems is the proper task of philosophy. Rather, wholes are demarcated by specific boundaries and used by historians as a tool in presenting the past. The primary object of historical study is the infinite number of these wholes.

As Horst Betz (1971, 1) points out, historicism does indeed play an important role in Sombart's conception of history; however, it does not reduce the conception to relativism. The relativizing influence of historicism is tempered by a further broadening of the concept of history with the establishment of quasi-universal structures. The notion that "society is mind" becomes tangible in Sombart's assertion that the manifold human relationships which society embodies result in two particular manifestations: language and "associations." Language, most simply, is the means by which humans are able to engage in relationships, but it also consists of a structure of grammar, syntax, and vocabulary. Associations are those institutions which humans create as an outgrowth of their relationships. By highlighting language and associations, society becomes much more than an amalgam of actions and motives, but consists of structures that are relevant to social behavior. As such, the two embody basic ideals of social reality and provide a common denominator for relations among humans. While these two provide the basis for studying society, they are endowed with distinctly ontological properties which contribute a stability of universality to the field of history.

The converse of Sombart's statement, "all mind is society," reflects the notion that humans do not create society anew and each generation confronts an already existing social structure. Because society outlasts the single individual, the human mind is shaped by these seemingly timeless structures, or as Sombart (1949, 190) stated, "without society the individual would be speechless and mindless." Human relationships – past and present – are fulfilled in and through language and the various associations of society; that is, they provide a determinative context to human life. While they originally arose from society, they now "contain" society by establishing parameters for human relations and, as such, exist on a different plane than society. While associations are substantively different in character than thoughts or human relationships, due to society's dynamic nature they are not rigid, unchanging

149

structures and thus remain susceptible to evolutionary or paradigmatic change, albeit over extended periods of time.

Given the rehabilitation of history, what is its relation to theory? Although history *qua* society is constructed as an empirical field, contrary to the natural science methodology, history is not reduced to the "historical," or mere sensory experience. Rather, as shown above, it consists of actual-lived reality. However, because Sombart (1929, 3) cautioned that "theory is the prerequisite of any scientific writing of history," it is necessary to use theory as it provides a measure by which to determine the relevance or meaning of past reality. As opposed to deductivists, who interpret history according to their theories, Sombart conceives of theory inductively, that is, as the crafting of general concepts from the particular facts of history. These concepts, in turn, are heuristic and aid the scientist in gaining insights into history. In further contrast to deductive theory, Sombart views these concepts or theories as works in progress, not as concrete, timeless laws.

Utilizing a distinction similar to the mind–psyche dichotomy, Sombart distinguished between two components of theory: the esoteric and the exoteric. Esoteric theory concerns the mental conception of the separate spiritual fields or, in Sombart's words, the "science of the logic" or "dogmatics" (Sombart 1949, 190). Because it is internal to the individual, like a "psyche," it cannot be known by other individuals. On the other hand, exoteric theory concerns the "sociality of the spiritual domain" and provides the "social-group theory of the separate spiritual fields" (ibid.). As exoteric theory is concerned with "sociality," or human relationships, it is derived from an analysis of society, specifically that which is known through language and associations. Sombart further distinguished two components of exoteric theory: special and general theory and, because history, as a separate discipline, is concerned with the particular, it can never be completely expressed in terms of a general significance. Therefore, history is conceded to special theory, or theory of the particular. Products of special (historical) theory are those historical monographs which detail the development of single cases, for example the history of the Bank of England or the history of English banking. However, situations and events do recur under similar conditions and exhibit similarity of features. General theory, derived from a serious study of special/historical theory, provides a framework which highlights those general characteristics to be "grouped together, given a collective label, and treated as a whole" (Sombart 1929, 18). Imbuing general theory with a scientific quality, Sombart likened their derivation to "that of the mathematician who takes out the letter recurring in all values and places it before a bracket, so that he says a(b + c + d . . .) instead of ab + ac + ad . . . " (ibid.).

Sombart's concept of economic system provides the clearest example of the type of general theory that is appropriate for studying society. The primary principle underlying the concept of economic system reflects the societal orientation of his particular notion of human relationships in that it consists of "a mode of satisfying and making provisions for material wants" (ibid., 14), and is mediated through human relations. Sombart outlined three constituent elements which he found to be basic to every economic system: an economic outlook or economic spirit; methods of organization and institutional structures which allow for regulating human relations to one another; and a definite level of technological development. Within each element there is a very limited number of possible variations and, among all three, permutations. For example, Sombart listed only three possible types of economic outlooks: the money-making principle; traditionalism (rationalism); and solidarity (individualism). However, these elements together provide a system comprehensive enough to grasp every aspect of economic life, and "general enough to be applied to every conceivable economic institution from the most primitive to the most highly developed" (ibid., 17). The economic system, in turn, allows for the myriad of human economic relationships to "be comprehended as a unit, wherein each constituent element of the economic process displays some given characteristic" (ibid., 14).

Through the concept of economic system, Sombart illuminated general characteristics of economic relationships and, when applied to history, those characteristics which are common throughout the system's historical development. To each economic system corresponds a particular economic epoch which means "a stretch of time during which an economic system is actually realized in History, or during which an economic life reveals features belonging to a definite economic system" (ibid., 15). Therefore, the application of one specific economic system to the history of Europe – such as capitalism – would attempt to identify "economic phenomena, which lead to the development of 'modern capitalism' and are essential to it." The purpose of such an investigation would not be to highlight differences between countries, but rather to isolate phenomena that "can be regarded as common to *all* European nations" (ibid., 19, original emphasis).

NOÖ-SOCIOLOGY AND SCIENCE

Sombart provided the rehabilitated relationship between history and theory as an alternative methodological foundation for economics. The character of the foundation is broader than the natural science-based economics because it draws upon, rather than imposes upon, social reality and seeks to include all that is exogenous to abstract deductive theories. With this foundation, Sombart sought to undertake theoretical analysis of associations abstracted from history. The new methodology was not limited to the sphere of economics, however, but was fundamental to Sombart's larger methodological project, that is, the establishment of an overarching science of society, *noö-sociology*. It is important to state at this point that noö-sociology is not to be confused with what we now associate with the discipline of sociology. For Sombart, the term sociology encompasses "the doctrine of human association in its broadest sense" (Sombart 1949, 178). Because human associations arise from the myriad of human relationships – the state, the law, economics, family – each different realm has a unique historical and theoretical component. Therefore, economics as the study of only one aspect of human relationships represents just one branch of noö-sociology.[7] Yet, because all branches of noö-sociology share a common methodology, their theories would be commensurate in a way unfamiliar to the contemporary social sciences. Further, in much the same manner as "associations," the product of history and theory produces a quasi-ontological object, that of culture. For example, the culture of an economic system – such as the culture of modern capitalism – represents a unique realm of essential characteristics which express, and are expressed in, an immanent historical process. Culture possesses objective value in the same way that empirical reality does for natural scientists, and while culture arises from the economic realm of human relationships it is not irreducible to them. Each realm of human association has culture as its object, and, in economics, one can speak of a specific culture as a prerequisite for a particular economic system.

What makes the content and methodology of noö-sociology more appropriate for the study of society? Sombart demarcated the scope and aims of noö-sociology with a critique encompassing *all* contemporary sociologies, which he groups into six main schools: the natural-law or normative; natural science; historical; historical philosophical; formal; and the German school of sociology. All six are rejected as true studies of human association because they have either chosen the wrong content or an incorrect methodology:

> In all six sociologies we criticized the following: either they set a task for sociology which belongs to other disciplines, such as ethics, history, or historical philosophy, or they chose as the object of sociology something which did not exist, as in formal sociology; or, finally, having chosen the correct objective and the correct goal, they employed a method, the natural science method, which was not suited to their objective.
>
> (Ibid., 189)

To put it another way, Sombart stated that these types of sociologies either separated "mind" from society or ignored the fact that all mind is society. Noö-sociology, however, offers the possibility of a more appropriate science of society because it is based on the concept of culture which combines the "spirituality" of society and the sociality of the mind into one concept. Culture, therefore, represents the objectified human in its manifold social relationships. Unlike the physical world of natural science methodology, culture does not provide concrete, timeless structures for study. Rather, culture is a constant interchange between "associations" and human action. Yet, as noö-sociology purports to be a science of society, Sombart's rejection of previous sociologies raises the question as to the specific scientific character of noö-sociology. In this he is emphatic that noö-sociology "has nothing to do with a total or universal science" (ibid., 190). As a study of human society, of which the observer is also a participant, the attempt to derive natural, universal laws is a futile one, and he stated that:

> since we know what the play is about, there is no need to describe, measure, and weigh the events and conditions in their outer form and then attempt to reduce the results of our casting-about to a few formulas or so-called "laws," which, moreover, would be of no use, since we do not know how to classify cases under them.
>
> (Ibid., 192)

For Sombart, the complex nature of human relationships as well as the irreducibility of mind and culture to material forces makes it impossible to make absolute judgments. But he did consider noö-sociology and, in particular, the study of each realm of human relationships, as sciences in the sense that they provide generally valid knowledge of reality. The scientific character and purpose of noö-sociology rests on the principle underlying the metaphor of the "play" given above, which illustrates the accessibility and understandability of the knowledge that is gained. Essentially, "we understand culture because we made it" (ibid.), based on the assumption that there are distinctly different ways of knowing the realms of nature and culture. While the natural sciences also aspire to a general validity for its conclusions, because its object is separated from mind it is impossible ever to truly know or understand from mere observation. However, noö-sociology utilizes the concept of *verstehen*, which for Sombart did not separate mind from society and encompasses the understandability of culture, to undergird its methodology. As the subject is human mind and the object is objectified mind, or culture, the unique capacity of *verstehen* rests on the presumption that "like understands like" and results in the immanence of the knower and the knowable.

CONCLUSION

Even with only the cursory overview provided above, the systematic nature of Sombart's methodology suggests that the contributions of the German Historical School represent more than mere historical monographs. Indeed, Sombart's noö-sociology is evidence of an earnest, and rather sophisticated, attempt to construct a more encompassing methodology for not only economics, but all of the social sciences. It is plausible to conclude, therefore, that the historical narrative which excludes Sombart, and by extension other "heterodox" contributors or perspectives, is untenable and in need of rehabilitation. Whether or not these contributors ultimately provide an alternative, or at least a complement, to economic orthodoxy remains to be seen. Nonetheless, it is clear from this discussion that the omission of the German

Historical School from the discipline's narrative has eliminated a perspective that might be helpful for more comprehensively incorporating the inter-dependency of the social, political and cultural realms into the currently narrow confines of economic theory.[8] However, unless the disciplinary narrative is questioned and investigated more thoroughly, an open dialogue about alternatives or extensions to neoclassical theory will continue to be discouraged. Rather than succumbing to a philosophy of science which seeks a "superior" methodology, though, such a re-investigation of the discipline's intellectual heritage should have as its primary objective the encouragement of an eclectic variety of perspectives within the discipline. Such openness could be achieved by adopting a more critical and honest understanding of the discipline's history. Because the selection of scientific practices and viewpoints is rooted in the historical narrative, a re-examination of these choices would allow the opportunity to decide for ourselves whether they were the right choices in the first place, and whether they remain the right choices for our current practice.[9] Investigating the historical narrative in this manner opens up methodological possibilities and thus allows the practitioner to expand the range of how they view their role in economics. To paraphrase Thomas Kuhn (1970, 1), history – if viewed as a repository for more than anecdote, chronology or proof – could produce a decisive transformation in the image of economics by which we are now possessed.

NOTES

1 The author wishes gratefully to acknowledge and thank, without implicating, Horst Betz, Richard Gaskins, Arjo Klamer, an anonymous referee and the participants of the 1995 History of Economics Society annual meeting for their review of and comments on the paper. Many thanks also to the Association for Evolutionary Economics for awarding the 1995 Institutionalist Essay Prize to an earlier version of the paper.
2 In a compelling article entitled "Division and difference in the 'discipline' of economics" (*Critical Inquiry*, 17 (autumn 1990): 108–39), Jack Amariglio, Stephen Resnick and Richard Wolff rightly point out that the notion of a unified discipline of economics is an illusory one. However, in a field of competing conceptual schemata, one perspective has acquired dominance. In a similar manner, the narratives within the discipline differ in many respects, but one narrative has been essential in providing a historical "foundation" to the efforts of the dominant perspective in asserting boundaries within economics.
3 For two recent and richly detailed accounts of this period, see Dorothy Ross, *The Origins of the American Social Sciences* (Cambridge: Cambridge University Press, 1991) and Peter T. Manicas, *A History and Philosophy of the Social Sciences* (Oxford: Basil Blackwell, 1987).
4 Blaug, (1985). See, for example, p. 547 where, in summarizing Wicksteed's *Lectures*, Blaug urges the reader to "note in particular the incisive critical comments on the German Historical School."
5 The publication of Alan Bloom's *The Closing of the American Mind* (New York: Simon

& Schuster, 1987) and Victor Farias' *Heidegger et le Nazisme* (Paris: Editions Verdier, 1986), focused attention on the participation of German philosopher Martin Heidegger in Nazi activities prior to the Second World War. At around the same time, it was revealed that Paul de Man, professor of comparative literature of Yale, had written a number of articles decades ago for a pro-Nazi newspaper in his native Belgium. For some of the context surrounding the use of political controversies in attacking the academic contributions of these theorists, see Michael Zimmerman's *Heidegger's Confrontation with Modernity* (Bloomington, IN: Indiana University Press, 1990), Roger Kimball's *Tenured Radicals: How Politics Has Corrupted Our Higher Education* (New York: Harper & Row, 1990), and David Lehman's *Signs of the Times: Deconstruction and Paul de Man* (New York: Poseidon Press, 1991).

6 See translator's note.
7 In *Die drei Nationalökonomien*, Sombart discusses in considerable detail the application of noö-sociological methodology to the discipline of economics.
8 This point has been made most persuasively by Horst Betz (1988, 429, and also 1994). One concrete example of how the ideas of the German Historical School might coincide with current reform efforts in economics is in Piore (1995). In this book, Piore talks about constructing a cognitive economics that resembles the theories of cognition embedded in Sombart's methodology. Yet Piore's cognitive economics lacks any substantive systematization, and Sombart's approach might inform such an effort.
9 In Ross (1991, 474) Dorothy Ross extends this piece of advice to historians, but it is equally applicable to those within other disciplines.

REFERENCES

Amariglio, Jack, Resnick, Stephen and Wolff, Richard (1990) "Division and difference in the 'discipline' of economics," *Critical Inquiry*, 17: 108–37.
Barber, William J. (ed.) (1988) *Breaking the Academic Mould: Economists and American Higher Learning in the Nineteenth Century*, Middletown, CN: Wesleyan University Press.
Barnes, Harry E. (ed.) (1948) *An Introduction to the History of Sociology*, Chicago: University of Chicago Press.
Betz, Horst (1971) "Scholarship and *Weltanschauung* in Sombart's work," *Journal of Economic Issues* 5(3): 1–11.
Betz, Horst (1988) "How does the German Historical School fit?" *History of Political Economy* 20(3): 407–30.
Betz, Horst (1994) "From Schmoller to Sombart," *History of Economic Ideas* 2(1/2): 331–56.
Blaug, Mark (1985) *Economic Theory in Retrospect*, Cambridge: Cambridge University Press.
Blaug, Mark (1986) *Great Economists before Keynes*, Cambridge: Cambridge University Press.
Dorfman, Joseph (1955) "The role of the German Historical School in American economic thought," *American Economic Review* xlv(2): 17–28.
Frisby, David (1984) *Georg Simmel*, Chichester, W. Sussex: Ellis Howard.
House, Floyd Nelson (1970) *The Development of Sociology*, Westport, CN: Greenwood House Press.
Kreiswirth, Martin (1992) "Trusting the tale: the narrativist turn in the human sciences," *New Literary History* 23(3): 629–57.
Kuhn, Thomas (1970) *The Structure of Scientific Revolutions*, Chicago: University of Chicago Press.

Manicas, Peter T. (1987) *A History and Philosophy of the Social Sciences*, Oxford: Basil Blackwell.

Mitzman, Arthur (1987) "Personal conflict and ideological options in Sombart and Weber," in Wolfgang Mommsen and Jurgen Osterhamel (eds), *Max Weber and His Contemporaries*, London: Unwin Hyman.

Piore, Michael J. (1995) *Beyond Individualism*, Cambridge, MA: Harvard University Press.

Plotnik, Morton J. (1937) *Werner Sombart and His Type of Economics*, New York: Eco Press.

Rogin, Leo (1933) "Werner Sombart and the natural science method," *Journal of Political Economy* 41: 222–36.

Ross, Dorothy (1991) *The Origins of the American Social Sciences*, Cambridge: Cambridge University Press.

Schnadelbach, Herbert (1988) *Philosophy in Germany, 1831–1933*, Cambridge: Cambridge University Press.

Schumpeter, Joseph (1954) *History of Economic Analysis*, New York: Oxford University Press.

Semmel, Bernard (1992) "Schumpeter's curious politics," *Public Interest*, no. 108: 3–16.

Snooks, Graeme D. (1993) *Economics Without Time: A Science Blind to the Forces of Historical Change*, Ann Arbor, MI: University of Michigan Press.

Sombart, Werner (1919) *Der Moderne Kapitalismus*, Munich: Duncker & Humblot.

Sombart, Werner (1929) "Economic theory and economic history," *Economic History Review* 2(1): 1–19.

Sombart, Werner (1930) *Die drei Nationalökonomien*, Munich: Duncker & Humblot.

Sombart, Werner (1949) "Sociology: what it is and what it ought to be," *American Journal of Sociology* 55: 178–93.

Swingewood, Alan (1984) *A Short History of Sociological Thought*, New York: St Martins Press.

Willey, Thomas E. (1978) *Back to Kant: The Revival of Kantianism in German Social and Historical Thought, 1860–1914*, Detroit, MI: Wayne State University Press.

10

CROMWELL'S OCCUPATION OF IRELAND AS JUDGED FROM PETTY'S OBSERVATIONS AND MARX'S THEORY OF COLONIALISM

Patrick J. Welch[1]

In August 1649 Oliver Cromwell, who would later and briefly be Protector of England, landed in Ireland to suppress a rebellion that had started in 1641. The expedition was prompted by reports of atrocities, Cromwell's belief that the profession of Catholicism was both a religious and a political act, and the fear that Ireland was a source of Royalist support and a potential embarkation point for invasion by England's enemies. What followed was a short and violent military campaign that lasted into May 1650, and a longer-running policy of plantation (granting land rights in Ireland to English settlers), transplantation (the removal of Irish landowners from their property, along with others), and transportation (the outright deportation of some from Ireland)[2] (Corish 1976a, 292, 337; Edwards 1973, 62–3; Howell 1977, 138–40; Gardner 1903, 79; Wedgwood 1953, 11).

Approximately two hundred years later, Volume I of *Capital* was published (1906). Here Marx presented a theory of colonialism that rests on the principle of primitive accumulation (the separating of individuals from the means of production with which they can carry on economic activity) and links primitive accumulation to brutality and religious factionalism, the supply of labor and creation of markets, and public debt and taxation issues.[3]

The English treatment of the Irish at the time of Cromwell is well characterized by the theory set out in *Capital*. The transplantation policy separated individuals from their means of production and was imposed largely on the agricultural sector of a precapitalist society. Those on whom it was imposed were clearly identifiable by their religious affiliation and, overall, the events of the period left a record of brutality. There were shortages of free labor and, in principle, Ireland provided an opportunity to expand markets. The colonial effort was underwritten by public borrowing, lenders were repaid with means of production expropriated from the Irish, and taxes were imposed on Ireland as well.

Parallels between events and policies in Ireland under Cromwell and the elements of Marx's theory of colonialism notwithstanding, Marx paid only passing attention to this episode in Irish history. This is curious for several reasons. For one, Marx showed great interest in modern Ireland in *Capital* and his correspondences.[4] He also referred to Holland's colonial system in 1648, and drew numerous examples from the Cromwellian and earlier periods when describing developments in England.[5] Finally, examining colonialism under Cromwell would have provided an opportunity to broaden the audience for the best-known works of Sir William Petty (1623–87), whom Marx described as the father of modern economics.[6]

One explanation for this omission is explored in this paper: that Ireland under Cromwell is an example of failed colonialism. While there was expropriation of the means of production and other pieces of Marx's model were in place, the outcomes did not support the view that colonizers gain at the expense of those on whom their policies are imposed.

In what follows, English policies toward Ireland at the time of Cromwell are judged using Petty's observations and Marx's theory of colonialism. The paper begins with a brief description of Cromwell's occupation and policies toward Ireland. Elements of Marx's theory of colonization, along with a discussion of conditions in Ireland that relate to each element, are set out in the second section. Concluding comments are presented in the third section.

Evaluating Cromwellian policies toward Ireland in this way provides a framework against which the policies can be judged, while at the same time testing whether the conclusions to which the framework purportedly leads necessarily follow. It also creates an opportunity to systematically examine Sir William Petty's writings on Ireland.

CROMWELL'S OCCUPATION AND POLICIES

The situation that awaited Cromwell in Ireland was one which pitted the Irish and, to a lesser extent, the "Old English" who migrated under earlier plantations against the English government and the "New English" who were to take possession of land in Ireland as a result of parliamentary policies enacted from 1642 through 1644 to help suppress the rebellion.[7] At issue were grievances over religion, the land itself, and access to the political process (Canny 1987, 198). According to Petty (1970 [?1672], 24), the rebellion grew out of:

> a desire of the Romanists, to recover the Church-Revenue, . . . and of the Common Irish, to get all the Englishmen's Estates; and of the 10 or 12 Grandees of Ireland to get the Empire of the whole.[8]

158

Elsewhere (ibid., 43) he wrote:

> The Old Protestants of Queen Elizabeth and King James' Plantation ... did not much love the New English; who came over since 1641, or rather since 1646. & 1648. because they envied the great Shares which they had gotten of the forfeited Lands from the Late Usurpers.

The parliamentary policies of 1642 through 1644 to help suppress the rebellion required the enactment of further policies during Cromwell's occupation if their commitments were to be honored. The Adventurers' Act of 1642 set aside 2.5 million acres in Ireland as payment to subscribers who made financial contributions to underwrite the suppression of the rebellion. An order in 1643 allowed soldiers serving in Ireland to receive payment in land, and in 1644 the English Parliament took fiscal responsibility for suppressing the rebellion, with the understanding that the debt would be paid with Irish land. By 1651 the claims granted under the Adventurers' Act had yet to be fully possessed, but following Cromwell's campaign, the possibility of acting on those claims appeared closer at hand (Corish 1976c, 360; Gardiner 1903, 80, 81)

Part of the problem in realizing the claims was that the plantation of English adventurers and soldiers in Ireland was tied to transportation and transplantation policies: the plantations could not go forward until the Irish soldiers were transported elsewhere, and the land on to which the pre-empted Irish property holders were to be transplanted could not be determined without knowing what land would be required to satisfy the plantation commitments (Simington 1970, ix). Many of the questions about those to be transported and transplanted were answered in the August 1652 Act for the Settling of Ireland, which classified the Irish according to their degree of guilt for the rebellion, their role in the government, and their religious affiliation. According to how persons were classified, the sanctions were execution, banishment or transplantation to a place to be determined by Parliament, and the forfeiture of all or part of their estates in return for land equivalent to a fraction of their original holdings in the place determined by Parliament.[9]

In July 1653, Cromwell instructed that the Irish were to be transplanted to County Clare and the province of Connacht (which together make up the area of western Ireland set off from the rest of the island by the River Shannon); and in September 1653, legislation primarily directed at granting forfeited land to the adventurers and soldiers confirmed that instruction[10] (Corish 1976c, 364; Simington 1970, vii–viii). It was this legislation that led to Petty's *Down Survey* (1967 [1851], vii–viii). The transplantation was declared complete in An Act for the Attainder of the Rebels in Ireland, passed in June 1657 (Corish 1976c, 368).

Writing specifically about the 1652 Act for the Settling of Ireland, but in a

159

way that could have included the 1653 instruction and legislation as well, Corish (1976c, 359) observed:

> This draconian legislation thus came to be directed almost exclusively against catholics, and was so framed that no person of any property could hope to escape ... [W]hile the emotional drive behind the land confiscation was a device to punish a people believed to be collectively guilty, there was a hard economic motive making it necessary to confiscate most of Ireland, and it can be stated quite simply: nothing less would satisfy the debts parliament had pledged against Irish land.

How did the suppression of the rebellion and the land policies under Cromwell affect the people and wealth of Ireland? Petty (1970 [?1672], 17–20) estimated the population of Ireland to be 1.466 million in 1641 and 850,000 in 1652. From this he concluded that 616,000 people – 112,000 English and 504,000 Irish – died in the rebellion.[11] Of these he further estimated that 412,000 died of the plague, 37,000 were slain English, and 167,000 others died "by the Sword and Famine, and other Hardships."[12] While those condemned to death under the 1652 Act were estimated at over 80,000 to 100,000, at most several hundred were executed (Corish 1976c, 360; Gardiner 1903, 82, 88; Simington 1970, ix, xxiv). Finally, and again according to Petty's calculations, 34,000 soldiers and 6,000 boys, women, priests and others were deported (Petty 1970 [?1672], 19).[13]

Petty (ibid., 20–1, 27) further calculated that it would have taken over £8 million to acquire all of the profitable land in Ireland in 1641, but that by 1653 those same acres were valued at £1 million. Livestock was worth over £4 million in 1641, but in 1652 Dublin imported meat from Wales because none was available domestically. In 1641, 2.3 million of 7.5 million usable acres in Ireland belonged to Protestants from earlier plantations and the Protestant Church. In 1672, Protestants and the Protestant Church possessed 5.14 million acres, five-sixths of the housing, nine-tenths of the housing in fortified towns, and two-thirds of the foreign trade.[14]

MARX'S THEORY OF COLONIALISM AND CONDITIONS IN IRELAND

Marx's theory of colonialism rests on the principle of primitive accumulation, and links primitive accumulation to brutality and religious factionalism, the supply of labor and the creation of markets, and public debt and taxation. These linkages provide a sensible framework for evaluating Cromwell's policies toward Ireland.

Primitive accumulation, brutality, and religious factionalism

Marx held that primitive accumulation, or the expropriation from individuals of the means of production with which they can engage in commercial enterprises on their own behalf, originates in the agricultural sector of either a domestic or a colonial economy, and is the vehicle through which feudal society is transformed into capitalist society and capitalist production begins (Marx 1906, 786, 787, 835). For primitive accumulation to occur and capitalist production to begin, persons stripped of their means of production must become free laborers in the sense that they have only their services to sell. He wrote (ibid., 840):

> So long ... as the labourer can accumulate for himself – and this he can do so long as he remains possessor of his means of production – capitalist accumulation and the capitalistic mode of production are impossible.

Primitive accumulation in a colonial setting was characterized as violent and sometimes reflective of religious factionalism. Marx (ibid., 833) noted, for example, that "Liverpool waxed fat on the slave-trade. This was its method of primitive accumulation," and elsewhere (ibid., 823) that:

> The discovery of gold and silver in America, the extirpation, enslavement and entombment in mines of the aboriginal population, the beginning of the conquest and looting of the East Indies ... signalized the rosy dawn of the era of capitalist production. These idyllic proceedings are the chief momenta of primitive accumulation.

More generally, he wrote that "the methods of primitive accumulation are anything but idyllic" (ibid., 785).

The relationship between primitive accumulation, colonialism, and religious factionalism is controversial. Pryor (1982, 527), writing on the classification of precapitalist economies, noted that Marx recognized factors such as war, famine, and pestilence, but not changes in religious views and ideologies, as basic causes of economic and social change. Marx, however, did revert to describing colonizers according to their religious viewpoints:

> Of the Christian colonial system, W. Howitt, a man who makes a specialty of Christianity says: "The barbarities and desperate outrages of the so-called Christian race, throughout every region of the world, and upon every people they have been able to subdue, are not to be paralleled by those of any other race, however fierce, however untaught, and however reckless of mercy and of shame, in any age of the earth."

> (Marx 1906, 824)

And elsewhere: "even in the colonies properly so-called, the Christian character of primitive accumulation did not belie itself" (ibid., 825).

As a practical matter, classes – particularly colonizer versus colonized – were as readily definable along religious and ethnic as along economic lines. Thus, it is instructive to allow that Marx's characterization of colonizers as religious people – a characterization which tended to be harsh – acknowledged that differences in religious persuasion, and specifically, prejudice, might influence colonial policies.

Marx's notion of primitive accumulation accompanied by violence and religious factionalism well describes the policies and attitudes of the Cromwell regime toward the Irish. Regarding violence, and as previously noted (p. 160), Petty estimated that 167,000 non-English died from force, famine, or other hardships resulting from the rebellion. "Gentlemen" who obtained pardons (probably from the Act of 1652) were required to wear a distinguishing mark on their clothing under pain of death, and those of "inferior rank" were to wear a black spot on their right cheek under penalty of branding or hanging (McGee 1863, 551).

Religious factionalism was clearly demonstrated in the way the transplantation policies were implemented. The Act of September 1653 granting forfeited land to the adventurers and soldiers confirmed the transplantation to Clare and Connacht of all Irish people who fell within the categories of the August 1652 Act for the Settling of Ireland. There was, however, disagreement over whether this meant all Irish people (as preferred by certain factions in the English army), or Irish landowners (as preferred by the old Protestants, who saw the need for tenants to remain behind to work the land) (Simington 1970, vii-viii).[15] What followed was a transplantation scheme that focused almost exclusively on Catholic landowners and their dependants. As reported by Corish (1976c, 361):

> The act of settlement of 1652 ... envisioned an almost universal confiscation of land held by catholics. It was clear that nothing less would meet the debt. The confiscation was confined to catholics.

There were approximately 3,000 landed Irish Catholics in 1641, according to Petty's estimates. Of these, about 1,900 received transplantation orders to Connacht. While less than half of these orders came from outside Connacht, they virtually eliminated Catholics as property owners east of the Shannon.[16] Nor was the expropriation of power from the Catholics limited to land: they also lost control of town corporations and were excluded from overseas trade. Tolerance of Catholics in Ireland by Cromwell was said to be an emotional, political, and economic impossibility (Corish 1976c, 369, 373, 381).[17]

Did the treatment of the Irish under Cromwell lead to primitive accumulation? It is clear that expropriation occurred, but did it so completely remove the means of production from the Irish that they had only their services to sell? Edwards (1973, 157) noted that:

162

Both the middle and lower classes, as well as the aristocrats, suffered directly from the confiscations and were forced to move away from their traditional homes or to work as labourers.

And Petty (1970 [?1672], 99–100), writing on whether the Irish were able to accumulate capital in their own behalf, thereby undermining the process of primitive accumulation, observed:

Why should they raise more Commodities, since there are not Merchants sufficiently Stock'd to take them of them ... ? And why should Men endeavour to get Estates, where the Legislative Power is not agreed upon; and where Tricks and Words destroy natural Right and Property?[18]

If primitive accumulation is taken to mean that individuals are left with only their labor services to sell in a market economy, then Cromwell's policies appear to have led to primitive accumulation. If, however, the success of primitive accumulation requires that persons stripped of means of production with which to carry out commercial activities on their own must actually sell their labor services to survive, then, for reasons set forth in the next section, the policies failed.

The policies also appear to have failed if measured by the number of English who actually took possession of the expropriated Irish means of production. Only 1,043 of 1,500 adventurers and fewer than 12,000 of nearly 35,000 soldiers receiving debentures actually settled, and in some cases intermarried with the Irish (Corish 1976c, 370, 372, 373; Petty 1970 [?1672], 6). Those who took possession of land often found it made desolate by the war. Fleetwood wrote in 1654 that there was "scarce a house left undemolished out of walled towns, nor any timber left undestroyed" (Firth 1964, 138). Bands of Irish soldiers who had not surrendered or emigrated terrorized the settlers, and in some areas the wolf population had grown to a menacing size: in 1652 emigrants were forbidden to take wolfhounds from Ireland (ibid., 138, 139; Gardiner 1903, 90). As for the transplantees to Clare and Connacht, the final day for departure was frequently postponed, and they were so slow in moving that disciplinary measures were instituted in March 1655. Some, anticipating confiscation, made private settlements of their estates in advance, or sheltered their property under someone else's name (Simington: xi–xiii, xix).

Primitive accumulation, the supply of labor, and the creation of markets

Marx arrived at strikingly different conclusions about the relationship of primitive accumulation to the availability of free labor under domestic as compared to colonial conditions. Primitive accumulation in countries such as

England and France was seen as creating a surplus of workers, many of whom would become vagrants subject to legislated sanctions, including scourging and branding. In the colonies, however, shortages of labor were seen as so severe that they created an ongoing conflict between the interests of the capitalists and those who worked for them, but who could, in time, acquire means of production of their own:

> [I]n the colonies . . . the labour market is always understocked . . . The wage-worker of to-day is tomorrow an independent peasant, or artisan, working for himself. He vanishes from the labour-market, but not into the workhouse.
>
> (Marx 1906, 843)

It is in this context that Marx discussed at length E.G. Wakefield's notions of "systematic colonization" and the "sufficient price" of land as underlying the preferred policy for solving the colonial labor problem:

> Let the Government put upon the virgin soil an artificial price . . . that compels the immigrant to work a long time for wages before he can earn enough money to buy land, and turn himself into an independent peasant. The funds resulting from the sale of land at a price relatively prohibitory for the wage-workers . . . the Government is to employ . . . to import have-nothings from Europe.[19]
>
> (Ibid., 846)

Labor market conditions in Ireland during and immediately following Cromwell's time are not completely clear. The shortages Marx visualized may well have occurred in the 1650s. The attitude among old Protestants, adventurers, and soldiers receiving land seemed to be that it was less costly to use Irish tenants than to settle English tenants, and that Irish labor was required if services were to be performed and livestock and crops were to be raised.[20] It appears that a large Irish population, including many old proprietors who became tenants on what was once their own land, remained behind following the transplantation and was in strong demand. On the other hand, Petty indicated that in 1672 only 380,000 out of 780,000 fit for work were actually employed (Corish 1976c, 364, 374; Firth 1964, 141; Petty 1970 [?1672], 11–13).

Why was there this high nonparticipation in the labor market when there was an apparently strong demand for Irish workers? One explanation is as Marx suggested: wage earners had become independent and had left the labor market. In this case, however, it seems they were leaving not to produce in markets for their own profit using newly reacquired means of production, but to subsist outside the market economy. Petty observed in *Political Anatomy* (1970 [?1672], 99) that:

> [W]hat need they to Work, who can content themselves with Potato's, whereof the Labour of one Man can feed forty; . . . when they can

every where gather Cockles, Oysters, Muscles, Crabs, &c . . .; can build a
House in three days? And why should they desire to fare better, tho
with more Labour, when they are taught, that this way of living is more
like the Patriarchs of old, and the Saints of later times.

And in *Political Arithmetic* (1751, 42) he wrote:

Ireland being under-peopled, and land, and cattle being very cheap;
there being every where store of fish and foul; the ground yielding
excellent roots (and particularly that bread-like root Potatoes) and
withal they being able to perform their husbandry, with such harness
and tackling, as each man can make with his own hands; and living in
such houses as almost every man can build; and every housewife being
a spinner and dyer of wool and yarn, they can live and subsist after
their present fashion, without the use of gold or silver money; and can
supply themselves with the necessities above-named, without labouring
two hours per diem.[21]

It appears that no policy similar to Wakefield's "sufficient price" was
introduced to lessen the economic self-sufficiency of the Irish. In fact, the
record suggests that many of the soldiers who received land sold it at a
discount (Petty 1970 [?1672], 20). However, a Wakefield-like mechanism is
described in *Political Arithmetic*, where Petty (1751, 60) wrote: "where the rent
of land is advanced . . . there the number of years purchase, for which the
inheritance may be sold, is also advanced."[22]

The self-sufficiency of the Irish also had implications for the creation of
colonial markets in Ireland. Marx (1906, 819–20) set out in a general way how
such markets would result from primitive accumulation applied to agriculture:

[T]he events that transformed the small peasants into wage labourers,
and their means of subsistence and of labour into material elements of
capital, created, at the same time, a home-market for the latter.
Formerly, the peasant family produced the means of subsistence and
the raw materials, which they themselves for the most part, consumed.
These raw materials and means of subsistence have now become . . .
transformed into articles of manufacture, to which the country
districts at once served for markets.

But based on Petty's above-quoted observations, the strong implication is
that the separation of the Irish from their capital through expropriation
and transplantation did not lead to the expansion of markets for English
products. More directly, he wrote (Petty 1970 [?1672], 82):

the Trade of Ireland, among $\frac{19}{22}$ parts of the whole people, is little or
nothing . . . Nor is above $\frac{1}{5}$ part of their Expence [*sic*] other than what
their own family produceth, which Condition and state of living cannot
beget Trade.

PATRICK J. WELCH

Primitive accumulation, public debt, and taxation

Of late seventeenth-century English colonial, debt, and taxation policies, and their relation to primitive accumulation, Marx (1906, 823–4) wrote:

> [T]hey arrive at a systematical combination, embracing the colonies, the national debt, the modern mode of taxation, and the protectionist system. These methods depend in part on brute force, e.g., the colonial system. But they all employ the power of the state . . . to hasten . . . the process of transformation of the feudal mode of production into the capitalist mode.[23]

Elsewhere, and more generally, he further wrote (ibid., 827) that:

> The public debt becomes one of the most powerful levers of primitive accumulation. As with the stroke of an enchanter's wand, it endows barren money with the power of breeding and thus turns it into capital.

Given colonial opportunities, primitive accumulation could be accomplished through private lending to the government (to help defray its costs of overseas adventures) in return for entitlements to real or other property in the colonies. Taxes imposed on the colonies would also create a revenue stream, allowing the government to meet its obligations to its creditors.

The honoring of commitments made by the English government when underwriting the debt for its activities in Ireland did separate the Irish from their means of production: the effect of the Adventurers' Act of 1642, of an order of 1643 granting land to soldiers, of the 1652 Act for the Settling of Ireland, and of Cromwell's instruction of 1653 was to transfer land into the hands of the English. However, while the debt-financing policies were expropriative, they appear to have been accompanied by tax policies that imposed a substantial burden on the adventurers who were the intended beneficiaries of the expropriations, and on others; while at the same time they failed to generate sufficient revenue to offset the government's costs of occupation.

From July 1649 through November 1656 England spent £3,509,396 on Ireland but recovered only £1,942,548 in revenue, leaving £1,566,848 as the debt of the English Treasury (Gardiner 1903, 89). And of the revenue recovered from Ireland, much may have come from the adventurers, who contracted to pay assessments, customs duties, and excise taxes (Ashley 1962, 91).

The primary sources of revenue were a monthly assessment, followed by rent on confiscated land and other property, and indirect taxes (Firth 1964, 165, 166). Because the population of Ireland was relatively small, its contribution of indirect taxes to the Treasury was relatively small as well, which led to an argument in Parliament over whether taxes on land should be increased (Ashley 1962, 92). However, a 1658 proposal to impose quit-rents on the forfeited land granted to the adventurers and soldiers was never

166

implemented: despite the smaller revenues generated in Ireland, it was already disproportionately taxed.

In this regard, Firth (1964, 168) noted that England and Wales paid less than four times as much per month in assessments than Ireland but were far more than four times as rich; and Vincent Gookin, the pamphleteer and acquaintance of Petty, is attributed as saying: "The tax sweeps away their whole subsistence, necessity makes them turn thieves and Tories; and then they are prosecuted by fire and sword for being so" (Gardiner 1903, 89). Petty's view (1751, 42, 43) was that because the Irish could subsist largely outside an exchange economy, a tax that was paid in flax rather than one which was levied on property and paid in silver would be more profitable.[24]

CONCLUSIONS

In his letter of November 29, 1869 to Dr Kugelmann, Marx wrote: "As a matter of fact, the English republic under Cromwell met shipwreck in – Ireland" (Marx and Engels 1936, 279). While providing no details for his opinion, Marx's views on colonial policies and their intended outcomes, as expressed in *Capital*, suggest how he would arrive at such a conclusion.

The expropriations may have significantly limited the ability of the Irish to carry on commercial activities on their own behalf, but many of the English who were eligible for plantation never took advantage of the opportunity to colonize the country. Nor does it appear that, following the expropriations, the Irish as a group were forced to sell their labor in order to survive; those who did may have bargained from a relatively strong position. The potential for newly created markets in Ireland appears to have been limited because many of the Irish subsisted outside of the exchange economy, and while the public debt policies of the English government were expropriative of the Irish, the accompanying tax policies appear to have been a burden to the adventurers and inadequate to meet the needs of the English Treasury.

The discussion of colonialism set out in *Capital* provides a sensible framework for analyzing the record and commentary on Ireland during Cromwell's occupation; and Cromwell's occupation provides one test case for evaluating the determinacy with which the proposed transition mechanism for moving society from the feudal to the capitalist epoch operates. Applying Marx's theory to Ireland under Cromwell also provides the opportunity to use, rather than simply to read, Petty's work.

NOTES

1 Thanks go to Tony Aspromourgos, A.W. Coats, Peter L. Danner, and an anonymous referee for helpful comments.
2 Oliver Cromwell (1599–1658) arrived in Ireland with an army of 12,000. Prior to his arrival, according to Petty's estimates, the British army numbered about 40,000 and the rebels numbered about 8,000 (Corish 1976b, 336; Petty 1970 [?1672], 23).

In 1650 Cromwell left Ireland but retained civil and military authority as Lord Lieutenant until 1652, when that authority passed to four commissioners. In 1654 authority passed to Lord Deputy Charles Fleetwood. It was Fleetwood who brought Sir William Petty to Ireland in 1652 as his personal physician and physician to the army (Firth 1964, 133; Petty 1967, 1).

Cromwell was installed as Protector in 1653 and held that title until his death in 1658. The following year his son, Richard, to whom the title of Protector passed, resigned, and his other son, Henry, left his post as Lord Deputy of Ireland (Corish 1976c, 356; Wedgwood 1953, 11).

3 Marx's presentation on colonialism is a special case of his more general theory of the development of a capitalist system and, arguably, could be described as a metatheory since it incorporates his empirical observations, views of history, and sociology, along with his constructions of the relations among economic variables. For reasons of expository convenience, however, it will be called a theory.

The theory of colonialism presented here is scattered throughout Part VIII of Volume I of *Capital*: "The So-called Primitive Accumulation." Of the topics relating to colonialism, only those pertaining to labor market conditions – and largely to the writing of Wakefield – are found in Chapter 33, "The Modern Theory of Colonization," which is the last chapter of *Capital*. This imbalance in a chapter formally devoted to colonialism is made all the more interesting by the question of whether the chapter was written out of concern over censorship, or as an integral part of Marx's analysis (see Rodriguez Braun 1987).

4 An extensive treatment by Marx of modern Ireland is found in Chapter XXV of *Capital* (1906, 767–83). Reference is also made to modern Ireland in his letters to Engels dated November 2, 1867 and November 18, 1869; to Meyer and Vogt dated April 9, 1870; to his daughter dated April 11, 1881, and in his "confidential circular" written to the General Council about December 1, 1869 and discussed in his letter to Meyer and Vogt (Marx and Engels 1936, 228, 265, 288–90, 391–92; 1968, 258–9). Brief reference is made to Cromwell in *Capital* (Marx 1906, 792, 821n), a letter to Engels dated November 30, 1867, and a letter to Kugelmann dated November 29, 1869 (Marx and Engels 1936, 228–9, 278–9). Engels wrote to Marx on October 24, 1869 that he was "still to work through the Cromwellian period" (ibid., 264), and Engels and Marx communicated on November 29, 1869 and December 10, 1869 about the work of Sir John Davies, Solicitor-General and Attorney-General in Ireland from 1603 through 1619, who applied English law to the colony and was an important predecessor to Cromwell in the formation of Irish policy (ibid., 274–6, 280–2; see also, Pawlisch 1985, 3–4).

5 See Marx (1906, chs xxvii and xxviii, and p. 826).

6 The opening sentence of Chapter 1 of Marx's *Theories of Surplus Value* reads: "The founder of modern political economy is Sir William Petty, one of the most gifted and original economic investigators" (Marx 1952, 15). His view of Petty is noted by Schumpeter (1966, 210n).

7 Plantation was pursued by Mary Tudor (1556), Elizabeth I (1586), and James I (after 1603). James was the first monarch to consider plantation in a systematic way (Edwards 1973, 157–62).

8 These desires can be traced in part to a policy of Charles I granting the Irish concessions, or "graces," on land and religion in return for the payment of £120,000. The sum was paid but the graces were never forthcoming. Legislation in 1641 effectively blocked their ever being granted (Edwards 1973, 58–60).

9 In one group were those inciting or contributing to the rebellion before October 1642, clerics involved in the rebellion, those found guilty of murdering civilians and English soldiers or fighting after the passage of the Act of Settlement, and 105

named individuals. These were to be executed and their estates confiscated. High-ranking officers in the Irish government not included in the first group were to be banished and their estates, along with the estates of all others who did or would have laid down their arms in the rebellion, were to be forfeited. The wives and children of the banished officers and the others who forfeited their estates were to be transplanted and receive the equivalent of one-third of their holdings at a place to be decided by Parliament. Catholics not included in the previous categories but not supporting the English government were to forfeit one-third of their estates and be transplanted to a place to be decided by Parliament, where they would receive the equivalent of two-thirds of their holdings. Other persons were to forfeit one-fifth of their estates, and persons of "an inferior sort" whose posses-sions were minimal were free on pardon, provided they transported themselves elsewhere (Simington 1970, xvii–xviii; see also Corish 1976c, 357–9; Gardiner 1903, 82–4).

10 Connacht comprises Galway, Mayo, Roscommon, and Sligo counties. The Irish were not to settle in port towns or garrisons, or within four miles (later one mile) of the Shannon or the sea. This suggests that Clare and Connacht were chosen for transplantation because the river and the sea effectively separated them from the rest of the island (Corish 1976c, 364, 367; Edwards 1973, 164).

11 Petty's attitude toward the Irish is not clear. On the one hand, he valued the Irish who died in the rebellion at the rate set for slaves (Petty 1970 [?1672], 21), and in his Author's Preface to *Political Anatomy* observed:

> as Students in Medicine, practice their inquiries upon cheap and common Animals, and such whose actions they are best acquainted with, and where there is the least confusion and perplexure o Parts; I have chosen Ireland as such a Political Animal, who is scarce Twenty years old; where the Intrigue of State is not very complicate and with which I have been conversant from an Embrion.

On the other hand, he called the Irish "men of admirable success and courage" (ibid., 24).

Adam Smith's position on the Irish is not altogether clear either. For example, he wrote (1937 [1776], 161):

> The chairmen, porters, and coal-haulers in London, and those unfortunate women who live by prostitution, the strongest men and the most beautiful women perhaps in the British dominions, are said to be, the greater part of them, from the lowest rank of people in Ireland.

12 Of the survivors, Gardiner (1903, 90) recorded a quote attributed to one of the commissioners:

> Frequently, some are found feeding on carrion and weeds, some starved in the highways, and many times poor children who lost their parents, or have been deserted by them, are found exposed to, and some of them fed upon by, ravening wolves and other beasts and birds of prey.

13 Some accounts placed the number of Irish deported at 100,000 (McGee 1863, 550).

14 *Political Anatomy* is thought to have been written in 1672 (1970, vi). Thus, there is some question about when data reported for 1672 were actually collected.

15 A commission established to examine delinquencies in transplantation dealt only with landholders, which suggests that the transplantation of others was either delayed or not pursued. Part of the disagreement over who should be transplanted

involved two pamphleteers: Vincent Gookin, who anonymously wrote *The Great Case for Transplantation* in January 1655, and Colonel Richard Lawrence, who responded with *The Interest of England in the Irish Transplantation* in March of that year. Gookin opposed a general transplantation and incorporated arguments supporting his position that were provided, also anonymously, by Petty. Lawrence responded that the transplantation would apply only to landholders and those bearing arms (Gardiner 1903, 100–4; see also Canny 1987, 198–9; Ellis 1975, 125–9).

16 By one estimate, 90 percent of the land was in Catholic hands in 1603, 59 percent was in Catholic hands in 1649, and 22 percent in Catholic hands in 1685 (Edwards 1973, 165).

17 The brutality and religious factionalism directed toward the Irish were not reserved for those to be colonized. The Irish were, in some senses, treated no differently by the English than were the English themselves. Marx (1906, 806–8) spent several pages describing penalties, including scourging and branding, that dated from the time of Henry VII and were imposed on beggars and others not working. More broadly, and referring to conditions in France and the Netherlands as well as in England, he concluded (ibid., 808–9):

> Thus were the agricultural people, first forcibly expropriated from the soil, driven from their homes, turned into vagabonds, and then whipped, branded, tortured by laws grotesquely terrible into the discipline necessary for the wage system.

The relationship between expropriation and religious affiliation, particularly Catholicism, in England itself was also noted by Marx, who wrote (ibid., 792):

> The process of forcible expropriation of the people received in the 16th century a new and frightful impulse from the Reformation, and from the consequent colossal spoilation of the church property.

While there was, apparently, more religious tolerance in England during Cromwell's administration than at other times, it did not extend equally to Anglicans and Catholics (Wedgwood 1973, 88, 89, 111; see also Marx 1906, 821n).

18 Petty was probably describing conditions in Ireland closer to 1672.

Primitive accumulation and the creation of surplus value in Ireland were hinted at by Petty in *Political Anatomy* (1970 [?1672], 86), where he wrote that trade was the way to obtaining riches and power:

> Not only by getting Commodities out of the Earth and Sea; by ploughing, fishing, Mines, Vecture, &c. *by getting away those Commodities from them, who first got them out of the Earth and Sea, as aforesaid* [emphasis added]. And not only, or at all encreasing the whole Wealth of the Nation, but one's own former share and proportion of the whole, tho diminish'd.

(See also (ibid., 86–7) for a numeric example.)

Marx devoted the first chapter of *Theories of Surplus Value* to an analysis of passages from Petty's *Treatise of Taxes and Contributions* that could be argued as developing that theory, and quoted in a footnote (1952, 16n) a passage from *Political Anatomy* relating to the measure of value. He did not mention the above-quoted passage, which appears to be more on point to the surplus value concept. This quote of Petty's, especially where he wrote: "And not only, or at all encreasing the whole Wealth of the Nation, but one's own former share and proportion of

170

the whole, tho diminish'd", is open to interpretation. On the one hand, it could refer to the passing of the goods to tradespersons and others whom the Physiocrats put in the sterile class because they did not add to value. (Marx (ibid.) commented on the "Physiocratic ring" of Petty's discussion of value.) On the other hand, the reference to increasing "one's . . . share . . . of the whole, tho diminish'd" could be seen as hinting at exploitation and crisis.

One also wonders if Smith noticed Petty's reference to the "Wealth of the Nation."

19 Kittrell (1973, 90) noted that Wakefield later abandoned the notion of using the proceeds from colonial land sales to import labor in favor of using the proceeds to offset colonial expenses.

20 Dependence on the Irish was not unique to Cromwell. Those with plantation rights in 1610, for example, found it less costly to use Irish tenants than to introduce English settlers (Clarke 1976, 201, 203).

21 Of the housing of the Irish, Petty (1970 [?1672], 27) observed that they "live in a brutish nasty Condition, as in Cabins, with neither Chimney, Door, Stairs nor Window."

22 See also Petty (1751, 63) for a numeric example. The quote is from a proposal to depopulate Ireland and the Scottish Highlands. This position is consistent with his earlier support of Gookin's opposition to a general transplantation of the Irish (see note 15 above). The opposition stemmed in part from the fear that the transplantation would intensify the hostility between the English and Irish (see Ellis 1975, 125–9). Rather than separate the Irish from the English, Petty proposed in *Political Anatomy* (1970 [?1672], 29–31) to homogenize the two groups by transporting English to Ireland and Irish in the other direction. During the writing of *Political Arithmetic*, however, he must have seen Ireland as such a drain on the English that he proposed its depopulation: a proposal put forth "rather as dream or refvery [*sic*], than a rational proposition" (Petty 1751, 59). His depopulation recommendation, like his proposal in *Political Anatomy*, would have had the effect of homogenizing the populations.

23 Marx did not limit his discussion of public debt and taxation to their roles in colonial policy.

24 Petty was writing of conditions in the 1670s.

REFERENCES

Ashley, Maurice (1962 [1934]) *Financial and Commercial Policy Under the Cromwellian Protectorate*, New York: Augustus M. Kelley.

Canny, Nicholas (1987) "Identity formation in Ireland: the emergence of the Anglo-Irish," in Nicholas Canny and Anthony Pagden (eds), *Colonial Identity in the Atlantic World, 1590–1800*, Princeton, NJ: Princeton University Press.

Clarke, Aidan with Edwards, R. Dudley (1976) "Pacification, plantation, and the Catholic question, 1603–23," in T.W. Moody, F.X. Martin, and F.J. Byrne (eds), *A New History of Ireland*, vol. III, Oxford: Clarendon Press, 187–232.

Corish, Patrick (1976a) "The rising of 1641 and the Catholic confederacy, 1641–45," in T.W. Moody, F.X. Martin, and F.J. Byrne (eds), *A New History of Ireland*, vol. III, Oxford: Clarendon Press, 289–316.

Corish, Patrick (1976b) "The Cromwell conquest, 1649–53," in T.W. Moody, F.X. Martin, and F.J. Byrne (eds), *A New History of Ireland*. vol. III, Oxford: Clarendon Press, 336–52.

Corish, Patrick (1976c) "The Cromwellian regime, 1650–60," in T.W. Moody, F.X.

Martin, and F.J. Byrne (eds), *A New History of Ireland*, vol. III, Oxford: Clarendon Press, 353–86.

Edwards, Ruth Dudley (1973) *An Atlas of Irish History*, London: Methuen.

Ellis, Peter B. (1975) *Hell or Connaught!*, New York: St Martin's Press.

Firth, Charles H. (1964) *The Last Years of the Protectorate*, vol. II, New York: Russell & Russell.

Gardiner, Samuel R. (1903) *History of the Commonwealth and Protectorate*, vol. IV, London: Longmans, Green.

Howell, Roger Jr (1977) *Cromwell*, Boston, MA: Little, Brown.

Kittrell, Edward R. (1973) "Wakefield's scheme of systematic colonization and classical economics," *American Journal of Economics and Sociology* 32(1): 87–111.

Marx, Karl (1906) *Capital* vol. I, ed. F. Engels, trans. Samuel Moore and Edward Aveling, Chicago: Charles H. Kerr.

Marx, Karl (1952) *Theories of Surplus Value*, trans. G.A. Bonner and Emile Burns, New York: International Publishers.

Marx, Karl and Engels, Friedrich (1936) *Correspondences*, New York: International Publishers.

Marx, Karl and Engels, Friedrich (1968) *On Colonialism*, Moscow: Progress Publishers.

McGee, Thomas D. (1863) *A Popular History of Ireland*, New York: D. & S. Sadlier.

Pawlisch, Hans S. (1985) *Sir John Davies and the Conquest of Ireland*, Cambridge: Cambridge University Press.

Petty, Sir William (1970 [?1672]) *The Political Anatomy of Ireland*, Shannon: Irish University Press.

Petty, Sir William (1751) *Political Arithmetic*, Glasgow: Robert and Andrew Foulis.

Petty, Sir William (1967 [1851]) *The History of the Survey of Ireland Commonly Called the Down Survey*, New York: Augustus M. Kelley.

Pryor, Frederic L. (1982) "The classification and analysis of precapitalist economic systems by Marx and Engels," *History of Political Economy* 14(4): 521–42.

Rodriguez Braun, Carlos (1987) "*Capital*'s last chapter," *History of Political Economy* 19(2): 299–310.

Schumpeter, Joseph A. (1966) *History of Economic Analysis*, New York: Oxford University Press.

Simington, Robert C. (1970) *The Transplantation to Connacht*, Shannon: Irish University Press, for the Irish Manuscript Commission.

Smith, Adam (1937 [1776]) *The Wealth of Nations*, ed. Edwin Cannon, New York: Random House.

Wedgwood, Dame Cicely V. (1953) *Oliver Cromwell*, London: Duckworth.

Wedgwood, Dame Cicely V. (1973) *Oliver Cromwell*, new edn, London: Gerald Duckworth.

172

11

VINCENT DE GOURNAY, OR *"LAISSEZ-FAIRE* WITHOUT *LAISSEZ-PASSER"*

Pascale Pitavy-Simoni[1]

INTRODUCTION

The constitution of economic liberalism first took shape in France in the eighteenth century. This liberalism went together with a strong rejection of free trade. This conclusion, borne out by my research, leads to an important question: Can one concurrently advocate liberalism and protectionism? A French economist of the eighteenth century, Vincent de Gournay, answered this question: liberalism and protectionism can coexist.

There are those who have thought that Gournay's liberalism was unadulterated, reflected in the famous maxim *"laissez-faire, laissez-passer"* which was attributed to him.[2] This, however, is a mistake and I will show that Gournay deceived us, for his brand of liberalism was protectionist. This maxim must be corrected and rewritten to become *"laissez-faire* without *laissez-passer."* The paradox of a protectionist liberalism has never been subject to criticism because the document which would have elucidated it has been hidden away and unpublished for more than two centuries.

It all began in the middle of the eighteenth century when Vincent de Gournay undertook the translation of Child's *A New Discourse of Trade* and Culpeper's *A Tract against Usury.*[3] The annotations and commentaries which he added to these translations make up what is called the *Remarques.* These *Remarques* went unpublished during Gournay's lifetime[4] and the two translations alone were published in 1754. It was not until two centuries later, in 1983, that the *Remarques* were published,[5] having been found by Takumi Tsuda.[6] Thanks to this wonderful find, the understanding of Gournay's thought was able to go beyond mere speculative analysis.

When Sécrestat-Escande wrote about Gournay at the beginning of the twentieth century without the benefit of reading the *Remarques,* he was aware of the theoretical vacuum this represented: "In any case, we will probably never have a real grasp of the Superintendent of Commerce's true doctrine unless we find the notes which must have accompanied his translation of Child."[7] The approach to Gournay's thought at that time was to assimilate it to authors affiliated to his group[8] and whom Gournay would have influenced directly in the writing of their works. The most important among these writers are: Cliquot Blervache, *Dissertation sur les effets que produit le taux de l'intérêt de l'argent sur le commerce et l'agriculture* (1755) and *Mémoire sur les corps de métiers* (written under the pseudonym M. Delisle in 1757); and l'abbé Morel-let, *Réflexions sur les avantages de la libre fabrication et de l'usage des toiles peintes en France* (1759). Apart from these two thinkers, there are a few other remnants of Gournay's own writings: a *Mémoire* addressed to the Lyon Chamber of Commerce concerning the suppression of the communities,[9] and letters sent to Trudaine, who was the Superintendent of Finance, and to Choisel.

Whereas Sécrestat-Escande exhibited caution when using Cliquot's and Morellet's writings,[10] Gustave Schelle is decidedly freer with his interpret-ation.[11] Schelle is in fact the last author in a line of economists beginning with Turgot who "betrayed," to use Takumi Tsuda's expression, Gournay's thought.[12] The *Eloge*, written in 1759 by Turgot, is the first important document which contributed to creating the legend of Gournay as the unconditional advocate of "*laissez-faire, laissez-passer.*" In fact, it would seem that Turgot inextricably meshed Gournay's thought with his. This is especially apparent in Turgot's muting of the protectionism of foreign trade so forcefully expressed in Gournay's defense of a Navigation Act. In his *Eloge*, Turgot even alludes to principles of free trade[13] despite their undeniable absence from Gournay's thought.

This betrayal will thus be the starting point for the reconstruction of Gournay's reasoning, which will be based directly upon his writings and not upon speculative or mistaken readings of these writings. Thus I will show that Gournay's thought was "*laissez-faire* without *laissez-passer.*"

The paper is consequently divided into two main parts. In the first, I will explain why Gournay wanted to free production from the hindrances imposed by the mercantilist – or more specifically Colbertist – straightjacket: the corporations, or corporate bodies, and regulations. This is *laissez-faire*, an expression of the freedom of labor and manufacture. In the second part, I will discuss *laissez-passer* by distinguishing domestic trade from international trade. Whereas a domestic application of *laissez-passer* does not create any interpret-ative problems in terms of economic liberalism, its international application is seriously compromised in Gournay's defense of a Navigation Act. This is why, in light of my desire to reconsider the "betrayal" of Gournay, I will devote most of the second part to an analysis of this refusal of *laissez-passer*. I will then show how protectionism is part and parcel of economic liberalism.[14]

THE DOCTRINE OF *LAISSEZ-FAIRE*: FREEDOM OF LABOR AND FREEDOM OF MANUFACTURE

It is fundamental that Gournay gave new meaning to the concept of wealth in 1754. In fact, never before had emphasis been placed solely on production:

Wealth does not lie in gold and in money but rather in what land and industry produce ... Gold and money are but merchandise in all trading nations, and until we see them in the same light we shall not be able to consider ourselves as being amongst the most insightful nations on trade.[15]

Wealth thus flows from production.

This emphasis on production as the foundation of wealth prompted Gournay from then on to reflect upon the need to reorganize production. The author's liberalism is at that point well summarized in the maxim *"laissez-faire."* Gournay believed in effect that production, which is to say labor and manufacture, had to be freed from the hindrances and regulations that Colbert had established. I will address these two aspects of the reorganization of production through the question of the struggle against the corporations and regulations.

The origins and economic consequences of corporations

To point out the benefits of *laissez-faire*, Gournay based his argument on elements which have been synthesized into one central idea: The conflict between private interest and general interest can only be resolved within an economy based on competition.

The origin of corporations: a conflict between private and general interest

In his *mémoire* addressed in 1753 to the Lyon Chamber of Commerce, Gournay traced the origin of the corporations in Lyon[16] and the internal and external economic consequences of their monopolies.[17] The first corporations dated from the time of Francis I and, according to Gournay, must have been given a free hand to have developed so successfully. Fearing competition, they subsequently merged. The prospect of too many competitors, from the point of view of those manufacturers already established, would be bound to entail a loss in profits. This in turn led to the creation of communities to which access was made more and more difficult:

> In the first place, they [the manufacturers] decided to group together in a class or a community those workers who had specialized in one aspect of the factory's production. They then made entry to each of these classes more difficult by creating the position of master craftsman which was earned by long periods of apprenticeship prolonged by the *"compagnonnage."*[18]

(Vincent de Gournay 1753, 140)

By restricting free access to labor, the corporations made the weight of their private interests felt and subverted the effects of competition. The state, however, believed that by backing the private interests of the

175

corporations, it was also fostering the general interest. This misapprehension, according to Gournay, was due to its ignorance:

> The various manufacturers, having established a common body of laws dictated by private interest, sought confirmation of these laws from the government. Their task was facilitated even more by the fact that it was easy to convince a government which had no knowledge of trade that what was sought for the particular interest of each community was for the good of the overall population and of trade in general.
>
> (Ibid., 140)

We can see from this the importance that knowledge had for Gournay, a theme which became a leitmotif throughout his work. Without knowledge, the government can only err and its economic policy will reflect its ignorance. The government therefore acted to "the detriment of the general good of commerce unwittingly" (ibid., 147). Gournay's appraisal of the state as being but an ignorant actor must be nuanced by the fact that it was also to the advantage of the state to back these monopolies because these communities lent money in times of need.

When the state intervenes in the economy by granting privileges it prevents competition from taking root. Competition, however, played an essential role for Gournay, in that it promoted compatibility between the interests of the individual and of the nation. Gournay was convinced that the liberal model is the only viable one for society and thus argued for *laissez-faire*. This is what I will show by analyzing, with Gournay, the negative economic consequences of corporations.

The negative economic consequences of corporations

To shore up his critique of corporations, which is to say the impossibility of working in conditions of freedom and desirable competition, Gournay described the economic effects of these communities. I shall present his position under three points. The first, which he deemed critical, is the increase in the price of commodities in the country:

> Our monopolies and restrictions mean that at a comparable quality our fabrics cost us more than they do abroad ... The manufacturers, by making access to the position of master craftsman more difficult have also reduced their numbers and therefore found it easier to raise the price of their fabrics, and pass off the cost of their luxury and expenses upon these fabrics, which makes them considerably more expensive. In other words, in an effort to make as much money as possible the number of people involved in commerce in Lyon has been kept to a minimum. This can only be done by jacking up the price of the merchandise.
>
> (Ibid., 150–1)

Gournay justly pointed out that the direct consequence of this increase in the price of commodities was a decrease in domestic consumption.

This in turn led (and herein lies Gournay's second argument, which compared France to other countries, notably England and Holland) to a drop in exports and perhaps even an increase in imports from these countries for certain goods. These countries, because, according to Gournay, they understood the importance of competition for industry, offered prices which were a lot more competitive than French prices, given that they were unaffected by restrictions or laws imposed by monopolies:

> While Lyon sustained the greed of its communities, it repelled commerce and favored the trade of London and Amsterdam where foreigners were welcome and were both master craftsmen and merchants. In these cities they increased the number of mills and lowered prices whereas the price of our fabrics made by an ever smaller number of people increased. It is a maxim borne out by truth that the multiplicity of people involved lowers the cost of salaries and boosts trade.
>
> (Ibid., 145–6)

Gournay backed up his argument with striking figures:

> The English have made out so well that today they only buy 5,000 French pounds worth of silk and lace whereas in 1685 they bought 12 million French pounds. The Dutch barely buy a million compared to 8 million in 1688. If you take into account the fact that both nations now furnish us, the amazing difference for our trade balance becomes apparent.
>
> (Ibid., 149)

Finally, Gournay pointed out one last consequence which he saw as undoubtedly the most serious: restrictions affecting the liberty of labor led to workers emigrating[19] to countries where the freedom to work was paramount:

> Such laws, which could only create an ever-increasing number of impediments, added to a worker's hardships and made the practice of his profession increasingly unpleasant. Disgruntledness reached such proportions that other nations became aware of this and attracted dissatisfied workers with promises and rewards. This new transmigration of our workers to foreign countries increased the number of our competitors which further weakened our manufacturing capability. This weakening further diminished competition at home and made labor and fabrics more expensive, which in turn gave foreigners new advantages over us.[20]
>
> (Ibid., 148–9)

PASCALE PITAVY-SIMONI

The loss of this labor force was thus felt doubly hard. Not only was English industry reinforced by the acquisition of new skilled workers but, as Gournay pointed out, France was weakened:

> How could we not be at a disadvantage with regards to the English and the Dutch given that they don't have a system of master craftsmen and forced apprenticeships especially in the silk industry? Aren't these different rites of passage just obstacles which impede industry and emulation and favor foreigners?

(Vincent de Gournay 1983, 99)

The problem with French industry, according to Gournay, was a lack of competition and the loss of precious know-how. Furthermore, this loss of know-how also caused a loss of potential consumers. The key role of consumption was not lost on Gournay: "If a thousand Genoans were to decide to settle in Lyon, what could be better for the King, who would thus acquire a thousand new subjects, for our lands which would acquire a thousand new consumers and for the city of Lyon which would acquire a thousand new citizens" (Vincent de Gournay 1753, 149). Here he echoed the argument developed by Boisguilbert, notably in his works *Détail de la France* and *Factum de la France*.[21]

Therefore, all that spurns work and all that favors monopolies was condemned. Gournay's struggle against monopolies was thus inspired by the defense of freedom of labor. What Gournay denounced in the communities of private interest was the inactivity to which they condemned workers. The idea of labor was fundamental to Gournay in that the increase of a nation's wealth depends on it:

> The State becomes richer when everyone is employed. By providing gainful occupation to a great number of men one strengthens the State ... The greatest of all evils is to deprive men of work and thus deprive the State of its part of the fruit of their work.

(Ibid., 152–3)

Gournay's attachment to freedom of labor thus well defined the specificity of his liberalism and, more generally, the specificity of French economic liberalism. It rested on the proposition which, if not Gournay's, nevertheless summarizes his thought: one must *laissez-faire*, which for Gournay meant freeing labor of its hindrances and eliminating the corporations: in short, reorganizing production along the lines of competition.

Laissez-faire in relation to labor enabled a link to be established between a definition of wealth based on production and the status of men. In other words, *laissez-faire* must be applied to the individual as a social element. This, however, presupposed that the state would not intervene by granting exclusive privileges but rather would let competition decide. Then, and then only, would individuals be in a position to define their best interests, and this would, in conditions of freedom, lead to the general good. One finds echoes of Gournay's *laissez-faire* in Turgot's article "Fondations' in the *Encyclopedia* of Diderot and d'Alambert:

> One does not have to reflect much to convince oneself that society's first type of needs [humanity's general needs] are not of the nature to be satisfied by foundations or by any other gratuitous means; and in this respect, the general good must be the result of each individual's efforts acting in his own interest ... If men have an overwhelming interest in the good that you wish to create for them, *laissez les faire* (let them be), this is the great, unique principle.
>
> (Turgot 1986, 120–1)

This will to *laissez-faire* is also present in the debate over regulations. The reorganization of production in fact implied the freeing of manufacture since it suffered the same hindrances as did freedom of labor.

Repressive regulations opposed to competition

In the final analysis, regulations presented the same sort of problems as did the corporations. Furthermore, established with the aim of protecting the public from bad quality, they provided food for thought on the issue of the relationship between the private and the general interest, which, according to Gournay, was falsely presented.

Repressive regulations and over-zealous inspectors

These regulations affected primarily the wool and cotton industries. They forced mill-owners to have different quality stamps at different stages of production:

> The quality and source of utilized raw materials, the way of manufacturing the products and their dimensions had been established by regulations. Stockings had to be made with floss-silk and three-string metal rods; they had to weigh five ounces for men and three for women. Sheets had to be made with a certain type of wool and had to be of a certain width ... Sheets had to be stamped three times when they were still in linen cloth, when they returned to the mill and following the last preparation; they also had to bear a lead marker indicating quality.
>
> (Schelle 1984 [1897], 48–9)

As we can see, the regulations Gournay wished to attack were stringent.

As well as regulations, Gournay was after the inspectors. Gournay felt that they could sometimes be of use with counterfeit products but that they should in no way discourage manufacturers through fines and excessive confiscations:

> It has been a pleasure to witness your zeal and talent. However, these will be to the benefit of trade only if you handle manufacturers with care and if you avoid as much as possible disheartening them; experience will have shown them that whereas foreigners have eagerly taken our workers from us, they have displayed previous little interest in our inspectors. If we wish to keep them, we will have to treat them gently and with good manners.
>
> (Gournay, letter of January 22, 1753 [to an inspector student], in ibid., 65)

There is thus a fundamental conflict between knowledge of production and trade and the eagerness with which inspectors fined manufacturers. Cliquot, a member of Gournay's group, pointed out that "the council weights the usefulness of an inspector by the number of violations he uncovers" (Cliquot, *Considerations sur le commerce* ... , quoted in ibid., 66). Gournay and Cliquot both call for the abolition of regulations and inspectors. The conflict of interest between inspectors and manufacturers is ambiguous, however, because the manufacturers didn't complain about these regulations. The problem is in finding where the interest of each lies, and this will be the next point.

Competition, freedom of manufacturing and the general interest of the nation

The reaction of Gournay and Cliquot is a quite isolated case within society. With regards to

> the issue of knowing whether our inspectors and regulations which carry fines are useful or not to factories . . . I have tried to show that the *preconceptions* we have are pulling us away from the *true spirit of knowledge* of commerce and is as detrimental to the progress of industry as it is to an increase in the number of the King's subjects and an increase in his revenues; this is the state of affairs which has driven me to distance myself from the temerity of attacking an opinion which has been ensconced and consecrated for more than eighty years.
>
> (Gournay, letter to Trudaine, September 25, 1752, quoted in ibid., 55, emphasis added)

No one wanted to touch the regulations. Despite having to bear their cost,[22] the manufacturers saw in them the justification of their privileges and the perpetuation of their monopoly. For its part, the state was convinced that the quality stamps shielded the consumer from abuse and the potential dishonesty of the manufacturers. The manufacturers thereby took advantage of the legislators' ignorance by making them believe that these regulations promoted the general interest whereas they were but a way of defending the manufacturers' private interests and protecting their privileges:

> People are always prepared to point out the overall positive nature of free trade yet quick to emphasize the negative when it affects their specific interests and thus argue for exemptions with regards to their particular case. This has been the case with the manufacturers of Tours, of Lyon and of all the merchants and manufacturers in the kingdom who have been clever enough to persuade that all that served their interests actually promoted the general good whereas nothing, in fact, could be further from the truth.
>
> (Gournay, letter to the Intendant of Tours, July 3, 1754, quoted in ibid., 62)

The problem is identical to that with the corporations. Given the state's ignorance and the bias which could ensue, misleading arguments for the interest of the nation are invoked. In this way, all that hindered competition was called for by these manufacturers.

From then on, the problem created by the regulations was that factory prices were not competitive. The effects were felt within the country in terms of consumption, and also abroad, since French prices were not at all competitive compared to foreign industries which operated in conditions of total freedom. If the choice had to be made between the interest of the manufacturer, whose profit margin would shrink due to competition, and that of the consumer, that is to say all the King's subjects who made up the general interest, there was for Gournay no room for hesitation. He stated that the merchants' interest must no longer be paramount:

> we will only set up a form of commerce advantageous to the nation in general when we cease tending to the private interests of the merchant, of the communities, of a province; for it is only when a merchant earns little and makes do with low profits (a situation which will only be brought about by a high level of competition in his own country) that the nation will gain much.
>
> (Vincent de Gournay 1983, 315–16)

Faced with the standard argument (that the consumer must be protected from bad quality), Gournay wished to re-establish what he saw as the truth, explaining that the true general interest lay elsewhere. In other words, that the best weapon against dishonesty and high prices is competition. The term "competition" appears in each of Gournay's letters: "The greed we endlessly hold against our traders is a necessary quality and will always be to the benefit of the State as long as they compete against each other. Competition is the best barrier to bad faith: an honest merchant will force a thousand scoundrels despite themselves to trade honestly" (Letter to Trudaine, March 15,

181

1754, quoted in Schelle 1984 [1897], 68). In another letter, Gournay further states: "This obsession [the quality of the raw material] impedes competition between wools; it is nonetheless true that the competition of the most inferior type inexorably limits the price of the most superior" (Letter to Trudaine, May 9, 1755, quoted in ibid., 59).[23]

Gournay's *laissez-faire* expressed well his liberal leanings. No law must hobble the production process, whether at the level of labor (the corporations) or of manufacturing (regulations). When Gournay called for the reorganization of production, he was in fact calling for a struggle against prejudice, that is to say favoring the true general interest over the private interests of each manufacturer or trader. His best and only weapon was to advocate the necessity of freeing labor and manufacturing; in other words, letting competition decide. As soon as competition was the guiding principle of society, each individual would be able to seek his or her own interest without undermining the general interest. However, the moment the regime imposed upon society was not one of freedom, there would be a conflict between private and general interests. Gournay's liberalism was based upon this principle. If there is competition, each individual's interest will be that of the nation: "This was the source of Gournay's conclusion that when the interest of individuals coincided exactly with the general interest, it was best to let each man do as he wished. He further thought it impossible that within conditions in which commerce was left to its own devices,[24] private interest would not concur with general interest" (Turgot 1966 [1844], 270).

Having analyzed the content and the economic stakes of *laissez-faire*, I will now turn to *laissez-passer*. We will see how and especially in what way the Gournay who is presented as the author and unconditional advocate of *laissez-passer* does not exist.

GOURNAY: ADVOCATE AND CRITIC OF *LAISSEZ-PASSER*

In order to have a real understanding of *laissez-passer*, it is necessary to distinguish between domestic trade – which Gournay wished to unfetter – and international trade – which he wished to control. I will deal with each separately while focusing on *laissez-passer* in relation to international trade. After briefly presenting Gournay's position on *laissez-passer* as it applies to domestic trade, I will show that his position on international trade can be expressed as *laissez-faire* without *laissez-passer*.

Laissez-passer and domestic trade

There were two preconditions for a flourishing domestic trade in France and for it contributing fully to the wealth of the nation. First of all, domestic trade must be unhindered. Gournay believed that the free circulation of commodities would only make sense – and this was the second condition – if money could also circulate freely. Gournay shored up his arguments with his theory on interest rates, which I will presently explain.

Free trade and wheat stores

"It is a fundamental maxim that for trade to flourish, it must be free" (Vincent de Gournay 1983, 106). This freedom of domestic trade was to be attained, and it entailed for Gournay a struggle against preconceptions. More specifically, Gournay said that we must stop thinking that it is up to the state to create wheat stores; individuals must do so: "No one will dare to so as long as we remain biased and while any man who creates wheat stores is considered odious" (ibid.). The bias was based on the belief that only the state, through its stores, could regulate the price of wheat. Gournay believed, however, that only freedom could sustain prices in times of abundance and prevent their skyrocketing in times of dearth: "Granting all the freedom to trade in wheat . . . will sustain the price of wheat in time of great abundance. This freedom will never make wheat expensive in time of scarcity, which is what we fear of monopolies" (ibid., 108). There are no grounds, according to Gournay, to fear monopolists since the competition engendered by freedom is accompanied by their disappearance: "Concentration leads to monopoly but since freedom prevents concentration it also prevents monopoly" (ibid., 109).[25] Gournay thus called for the free circulation of commodities. For this freedom to be effective, however, it must go hand in hand with a good currency circulation, which is only conceivable if interest rates are low. The consideration of interest rates thus becomes paramount for Gournay and carries over directly into his conceptualization of domestic trade.

Interest rates and currency circulation

According to Gournay, the inertia of French commerce could be explained by high interest rates. Commerce would flourish anew when a decrease in interest rates enabled money to flow rather than be hoarded. A decrease in interest rates would therefore be considered the determining factor for the wellbeing of commerce and, by extension, would become the foundation for all other forms of wealth: "Lowering interest rates is the source of wealth" (ibid., 364).

High interest rates encourage greater investment in money than in commerce: "High interest rates making money more valuable than commodities, one will hold on to money until that point when one forecasts that the value of commodities will exceed that of money" (ibid., 40–1). High interest rates would thus divert money away from commerce, given the security of financial investment. The profit–risk ratio will always be superior to that of commerce:

The security of finance contributes much to the scarcity of money in commerce. There is always an element of uncertainty in commerce due to the possibility of loss stemming from innumerable hazards and even more from one's own inability or inexperience. There is no room for doubt that one will prefer the security of a risk-free and effortless investment and where one's inexperience and possible mistakes are not be feared, to the risk of loss in commerce.[26]

(ibid., 298)

This preference for finance, whose origin was interest rates with a guaranteed return of 6 per cent as compared to trade which generated less and had an element of risk, considerably prejudiced the country's economic well-being. Gournay was convinced that the state could not enrich itself if it favored financial investments over investments in trade. In so doing, the state generated unproductive investments:

The state can only base itself on the wellbeing of the multitude . . . and the multitude cannot engage in finance whereas it can in commerce. It is thus greatly unfortunate to have allowed the genius of the nation to invest itself so exclusively in finance, on which the state can never depend, to the detriment of agriculture and commerce which are and will eternally be the source and power of the state.

(ibid., 308)

The only cure for unproductive investment, therefore, consists in lowering interest rates.

Domestic trade must therefore be free but it must also be aided by a policy of low interest rates.[27] If there is an element of *laissez-passer* in Gournay's work, it is to be found here.

With regards to foreign trade, Gournay was undeniably protectionist. The irrefutable proof of this is his sustained defense of a Navigation Act. I will now present a vision of an economy without *laissez-passer*.

THE REJECTION OF *LAISSEZ-PASSER*: THE NAVIGATION ACT

In concrete terms, Gournay's reaction against *laissez-passer* manifests itself in his support of a Navigation Act. This act required a ban on "the shipping of food supplies and merchandise and the delivery of sugar, coffee, and other products by ships flying a foreign flag and whose crews were not at least three-quarters French" (Vincent de Gournay 1983, 34). The aim of this act was to protect French commerce from beginning to end, that is to say from production to transportation. Gournay wanted to limit imports but also ensure that the carriage of wares would rely mostly on French shipping:

184

The nation is losing in wheat and tobacco which we receive from the English, in the freight we pay to the Dutch for the shipping of naval supplies and in wares their ships bring us which are not Dutch products. The freight we pay to our ships for wares shipped costs the nation nothing; but that which we pay to foreigners is pure loss.

(Ibid., 286)

It is a "well thought out Navigation Act" that Gournay wished for. The term "well thought out" is in fact almost entirely associated with the Navigation Act (see ibid., 24, 30, 104, 106, 401, 402). This is not fortuitous and it is essential to understand what it meant to Gournay. It is not the act in and of itself which was important but the reasons why the author calls it so. There were two contradictory yet complementary aspects in Gournay's motivations. On the one hand, there was the desire to imitate the English where they have been right ("we must follow the lead of the English": ibid., 134), and on the other, the fear inspired by England and its economic power. It is this mixture of anglophilia and anglophobia[28] which conveys the twin aspects of Gournay's protectionism. It is a form of protectionism which I propose naming a protectionism of reaction, as opposed to a more aggressive approach which I qualify as a protectionism of intention.

This protectionism of reaction can be explained by the fact that Gournay was more of a practitioner than a theorist. His position as Superintendent of Commerce from 1751 to 1758 and his previous experience as a merchant, which took him to Cadiz, made of him a field man with both national and international experience. It enabled him to see with his own eyes the position of commerce in eighteenth-century France; and more specifically as compared to its great rival, England: "Through his daily contacts with industrialists, shippers and traders from all countries, he was able to appraise the consequences of the meticulous regulations in vogue in France by comparing the economic prosperity of the different countries" (Sécrestat-Escande, 1911, 11–12). During his stay in England,[29] Gournay observed, obtained information, and discovered the benefits of a protectionist attitude which he resolved, in reaction, to imitate:

Just as the English economist had sought the way in Holland to strip that country of its hegemony, Gournay sought in Child's work, eighty or ninety years later, the secrets to overtake England. Gournay considered the period beginning in 1650, when the second Navigation Act was promulgated, to 1700 as the one in which England gained the upper hand on France.

(Tsuda 1983, 470)

By explaining Gournay's reactive protectionism, it is this *laissez-faire without laissez-passer* that I will present and analyze. Gournay recommends using the knowledge and the experience acquired by the English while at the same time

185

being wary of it. There are thus two feelings present in Gournay's thought and in the use of the term "well thought out": imitation and prudence. I will study each of these two aspects.

An Act of Imitation

The desire to imitate the English can be explained by two reasons. First of all, I believe that there was some admiration for the prosperity and growth of that country. Gournay would not have shown such vigor and precision in his study of England if he hadn't felt a touch of admiration with regards to its economic principles. England was in fact France's main rival in the middle of the eighteenth century. Gournay therefore seems attracted to a country he fears. This led him to ask himself why France didn't have a Navigation Act if England had one: "There is no country in Europe which needs a Navigation Act more than we do if we are to rebuild our navy, increase the number of sailors and back our trade ... Who will stop us imitating them by extending our shipping?" (Vincent de Gournay 1983, 187).

Nevertheless, it seems to me that the idea of imitating the English is more pernicious: if France wants to be England's equal, it must do as England does:

It is only by becoming like them in all ways that we can reach the same goal. To stubbornly refuse undertaking the changes foreigners are imposing upon us, and whose positive effects we can see in their countries, is to accept more and more letting them have our resources and to happily concur in our ruin to make them rich.

(Ibid., 320).

There was therefore a lot more in this desire to imitate the English than the basic idea of following a model. It was imperative that France adopt the same protectionist principles, and thereby an act of navigation, if it was not to see its economy sink, to the benefit of England's: "There is no other way to multiply [livestock] at home but to follow the lead of the English, which is to say block entry or impose heavy tariffs" (ibid., 134). France therefore had no choice and, given this situation, Gournay had no qualms about becoming protectionist. The will to imitate the English therefore conveyed the need for readjustment. The existing forces must be rebalanced. For Gournay, it was not therefore, as I see it, a desire to be superior but to be equal and to restimulate, through maritime trade, domestic growth.

Gournay's position can be considered as legitimate if we see it in the context of his time. France was caught up in a spiral of protectionism imposed by the other nations of Europe. If France wished to remain an economic power within Europe yet without seeking hegemony, it had to adopt an identical approach or else be smothered by the others.[30] Gournay's protectionism was thus, as I have pointed out, one of reaction rather than of conviction or intent, which nevertheless does not mitigate it in any way.

There is still a slight difference between the wish to imitate a country and being so wary of it that one turns one's competitors into veritable enemies. The following quote exemplifies this: "it would be bad form for England to take offense [at a Navigation Act]; England which will not even accept a letter delivered by a French ship . . . Furthermore, can England take offense at our doing what they did first? That we should seek to build our greatness, our power on the same foundations which contributed so much to England's?" (ibid., 186).

In line with what I interpret as a feeling of anglophobia, it seems to me that Gournay's language because progressively tougher to the point of militancy. England was gradually becoming a rival in an almost military connotation of the word. The Navigation Act was therefore also a means of preparing for an adversary, and hence related to an act of prudence as defined by Child: "It is one of the most excellent and most prudent laws ever passed in England" (Child 1983 [1671], 173).

"One of the most prudent laws": an act of prudence

There are two aspects to this prudence: a trade aspect and a military aspect, both being perfectly complementary for Gournay. Commercial prudence was called for essentially with regards to wheat, the most difficult point of negotiation with the English at that time. Gournay bitterly regretted the time when France supplied wheat to England as opposed to receiving large quantities at high prices:

> Ever since they have inundated us with wheat and we don't supply any to them, such laws [Navigation Act] have become imperative if we are to restore agriculture . . . We must impose tariffs on foreign wheat entering the kingdom, and double or triple them when brought by foreign ships so as to favor our shipping over theirs.
>
> (Vincent de Gournay 1983, 122–4)

Therefore, in addition to the struggle against the deterioration of French trade, we find the desire to protect French shipping by granting it most of the freight.

Finally, to illustrate this prudence, I propose looking at one of Gournay's annotations which I find very revealing. Child explained that trade with England ("with us") must be made beneficial for other nations: "To make it in the other nations' interest to trade with us" (Child 1983 [1671], 275). Gournay reacted by suggesting replacing "with us" with "for them," which would then be to England's benefit and not to the benefit of the country doing business with England:

> The author states "to trade with us" and not "for them" whereas the truth of the matter is that when England supplies us with tobacco that

we could obtain from our colonies, they aren't negotiating with us but for us; it is the same when Dutch ships take our ships' place and we use them instead of employing ours. The Dutch are not trading with us, but for us.

(Vincent de Gournay 1983, 291)

Gournay's pun says much about the atmosphere of rivalry and prudence which existed between the two countries.

However, I believe that Gournay delved even further into anglophobia. His numerous military metaphors perfectly illustrate my interpretation of his protectionism and how the martial logic of the mercantilists kept its relevance for Gournay. It is no longer just a trade rivalry but a war in which one must prepare for a possible "invasion": "It is in our great interest to make our neighbors fear our navy and the invasions we could launch. It is the only way to suppress and contain a proud neighbor, always prepared to invade" (ibid., 372). It is imperative to master the art of "besieging":

The changes wrought by the spirit of trade, which has spread throughout Europe in the past fifty years, in those nations who are our rivals force us to fashion administrative laws just as the advances in the art of besieging made it necessary to reappraise the notions of attack and defense.

(Ibid., 212)

France must position itself in relation to England as the general of an army would:

We must preoccupy ourselves more than we have in a long time with what our rivals are doing. We must observe their operations and adopt ours to theirs or else resemble forever a general who arranges his troops for battle and employs them with no consideration whatsoever of the order, position, and movement of the enemy.

(Ibid., 317).

The relationship with England is thus a war in which "numbers must be repelled with numbers and force by force" (ibid., 300). The power and strength of a nation, however, flows from its wealth, and in this war it is wealth which is in opposition: "War today is a confrontation of wealth vs. wealth rather than man vs. man and therefore the victor will be that nation which has the most wealth and which will best be able to sustain war the longest" (ibid., 301).

Gournay's protectionism is thus marked by both anglophilia and anglophobia. This reactive protectionism probably would not have existed if all countries had adopted free trade.

CONCLUSION

French economic liberalism in the eighteenth century thus poses an import-ant question: Can one promote liberalism and not free trade? The answer is: yes. This position is explained in the writing of well-known authors, such as the Physiocrats, and others who are less known yet essential to the analysis of economic liberalism, such as Boisguilbert, Melon and Dutot. Whereas these thinkers are decidedly liberal with regards to domestic trade, they cease advocating total freedom when it comes to international trade. Boisguilbert advocates freeing exports by banning the import of grain except in times of shortage. As far as Melon and Dutot are concerned, free trade only makes sense within a protectionist framework guaranteeing the general interest. This enables Melon to legitimate privileged companies and the defense of a Navigation Act. Like Gournay, he believed that France must imitate Eng-land's protectionist logic. Finally, the Physiocrats also sought the imposition of certain restrictions on the freedom of international trade. In accordance with the principle of the exclusive productivity of agriculture, the Econo-mists took up a position against export industries and wished to limit imports to staple foods.

Gournay was no different. Therefore the maxim *"laissez-faire, laissez-passer"* must be rethought. Gournay put forth a restrictive and protectionist vision of international trade. The famous liberal maxim must therefore be read as *"laissez-faire* without *laissez-passer."*

NOTES

1 I wish to thank Philippe Le Gall and Annie L. Cot, whose advice helped me to improve this text, and Michael Zink, who helped me to work on my translation.
2 In fact, Gournay is assumed to be the author of this maxim. It was the marquis de Mirabeau who first publicly stated it, attributing it to Gournay in an article in the *Ephémérides*:

> Gournay was able, from the trade in which he was brought up, to extract those simple and natural truths, but which then were so strange, expressed in that one axiom he would have wished engraved on all barriers whatsoever: *laissez-faire, laissez-passer.* Receive, O excellent Gournay, this homage to your creative and propitious genius, to your righteous and warm heart, to your honest and courageous soul.
>
> (Mirabeau, *Ephémérides*, June 1755, quoted in Schelle 1984, 217).

In Gournay's writings, however, there is no trace of this maxim. It would appear, therefore, that Gournay's authorship is due to the oral propaganda he disseminated amongst his friends. (See August Oncken, *Die Maxime "laissez-faire et laissez-passer"*, Bern, 1886, quoted in Sécrestat-Escande 1911.)

3 Josiah Child, *Traités sur le commerce (A new discourse of trade)*, 1671; Chevalier Thomas Culpeper, *Traité contre l'usure (A tract against usury)*, 1621, trans. Vincent de Gournay, Amsterdam and Berlin: Jean Neaulme, 1754; re-edited Takumi Tsuda, Tokyo: Kinokuniya, 1983.

4 It seems that Machault, who was the Comptroller of Finance, advised Gournay to leave his work unpublished because of its statements critical of the state. However, and this is what is important, Gournay's contemporaries knew the *Remarques*. Turgot especially comes to mind; he wrote in 1754 the *Remarques sur les notes qui accompagnent la traduction de Child* in which he directly addresses positions developed by Gournay in his work (see *Oeuvres de Turgot*, ed. Gustave Schelle, vol. i, Paris, 1913–23, 372–6; see also the *Correspondence* of Grimm, Paris, 1877, letters of August 15, 1754, p. 398; of August 19, 1754, p. 144; and of March 15, 1755, p. 506.

5 Vincent de Gournay 1983.

6 Gournay's written work was presumed lost for more than two centuries. The *Remarques* which Gournay apparently entrusted to the abbé Morellet were later given, in unknown circumstances and at an unknown date, to the municipal library of Saint-Brieuc. They were found thanks to Takumi Tsuda's research.

7 Sécrestat-Escande (1911, 134).

8 For more information about Gournay's group, see Murphy 1992.

9 Vincent de Gournay 1753.

10 "But, as we have said, the ideas present in these works can only be attributed to him with the utmost caution" (Sécrestat-Escande 1911, 25). We will exhibit the same caution and will only use these peripheral writings to shore up or to back certain aspects of Gournay's thought and base it upon them. We will base ourselves only on the *Remarques*, the *mémoire* to the Lyon chamber of commerce, and Gournay's correspondence.

11 Schelle (1984, [1897]).

12 Takumi Tsuda, "Un économiste trahi, Vincent de Gournay", in Vincent de Gournay (1983, 445–85). "Turgot, after having read Gournay's *Remarques*, was in agreement with the principle of freedom and competition, but disapproved of the proposal to lower interest and promulgate a Navigation Act. He was to stand by this position his whole life ... Turgot thus preferred immortalizing Gournay's name as the pioneer of *laissez-faire, laissez-passer*, an already well-established physiocratic principle. Gournay's *Remarques* were not therefore lost as much as neglected" (481).

13 "All commercial operations having to be reciprocal, to wish to sell all to foreigners and buy nothing from them is absurd" (Turgot 1966 [1759], 274). We can see that this quote is also an attack on mercantilist principles.

14 The ambiguity of a refusal of *laissez-passer* amidst liberal reflections was taken up by Murphy as well. According to him, Gournay and his group advocate supply-side liberalism, which is to say for production and labor, but interventionism with regards to demand and especially all that concerns interest rates and currency circulation (see, Murphy 1992).

15 Vincent de Gournay (1983, 370, emphasis added). Wealth and production are here assimilated in a very clear fashion but I would like to point out that it is the only quote of Gournay's which does so. All quotes from Gournay's *Remarques* being taken from this edition, I shall no longer mention said edition.

16 The *modus operandi* of the Lyon corporations is representative of other corporations in the nation. Furthermore, this was the region in which Gournay worked most. His knowledge of the corporate system thus relies essentially on his experience with the corporations of Lyon.

17 One can point out that when Gournay evokes monopolies (see pp. 141, 142, 146 and 147 of his *Mémoire adressé à la chambre de commerce de Lyon*), he is in fact speaking about oligopolies, since it is several factories and not only one which hold the monopoly of supply. The term oligopoly did not exist in the eighteenth century and therefore I will use the term monopoly despite their being oligopolies.

18 The *compagnonnage* is an association of workers in the same trade promoting professional instruction and mutual assistance.

19 One can suppose, although Gournay doesn't make it clear, that the industries seeking to enter the market were equally affected by emigration.

20 One finds in Child's work confirmation of this emigration. England indeed profited from the perverse effects of the French corporate system. Child thus points out in the introduction to his *Treatise* the adverse effects of a policy of low salaries: "Good laws bring about an increase in the population which is a country's main wealth. If we cut back, by means of law, our people's price of labor, we will drive them away towards other countries to seek better salaries ... This is precisely the way we have gained ourselves a great number of France's workers" (Child 1983 [1671], 5–6).

21 "It is thus easy to see, through all that has been said, that to generate a lot of revenue in a commodity-rich country there is no need for a lot of money but only a lot of consumption. A million will thus have more effect than ten when there is no consumption for that million will renew itself a thousand fold" (Boisguilbert 1966 [1695], 619–20).

22 This was not always the case. Apparently certain mill-owners made arrangements with inspectors so as to obtain approval without inspection. It was even discovered officially that in Troyes in 1724 the cloth manufacturers were vetting their own sheets with the stamps of the inspectors.

23 The term "competition" also appears in a letter of January 3, 1744.

24 That is to say, in a state of competition.

25 Gournay defines a monopolist as "someone who seeks to group together and master all of a commodity to then sell it as expensively as possible" (Vincent de Gournay 1983, 108).

26 One can find in Culpeper's work the same appraisal of the preference for the more secure financial investment to investment in trade:

> To prove the degree to which high interest rates harm commerce, all one has to do is to observe how our traders, having amassed a relatively important fortune, will turn their backs on trade and lend their money to garner interest; they are tempted by the ease and security ... In other countries where usury is cheaper, they keep to their profession from generation to generation to become richer and in enriching themselves they enrich the State.
>
> (Culpeper 1983 [1621], 377–8).

27 This policy of low interest rates is difficult to interpret because the means recommended for its implementation stem from a hesitation. Gournay seems to be unsure whether he should opt for a liberal or an interventionist policy: should rates be allowed to drop on their own or, to the contrary, should this drop be brought about by applying laws designed to have that effect? Both interpretations are possible since Gournay gives elements applicable to both. Yet I don't think Gournay is contradicting himself in this hesitation between liberalism and interventionism. I believe that the arguments he puts forth are, to the contrary, complementary. Gournay's analysis is in fact twofold. The precariousness of France's economic situation and the wrongs to which France is increasingly subjected bring Gournay at first to advocate urgently active intervention by the state with the aim of a drop in interest rates (see Vincent de Gournay 1983, 141, or 371: one must make "haste" and not be "left behind." Once the urgency was dispelled, however, there is no doubt that Gournay's thought returned to the fold of liberalism.

28 Jean-Claude Perrot describes, through poetry contests in Normandy, France's

PASCALE PITAVY-SIMONI

opinion of England in the eighteenth century: "Les concours poétiques de basse Normandie (1660–1792): Anglophilie et anglophobie au XVIIIème siècle", in Perrot (1992, 305–31). He notably gives us a very interesting bibliography on this topic (p. 322 n38).

29 Gournay stayed in England between November 5, 1746 and the beginning of March 1747; see Tsuda, "Un économiste trahi, Vincent de Gournay," in Vincent de Gournay (1983, 455).

30 What can we think of Gournay's position with regards to Holland which didn't have a Navigation Act? If we were to be logical, France should not take protectionist steps against this country. Yet that is exactly what Gournay wished. According to him, France had no interest in humoring Holland, given that that country was able to take irreversible advantage of France under the Treaties of 1713 and 1739, while France was ignorant in matters of trade. In these treaties, economic reciprocity was advantageous to one party and illusory for the other. See article 6 of the Treaty of 1713, signed in Utrecht between France and the General States (Vincent de Gournay 1983, 403–4). Finally, because the initial positions were too unequal, competition couldn't take effect. Gournay refused to see France as the only nation in Europe to enrich Holland at its own expense and therefore displayed an unambiguous protectionism: "Why should we humour Holland? ... Let us remain friends, as long as it costs us nothing and as long as the enriching and the sustaining of its industry does not entail the sacrifice of France's wealth and the industry of its children" (ibid., 186).

REFERENCES

Baccalan, Isaac de (1903 [1764]) *Paradoxes philosophiques sur la liberté du commerce entre les nations*, édité par Sauvaire Jourdan, Paris: L. Larose.

Boisguilbert, Pierre de (1966 [1695]) *Détail de la France*, Paris: Edition de l'INED.

Child, Josiah (1983 [1671]) *Traités sur le commerce et sur les advantages qui résultent de la réduction de l'interêt de l'argent*, trans. from the English by Vincent de Gournay, Amsterdam and Berlin: Jean Neaulme, 1754; re-edited by Takumi Tsuda, *Remarques inédites de Vincent de Gournay*, Tokyo: Kinokuniya Co.

Cliquot Blervache, Simon (1753) *Considérations sur le commerce et en particulier sur les compagnies, sociétés et les maîtrises*, Amsterdam.

Cliquot Blervache, Simon (?1757/1753) *Mémoire sur les corps de métier*, under the pseudonym of M. Deslisle, The Hague.

Culpeper, Thomas Chevalier (1983 [1621]) *Traité contre l'usure*, trans. from the English by Vincent de Gournay, Amsterdam and Berlin: Jean Neaulme; re-edited by Takumi Tsuda, *Remarques inédites de Vincent de Gournay*, Tokyo: Kinokuniya Co.

Larrere, Catherine (1992) *L'Invention de l'économie au XVIIIème siècle*, Paris: Leviathan PUF.

Meyssonnier, Simone (1989) *La Balance et l'horloge: la genèse de la pensée libérale en France au XVIIIème siècle*, Montreuil: Editions de La Passion.

Murphy, Antoin (1992) "Vincent de Gournay et son groupe," in *Nouvelle histoire de la pensée économique, des scolastiques aux classiques*, vol. 1, Paris: Editions de la découverte, 199–203.

Perrot, Jean-Claude (1992) *Une Histoire intellectuelle de l'économie politique*, Paris: E.H.E.S.S.

Quesnay, François (1953) *François Quesnay et la physiocratie*, 2 vols, Paris: UNITE.

Sauvaire-Jourdan, F. (1903) *Isaac de Baccalan et les idées libre échangistes en France vers le milieu du XVIIIème siècle*, Paris: L. Larose.

192

Schelle, Gustave (1984 [1897]) *Vincent de Gournay*, Genève-Paris: Slatkine Reprints, reprint of the Paris edition of 1897.

Sécrestat-Escande, G. (1911) *Les Idées économiques de Vincent de Gournay*, Bordeaux: Y. Cadoret.

Tsuda, Takumi (1983) "Un économiste trahi, Vincent de Gournay," in *Remarques inédites de Gournay*, Tokyo: Kinokuniya Co.

Turgot, Anne Robert (1913) "Fragments d'économie politique: remarques sur les notes qui accompagnent la traduction de Child," in *Oeuvres*, vol. I, ed. Gustave Schelle, Paris, 372–6.

Turgot, Anne Robert, (1966 [1759]) "Eloge de Gournay," in *Oeuvres*, ed. Otto Zeller, Osnabrück: Eugene Daire, reprint of the 1844 edition.

Turgot, Anne Robert (1986) "Fondations," in *L'Encyclopédie ou dictionnaire raisonné des sciences, des arts et des métiers: articles choisis*, Paris: Flammarion.

Vincent de Gournay, Jacques Claude (1753) *Mémoire adressé à la Chambre de Commerce de Lyon*, édité par G. Sécrestat-Escande, Archives de la Chambre de Commerce de Lyon.

Vincent de Gournay, Jacques Claude (1983) *Remarques inédites*, texte édité d'après les manuscrits de la Bibliothèque municipale de Saint-Brieuc, Tokyo: Kinokuniya Co.

12

STORM OVER ECONOMIC THOUGHT

Debates in French economic journals, 1750–70

Philippe Steiner[1]

> In the cultivation of minds as in that of the earth, the first work is that of destruction. It is necessary to turn over the soil in order to destroy plants that are useless or harmful before flattering oneself that others will take root.
>
> *Ephémérides du citoyen*, 1772, t1, p. vi

From 1751 to 1783, among the francophone journals seven were interested in economy in a broad sense:

Le Journal œconomique (1751–72), Paris
Le Nouvelliste œconomique et littéraire (1754–61), La Haye
Le Journal de commerce (1759–62), Brussels
La Gazette du commerce (1763–83), Paris[2]
Le Journal de l'agriculture, du commerce et des finances (1765–74), Paris[3]
Les Ephémérides du citoyen (1767–72), Paris
Les Nouvelles Ephémérides économiques (1774–76), Paris

Several works have already drawn on this important documentary source[4] in order to give an account of French political economy, a field whose first vigor dates from this period.[5] Nevertheless, unlike some of these studies, we think that it is deceptive to arrange economic literature before 1763–5 around the fictitious center of physiocracy.[6] On the contrary, we think that it is a question of understanding how the very appearance of physiocracy is possible: among the different forms of economic thought that were born in the middle of the eighteenth century, how did it succeed first in entering into existing economic thought, and then in expressing itself as a current of autonomous thought? This reversal of perspective will lead us to consider physiocracy as one component of French economic thought among others, and it incites us to underline the closeness of the links existing between physiocracy and other forms of economic thought.[7] Only thus can the "new science of political economy" (Dupont de Nemours 1768b) be understood without using the deforming practice of retrospective history.

By basing our work mainly on economic journals, we will show, first, how French economic thought was structured in two currents; then, we will examine the specific position occupied by the Physiocrats' "new science of political economy." Finally, by studying several discussions of theoretical standpoints or some editorial choices made by the journals, we will see how the different discourses became interpenetrated, and how, even while criticizing the other currents, physiocracy stands in a strict relationship to them.

THE TWO CURRENTS OF ECONOMIC THOUGHT IN FRENCH JOURNALS, 1751–65

Weulersse (1910, I: 23–42) considered the development of economic thought in France between 1748 and 1756 to be a question of the onset of physiocracy; thus he speaks of the "pre-physiocratic" movement of this period. This approach has borne fruit, but it can no longer be maintained. Murphy (1982), Hoock (1987) and Meysonnier (1989) have shown that the economic literature of the period was not oriented essentially toward agriculture: on the one hand, the question of trade was debated much more often than that of agriculture, and on the other, the place of domestic or rural œconomy was much larger and its importance much stronger than the historians of political economy are ready to recognize.[8] Following the path . set forth by these scholars, a study of economic reviews shows, both before and after Quesnay's intervention, the existence of two great currents in French economic thought: œconomy and the Science of Trade.

In the first place, it is necessary to examine the importance attributed to "œconomy," the management of property.[9] Of what precisely is it a question and how is such a perspective related to our purpose? In order to answer this question, let us examine the review that has the explicit objective of treating this subject: the *Journal œconomique*.[10]

The first issue of the journal opens with a preface entitled "Plan of the *Journal œconomique*," which is concerned with providing œconomy with a place between the dignity of the sciences and the pleasure of *belles-lettres* (*Journal œconomique*, January 1751, 3):

> Between the occupations of men, the ones that are only presented under modest appearances are as worthy of our esteem by the work and industry that they require and the utility that they bring, as the most brilliant are of our praise by the beauty, correctness and elevation of spirit that they demand. Such is the character of the simple and wise Œconomy, which by means of agriculture, art and trade, procures for us an abundance of the wealth and all the commodities of life.
>
> (Ibid., 4)

195

This field conceals a treasure of knowledge:

> When an attentive spirit fastens on the aim of penetrating this veil of modesty and enters into the detail of its occupations, he is surprised by the constant attention that must be devoted to it, and the enormous amount of knowledge that is necessary to assure its success ... He even recognizes that the sciences are in continual commerce with it; some in order to make it the subject of their meditations, others to aid it by their knowledge.
>
> (Ibid., 5)

This linkage of the sciences and œconomy gives a first indication of the *Journal*'s orientation and the meaning of œconomy. A second indication comes with the statement of the fields treated by the *Journal*, which endeavored to publish "a collection of recent writings on agriculture, the arts and commerce, and of opinions that can provide new aid to those who take it up, and can enable them to increase the general good by working for their particular fortunes" (ibid., 6). The second aspect undertaken by the *Journal* clearly indicates its breadth of purpose and shows that, contrary to what is commonly believed, œconomy, from the beginning, had something to do with political economy in the modern sense of the term.

By following Linné, one of the most famous of the *Journal*'s authors, in the only article that he published there, the essential axis that brings together all the œconomic reflections of the time can appear in its full light. Linné develops a powerful perspective by indicating the links that, according to him, exist between the natural sciences, physics and œconomy.[11] He classifies the world of objects existing on the globe into two large categories: simple elements or substances, and the composite bodies formed from them; the first are studied by physics and the second by natural science. When discussing the category of the composite, Linné distinguishes among mineral, vegetal and animal realms; everything that man uses to satisfy his needs must necessarily exist in one of these forms, and from this established fact he defines the object of œconomy:

> The name "œconomy" is given to the science that teaches us how to prepare things for our use by means of elements. Thus the knowledge of these natural things and the action of elements on bodies, and the way to direct this action to certain ends, are the two points around which all of œconomy revolves.[12]
>
> (Linné 1752, 41)

Thus, to summarize and give a provisional conclusion about this aspect of economic thought, an entire current finds its unity in the act of linking œconomy with physics and natural science. Œconomy thus provides a rational guide for the behavior of the agent, who is considered as the agent of an enlightened husbandry of an agricultural property. This is a powerful means to raise the social status of the farmer and to indicate that his work involves something quite different from routine.[13]

Let us now consider the second great stream of economic thought: the science of trade – trade in general (*le commerce en général*) or political trade (*le commerce politique*). Here, we cannot rely only on journals because the two devoted explicitly to commerce – *Le Journal de commerce* and *La Gazette du commerce* – appeared on the French scene a little late, in 1759 and 1763 respectively. We thus also take account of what is presented in 1754 under the label "science of trade" or "political trade" in works written, for the most part, by the group centered upon Jacques Vincent de Gournay.[14]

The approach that François Véron de Forbonnais developed in his influential *Eléments du commerce* (1754) is fundamental for grasping what is meant by political trade. According to Forbonnais: "By trade, in the general sense, we understand a reciprocal communication. More specifically, it applies to the communication that men make with each other of the productions of their land and their industry" (Forbonnais 1754, I: 1).[15] In the latter sense, trade includes all the economic activities, as Forbonnais indicates by specifying its eight branches: agriculture, manufacturing, liberal arts, fishing, navigation, colonies, insurance, and exchange (ibid., 6). But beyond this general view, attention is brought to bear on the two levels on which trade can be studied:

> When trade is considered in relation to a political body, its operation consists in the internal circulation of the country's or the colonies' commodities, the exporting of their surpluses, and the importing of foreign commodities, whether in order to consume them or to export them again. When commerce is considered as the occupation of a citizen of the political body, its operation consists in buying, selling or exchanging merchandises that other men need, with the aim of making a profit.
>
> (Ibid., 6–7)

In the body of the chapter, Forbonnais makes explicit part of the connection between the two levels, and defines the level that concerns the statesman more precisely:

> To know how to trade and how to lead it are two very distinct things: in order to lead it well, it is necessary to know how it develops, and to know how to trade profitably, it is useless to know how it must be conducted. The merchant's science is that of the details with which he busies himself; the statesman's science is the advantage that can be drawn from these details. It is necessary thus to know them, and it is only through merchants that somebody can acquire knowledge about it: one cannot talk with them too much in order to learn; in order to take counsel, their advice must be allowed with caution.
>
> (Ibid., 87)

197

The statesman's objective will then be to become as informed as he can concerning the merchants' knowledge, but the ends for which this knowledge is necessary remain to be defined:

> The objective of trade in a state is to maintain in ease the greatest number of men possible ... The effect of trade is to clothe the political body in all the strength that it is capable of receiving. This strength lies in the population that its political wealth attracts to it, i.e., both real and relative wealth. A state's real wealth is the greatest degree of independence that it can achieve from other states in providing for its needs, and the greatest surplus that it ... can export. Its relative wealth depends on the quantity of money that its commerce attracts to it, compared with the quantity of the same wealth that trade attracts in the neighboring states. The combination of real and relative wealth constitutes the art and science of administering political trade.[16]
>
> (Ibid., 47–8)

In essential matters, Forbonnais fixes the terms of the debate for questions of trade in the 1750s.[17] First, the development of commercial activity makes it necessary for statesmen to consider it attentively.[18] Second, political trade relies on the merchant's knowledge and science, and for the statesman, there can be no question of legislating or intervening without becoming thoroughly conversant with the rules prevailing in this field.[19] Third, the statesman's science goes well beyond that of the merchant, since he takes all of commercial practice as his object.[20] Fourth, the statesman's principle of action is not that of the merchant: the goal of the first is to increase the state's wealth and power, while the second seeks only his own personal profit. This difference creates disagreements between the merchants' and the nation's or the statesmen's points of view, and therefore the leitmotif of all of the authors, with few exceptions,[21] is that the merchants' profits must always be distinguished from the nation's.[22]

QUESNAY AND THE "NEW SCIENCE" OF POLITICAL ECONOMY

When placing Quesnay in the context of French economic journals of the middle of the eighteenth century, it is necessary to begin by recalling the quite specific nature of his economic work. Quesnay published no book on political economy; *he only published articles.*[23] He left to others the task of collecting his scattered essays in order to present them as a unified work;[24] all the same, he allowed the Marquis de Mirabeau (1760, 1763) and P. P. Le Mercier de la Rivière (1767) to present the different elements of the new science in a continuous form, and he contented himself with supervising or writing anonymously some passages.[25] Consequently, Quesnay's writings

198

profit by being placed in their context: the reviews and the debates that brought them into print.

Quesnay's political economy is connected as much with œconomy as with the science of trade; it is not, however, related to each of them in the same way. Political economy is situated in relation to œconomy as political trade is situated in relation to the merchant's science. In both cases, the adjective "political" indicates the movement from the private to the public level, the level where all the national and international economic relations are situated. This homology, however, does not lessen an essential difference between the two oppositions. In the cases of œconomy and political economy, most authors consider that a continuity exists between the two levels.[26] On the contrary, with trade and political trade, as we have seen above, the authors underline instead the existence of possible difficulties because of differences between principles.

Quesnay is truly close to œconomy in his article, "Fermier," when he analyzes some specific methods of cultivation; in part,[27] his considerations can then be brought together with those concerning the "wise management" of an agricultural estate.[28] The fact that Butré, the calculating agronomist, published his empirical researches and evaluations in the *Ephémérides du citoyen* (1767, vols 9–12) also goes in this direction: "I busied myself with verifying, in various provinces with large and small cultivation, the calculations that have served as the basis of the *Economic Table* and of *Philosophie rurale*; by studying the large and small farms; by seeing everything myself in the greatest possible detail" (ibid., 12: 73; cf. also Perrot 1992, 217–36). Likewise, the *Journal œconomique* criticizes the physiocratic point of view by taking a text from Soisson's chamber of agriculture as a target and, on this occasion, the *Journal* upholds agricultural customs in the name of "œconomy of expenses" (*Journal œconomique*, May 1765: 250). Nevertheless, Quesnay was not interested in the attempt, associated with Linné, to transform œconomy into a science thanks to a conjunction with physics and the natural sciences; it is only something to which, it can be supposed, he gave the status of a useful technical phenomenon, but which remains secondary in his analysis.[29]

The link with the science of trade is much more considerable – and in view of the important development that characterizes this form of economic thought at this moment, it would be astonishing if it were otherwise (cf. Steiner 1997) – but this link is essentially critical. Quesnay's first writings that were intended for the *Encyclopédie* criticize political trade vigorously and reject two important aspects of it: first, he criticizes Forbonnais' distinction between the two circuits (national trade and international trade)[30] with the corollary that the circuit of external trade is essential – especially for the statesman – because it can provide an inflow of precious metals to the nation; second, he criticizes the dynamic role attributed to money – there again Forbonnais may serve as reference for understanding what the target is.[31]

This provides a first anchorage for what Dupont de Nemours calls "the new science of political economy" in relation to political trade. A second appears at the level of the articulation between political trade and political economy. We have seen that political trade is conceived of as superior to that of the merchant's science because the task of statesman consists of having a view of the whole of what the former does, as Forbonnais says so well (1754, 1). Turgot presents things in this same way when he speaks of Vincent de Gournay's different abilities. On this occasion, Turgot distinguishes the merchant's science[32] from the statesman's[33] by arguing that the first is subject to the incessant flux that animates the world of trade, while the second is elevated to the search for the causes of these endless movements. In the latter case, he says, trade is connected to political economy, the science cultivated by a new character, the philosopher.[34] A similar conception can be found in Morellet, another member of Vincent de Gournay's group, when, in 1769, he presents the articulation following which he offers to write his *Dictionnaire de commerce*. The majority of economic facts are relative, while "the interesting facts in the study of political economy are the general ones; for the specific facts, may be only exceptions to a contrary and general fact, cannot help discover principles" (Morellet 1769, 3). His *Dictionnaire* was also to include three categories of knowledge; the first two are of the order of these relative facts ("commercial geography"; "the object or substance of trade"); the third is centered on "the principles according to which trade must be conducted" (ibid., 27). But this is still not enough, since Morellet creates a new distinction. Indeed, he indicates that it is necessary to distinguish general knowledge that "leads and directs the merchant in the operations of trade common to all countries" (ibid., 325) and the part of the science of trade that returns in the frame of political economy:

> Other knowledge forms what we call the theory of trade in general. By this we understand the part of the science of political economy that is elevating itself above even the general operations of trade; studies on a large scale and abstraction made of all the details ... descend from causes to effects and try to ascend from effects to causes, strive to determine the best laws that can direct trade to bring about the greatest happiness of societies.
>
> (Ibid., 326)

These reflections, emanating from authors who were linked initially with political trade as it was developed in Vincent de Gournay's entourage, allow us to understand the particularity of Quesnay's and the Physiocrats' position. The latter rise to the level of principles and seek to elaborate the science of political economy, which means, if one pays attention to words, that they try to determine a small number of related principles, thanks to which political economy becomes a true science.[35]

This change of level appears very clearly if the tone of reviews marked by the physiocratic imprint (the *Journal de l'agriculture* and the *Ephémérides du citoyen*) is compared with that of other journals. Dupont de Nemours was the editor of the first of these reviews between August 1765 and November 1766, and although he multiplied the declarations of the kind that figured in the *Gazette du commerce* concerning the utility of contradictory reflections,[36] he frequently added long notes to the published articles when the authors' positions collided with his convictions.[37] When the abbé Baudeau presents the *Ephémérides du citoyen* in the first physiocratic issue of his journal, the tone is the same. The journal becomes the place for the expression of a school of thought that has the objective of propagating the truths of the science of political economy: "Political knowledge, which has been uncertain, problematic and arbitrary for too long, finally appears, in our time, to form a body of exact science, as simple as it is sublime, one with a never-failing stability, that will perhaps have some unhoped-for success" (*Ephémérides du Citoyen* 1767, i: 22). It is henceforth in relation to this science of political economy that the Physiocrats will evaluate economic publications and will devote themselves to the study of economic events (cf. Cusano 1991; Goutte 1994); they will act as if they constituted the only center of economic reflection.

THE DEBATES AND THE INTERRELATIONS BETWEEN DIFFERENT FIELDS OF ECONOMIC THOUGHT

We have seen three types of economic discourse occupying the field during this period. It is necessary now to examine what interrelations exist between them. Economic thought was not sufficiently institutionalized for each discourse to stay separate from the two others and to remain autonomous. On the contrary, the journals devoted to trade contain numerous reflections on rural œconomy, are very interested in the mechanical arts (the construction of machines) and therefore, in an aspect of physics – it is very explicit in the *Gazette du commerce (Paris)* in 1763; likewise, the *Journal œconomique* does not neglect questions relating to trade and commercial policy. An examination of some discussions and some critical moments in the journals' editorial lines will allow a finer grasp of the relations among the three discourses and the way in which physiocracy infiltrated the two that had preceded it, even before it sought to dominate them.

The best-known case is certainly that of the *Journal de l'agriculture, du commerce et des finances* stemming from the *Gazette du commerce* (Weulersse 1910; Sgard 1991). The *Gazette* was created in April 1763 as a way of offering to merchants information that could help them in their commercial activities, and to the public both useful information (retail prices) and the means of becoming familiar with the world of trade.[38] The editors of the *Gazette* seemed satisfied when they began the second year of their periodical;

nevertheless, the editorial of April 3, 1764 marks a slight modification. After thanking the numerous readers who had sent them information and reflections on trade,[39] the editors point out:

> We do not limit ourselves with putting the readers on the path of drawing these inductions; we have still sought to make them ascend to causes from effects that we set forth. We have shown that the laymen in foreign countries are concerned with public matters, that the Great and the small, the merchants and those who are not, all submit œconomic operations to the science of arithmetic; the general spirit that animates all of them is to diminish ceaselessly the sum of foreign raw material necessary to their consumption and to increase what they provide to other peoples.
>
> (Ibid., 210)

This modification is quickly effective when the *Gazette*, which was initially divided into two reviews (one for Paris and one for the provinces), was briefly unified in 1764, split again in April 1765 between the *Gazette du commerce*, which would set forth facts, and the *Journal de l'agriculture, du commerce et des finances*, which would deal with theoretical and doctrinal questions ("general views and principles") (*Journal de commerce*, September 1765, iv-v). It is true that the previous melding of the two aspects created dissatisfaction that quickly became perceptible to the *Gazette*'s editor.[40]

This is a first example that shows how, from a journal conceived in a rather practical spirit (technical information on the one hand, and general public information on the other) there was formed a theoretical review whose trajectory was immediately caught up in the discussions concerning physiocracy.[41] A similar phenomenon occurred in two other important journals of the period: the *Journal œconomique* and the *Journal de commerce*.

The case of the *Journal œconomique* allows the relations between œconomy and two other forms of economic thought to be considered. From the end of the 1750s, with the multiplication of publications, the *Journal* encountered difficulties in organizing overabundant material.[42] In January 1760, the *Journal* felt the need to explain its orientation, and it indicated that it did not intend to restrict itself to the practice of agriculture, trade and the arts, but also wished to approach "the principles and theory of œconomic science" (*Journal œconomique*, January 1760, 3). This declaration involves a specification and an extension of what the *Journal* understands by "œconomy":

> Let us now examine what the theory of œconomy consists of: the latter tends to make us happy, inasmuch as happiness is possible, by the prudent use of worldly goods, over which Providence has given us possession and dominion. But how can this goal be reached without a considered knowledge of the corporeal obstacles that form most

worldly goods? Now this knowledge is the study of physics. This science must therefore be regarded as the foundation of œconomy.

(Ibid.)

The *Journal* thus preserves what constitutes its directive line, namely the establishment of a strict link between œconomy and physics, but it is quite significant to see that, at the moment when the readers question the *Journal*'s orientation, it alludes to happiness, that is, it brings the fields of politics and political economy to the forefront.[43] By the beginning of 1763, the problem has obviously not been settled, since the preface contains some "Observations relating to the principal object of the *Journal œconomique*," in which the *Journal* recognizes that with the diversity of economic subjects, it is impossible to satisfy all readers, especially those who would like to find only articles in direct relation to the rural economy.[44]

It is not difficult to grasp what motivates this kind of consideration on the *Journal*'s part and the probable origin of the readers' reactions. The beginning of the 1760s saw the rise of what would soon become the physiocratic school,[45] and there were already questions about this school, since 1763 was the occasion for criticizing the general approach of "political-œconomic writers" guilty of having "led the public into error, for want of having paid enough attention to the different situations of countries, to the inhabitants' manners, to the true interests of each power" (ibid., July 1763, 306). An article in June, moreover, directs attention to the importance of taking the nature of the soil into account in order to reap the greatest harvest from it; the article is followed by a criticism of the advantages that Quesnay had accorded to cultivation with horses compared with cattle (*Journal œconomique*, June 1765, 249ff). In 1767, at the moment when the physiocratic school reached its peak, the *Journal*'s preface marks its reticence in relation to the political orientation given to the economic debates with physiocracy:

It can be acknowledged without difficulty that in the general œconomy, which comprises one of the largest parts of government, we cannot extend ourselves far without meeting respectable boundaries that we must cross . . . and we know too well that, in this part of our career, we walk over hot coals covered by deceptive ashes, in order to forget the precautions and reserve with which we must conduct ourselves. So, one must not expect that we have said everything that we would have wished said: the evident danger is equivalent to a physical impossibility.

(Ibid., January 1767, 3)

The ambiguity of the *Journal*'s position is especially apparent during the year before it ceased publication. Following an article by M. Verdier on the perfectibility of man, the *Journal* adds: "Does not œconomy, this first of the sciences that has occupied us for more than twenty years, include education

203

and morality considered under whatever aspect they may be? . . . Morality and education are thus among the objects and sciences of œconomy" (May 1772, 216). The issue for the following month devoted space to polemic, and M. Verdier denounced the "economist philosophers" for having lost the meaning of the term œconomy:

> For what reason have they misappropriated the meaning of the word "œconomy" in order to apply it to politics? Œconomy designates nothing other than the law of the house: i.e., the science and art of the father of the family. It is true that, in many circumstances, the usage has been transported to the political, but this is only to remind government of its only true legitimate origin . . . the principles of administering both of them are the same; the only differences are from the greater to the lesser.
>
> (Ibid., 249)

Although more ephemeral, the *Journal du commerce* is an interesting case because of its stronger theoretical orientation in favor of the science of trade and the hold exercised by a "mercantilist" reflection in terms of the balance of trade. This orientation appears especially in the series of articles devoted to European trade which open each issue of the *Journal*. These articles are intended to show how English political trade is aggressive, unjust and damaging to the interests of the European countries (French, of course, but also Dutch, Spanish or Portuguese). The editor of the *Journal*, however, takes the trouble to note that the series of articles devoted to Portugal has a precise origin in Herbert's *Essai sur la police générale des grains* (*Journal de commerce*, September 1759, 3). This remark takes on a new meaning when it is established that the reference to Herbert's work reappears in December 1760 at the moment when the editor introduces in his *Lettres sur le commerce d'Espagne* a discussion of the theory of prices, a field that had never previously been approached in a sustained fashion. The editor opposes two interpretations of the price variations: against Herbert, who argues that variations in the price of grain derive from the abundance or mediocrity of harvests, the author identifies the growth of the quantity of precious metal as the general cause of price variations. On this occasion, the *Journal* therefore discusses one of the most important theses to be found in Quesnay's first articles.[46] The author draws his theoretical reference from Cantillon (ibid., 13), but without making a well-specified use of Cantillon's theory of price formation, and tries to take into account the relation between Quesnay–Herbert–Chamousset's thesis and his own, which was evidently connected with the position already held by Bodin. A year and a half later, the question of prices resurfaced during the discussion of a question concerning fiscal policy. Is the tax on merchandise really paid by the final consumer? Yes, the editor answers, by pointing out that, on the occasion of this debate, "we have ascended to the origin of prices" (ibid., April 1762, 23). Therefore, once again, but this time in relation to the science of trade, we see economic thought being captured by physiocratic political economy, which, from the moment it infiltrates the debates, transforms them into discussions of its theoretical and practical propositions.

CONCLUSIONS

Two principal conclusions follow from this study of the economic journals (in the broad sense) that appeared in France at the beginning of the second half of the eighteenth century. On the one hand, it reveals the extent of the field covered by the terms œconomy, science of trade and, finally, political economy. The first two discourses are relatively structured, possess the embryos of theorization, and are open to discussion with the third. On the other hand, it throws light on the historical situation in which modern political economy appears with physiocracy. The latter maintains contact with other forms of economic discourse – and this is not an aberration, for it was without doubt necessary in order to make itself understood and to show that the propositions advanced by Quesnay and his disciples could answer questions that had already been asked and in terms that remained understandable to their contemporaries. This means that the new school did not appear in an unfavorable situation – as Dupont wished to make us believe (*Ephémérides du citoyen* 1769, I: xii–xv; 1768, 1, 8–10) – or in a theoretical and doctrinal void, and that it was incapable of infiltrating the discourse of the moment. The study of the journals shows that the contrary is the case, and from the point of view of the history of sciences, this situation constitutes an essential element without which physiocracy would simply not have been able to reach its full powers.

NOTES

1 I thank Paul Wendt for his comments on the first draft of this paper, delivered as a communication during the 22nd meeting of the History of Economics Society at the University of Notre Dame.

2 First published under the name *Gazette du commerce* in two distinct forms, one for the provinces and the other for Paris, it was unified in January 1764; it became the *Gazette du commerce, de l'agriculture et des finances* in June 1765; and then the *Gazette d'agriculture, commerce, arts et finance* in January 1769.

3 This *Journal* is linked with the *Gazette*: the first would set forth "general views and principles," and the second would "state the facts" (*Journal de l'agriculture*, September 1765, iv–v, xvi; June 1770, 16). It became the *Journal de l'agriculture, du commerce, des arts et des finances* in 1769.

4 We will not describe these journals – studied only from 1751 to 1770 – because brief but clear accounts can be found in the work published under the editorship of Jean Sgard (1991).

5 It is necessary to mention first the work of G. Weulersse (1910) and the more recent works of historians as S.L. Kaplan (1976) and J.C. Perrot (1992).

PHILIPPE STEINER

6 Let us recall that the term "physiocracy" only entered the scene at a fairly late date and that it owes its existence to publications by two disciples that were characterized by active proselytism: Dupont de Nemours and the abbé Baudeau (Weulersse 1910, I: 128). In other respects, and these two points are linked, Weulersse's classic study of physiocracy shows the slowness with which the school was formed: before 1763, the "school" was almost reduced to two figures: Mirabeau and Quesnay. It shows as well that the school only takes on its first vigor with, on the one hand, the series of articles that Quesnay published in *Le Journal d'agriculture* (which was then edited by Dupont), and then, after the departure of the latter, in the *Ephémérides du citoyen*, which Baudeau had just put at the school's service; on the other hand, with the publications to which Quesnay gave his endorsement or his aid: the book published by P.P. Le Mercier de la Rivière (1767), a collection of articles published by Dupont under the title of *Physiocratie*, and so on.

7 This remains true even if we limit ourselves, as will be the case throughout most of this work, to the writings of François Quesnay himself.

8 There are very few studies on this question. See, however, the work of J. M. Barbier (1981) as well as K. Tribe's remarks (1978).

9 The *Dictionnaire* compiled by M. Robinet defines the agent (*œconome*) as: "The one who manages and administers anything whatever, whether it be a house, goods, etc. with the appropriate order and intelligence" (Robinet 1777–83, XVII: 28). Œconomy, however, thus has the sense of management or of judicious expense as opposed to an attempt to minimize monetary expense: "To believe that œconomy consists positively in saving money and other useful material would be a mistake. Saving can be as opposed to economy as prodigal spending. The virtue that we are speaking of is an appropriate use of stock, an industrious means of perpetuating it, in order to be always within reach, not only of not diminishing one's expense, but even of increasing it." This specification explains why physiocratic ideas concerning agricultural advances were easily grafted onto this part of French economic thought. Another meaning can be found when the *Journal de commerce* refers to an "economic plan" that allows improved production techniques to be financed (January 1759, 45) or to an "economic system" that allows expenses and the management of public finances to be rationalized (June 1762, 38).

10 The *Nouvelliste œconomique et littéraire* will be relied upon to a much lesser extent, for this journal, as the second part of its title indicates, is more literary than œconomic.

11 The importance that we give to Linné's article does not derive only from the author's notoriety. The *Journal* contains numerous references to this article. As early as October 1753, a new article entitled "Sur l'accord de la physique et de l'œconomie" reinforces Linné's point of view, and this article is taken up again in the first instalment of the *Nouvelliste œconomique et littéraire* (July–August 1754); in January 1755, the *Journal*'s preface notes "the infinity of works filled with œconomic discussions" (ibid., 11) and among those that are mentioned in the first rank of importance are the *Encyclopédie*, Duhamel de Monceau's agronomy, C. Dupin's *Mémoire sur les blés* and Linné's article (ibid., 18); in 1757, the *Journal*'s preface recalls: "We have often demonstrated in our journals the intimate linkage between physics and œconomy" (p. 40); at the moment when the *Journal*'s orientation is questioned, the preface of January 1760 specifies that "the theory of œconomy tends to make us happy, insofar as such a state is possible, by the prudent use of earthly goods, over which Providence gives us dominion and possession. But how can we succeed in this goal without a considered knowledge of the tangible obstacles that form the mass of these tangible goods? Now this knowledge is the fruit of the study of

physics. This science must then be regarded as the foundation of œconomy" (p. 3), and so on.

12 There is an evident connection here with some founding reflections of political ecology (cf. Christensen 1989).

13 This is often the motive of the *Journal*'s considerations, as, for example, in the "Lettres sur agriculture" published in January 1751, where the agent (*œconome champêtre*) is qualified by the knowledge and the fact that he does not work directly, but that his task is that of a contractor making others work: "One no longer requests from the agent [*œconome champêtre*] as much of practice as of theory. It is no longer a question of his laboring in his field, working on the farm, cutting in the woods, digging in the garden. Far from subjecting himself to any of this work, I prescribe for him to do nothing; he works enough when he makes others work" (p. 41).

14 On this aspect of things, see the works of Murphy (1987) and Meysonnier (1989).

15 This definition appears again in the *Journal de commerce* in a review of Mirabeau's *L'Ami des hommes* (*Journal de commerce*, February 1759, 105) and in Robinet's *Dictionnaire* when he gives the first chapter of Forbonnais' book under the entry "commerce" (Robinet 1777–83, xii: 419ff).

16 We cannot expand here on the principles of the science of trade that can be found in Forbonnais' writings (see, for example, Forbonnais 1753, i: 7–8 or 1754, i: 52–4), the *Journal de commerce* (July 1760, 26–32) or in its main editor's book (Accarias de Serionne 1766).

17 Beyond even what can be found in Cantillon's work – written around 1728–30 and published in 1755 – which certainly constitutes an important reference for all of these authors, especially in the *Journal de commerce*, but which remains much less precise in its definition of trade in general.

18 Forbonnais devotes his *Réflexion sur la nécessité de comprendre l'étude du commerce dans celle de la politique* to drawing the consequences of this fact: "My intention is to make those who are being prepared by work and application to enter a political career understand that they cannot safely neglect the study of commerce and finances ... Without attaching myself to a choice of new ideas; I will content myself with collecting the general principles that will serve as the center of what I have to speak about" (Forbonnais 1764, 217–18). This theme often figures in the works of authors interested in political trade (for example, Le Blanc 1754; Lacombe de Prezel 1760) as well as in the journals: "Wealth has an influence and a power over the fortune of states that it did not have formerly. The gold and silver that trade procures have become the most certain ammunition both for attack and for defense. Finally, the author proves very well that, today, wealth alone constitutes the relative power of states, and that there is no rich and powerful state without trade" (*Journal de commerce*, January 1760, 113).

19 "The good merchants are not pure spectators in the widespread fashion in recent studies of trade. They read the research of men of letters, the observations of philosophers and politicians; they also write themselves and, uniting theory with practice and a long experience, they enrich the public with knowledge that is all the more valuable in that it is marked by the most rigorous exactitude" (*Journal de commerce*, February 1760, 111). The *Journal de commerce* even evokes the merchant's accession to the level of administering trade: "This same merchant, called to administer a state's trade, will have even more elevated views; he will embrace the whole of trade, and without delivering himself to mercantile details, he will see all of its resources; the means of extending or of restricting it according to need; he will ceaselessly keep his eye open toward agriculture, toward grains, toward all

PHILIPPE STEINER

branches of foreign trade, toward balance of trade finally, and the means of turning it to his advantage" (ibid., January 1759, 58–9).

20 This motivates, for example, the way in which Turgot, as early as 1751, envisions political geography (cf. Turgot 1751); a geography about which the *Journal œconomique* says: "Geography is a truly œconomic science, since by presenting us the map of the world and the respective situation of its parts, it is extremely useful to trade" (January 1759, 8). Turgot also discusses this object in his "Eloge de Vincent de Gournay," when he gives a very long definition of the science of trade by enumerating what enters respectively into the merchant's and the statesman's points of view in such a way as to compliment de Gournay for having known how to combine them (Turgot 1759, 596–7). Such a perspective appears again in a letter addressed to the *Gazette du commerce (Province)* from a writer who criticizes the journal's organization; he suggests a division into four parts: (a) general ideas on economic matters and principles of commercial interest; (b) data on imports and exports and the movement of commercial ships; (c) the rates of exchange and of government stock; (d) the prices of merchandise. And finally the writer adds: "The statesman would read all of them because he would easily perceive their mutual relation and he could draw deductions from them that would be of some help in balancing the states' interests" (*Gazette du commerce (Province)*, December 10, 1763, 312).

21 Turgot occupies a place apart in this context, since, quite frequently, he links the general with the particular interest when a perfect freedom of trade exists: "It is impossible that, when trade is left to itself, the particular interest will not contribute to the general"; "under all points of view under which trade can concern the state, the particular interest left to itself will always produce the general good more certainly than the operations of government, which are always faulty and are necessarily directed by a vague and uncertain theory" (Turgot, 1759, 602, 606). In this case, the distinction between the two types of profit no longer has any place.

22 As Forbonnais defines political trade by the state's power in terms of the population level and activity, on the one hand, and the relative quantity of precious metal on the other, there is a good trade (which increases these quantities) and a bad: "In order to be convinced of it," he says, "the merchants and the state's profit must be distinguished" (Forbonnais 1754, 1: 49). The *Journal de commerce* takes up this theme again in an article about freedom of trade in painted linen (*Journal de commerce*, February 1759, 29–30, 46, 57–8). More generally, this *Journal*, on the occasion of a review of the work of Lacombe de Prezel (1760), addresses the reproach: "The author lends to merchants some political motives that we cannot adopt. Trade does not direct its steps to such principles. The spirit of profit is its only compass" (*Journal de commerce*, August 1760, 145).

23 This particularity does not proceed from any aversion of Quesnay's toward publishing books. As physician and surgeon, Quesnay expressed himself abundantly by this means.

24 We are thinking, of course, of the volumes published by Dupont de Nemours and entitled *Physiocratie*.

25 We are thinking especially of the very important Chapter VII of the *Philosophie rurale* devoted to the relation between the different expenses.

26 "The domestic economy can be regarded as parallel to the political economy, two lines having the same direction and differing from each other only in that one relates to a larger frame. However sublime be the objects that the political system of states embraces: a father in his family, a lord at the head of his estate, a sovereign on the throne – all represent equally the cares of an attentive master who directs the members, gives activity to them, by maintaining a just equilibrium in

208

their strength" (M. Robinet 1777–83, xvii: 31–2; cf. also the physiocrat G. Grivel's article "Economie" in Démeunier 1784–8, ii: 184–5).

27 This restriction proceeds from the fact that it is not possible to consider the alternative cultivation with cattle/cultivation with horses from only a technical point of view; in effect, the way in which Quesnay presents the two branches of this alternative demonstrates that it is a question also of an economic appreciation, i.e., making the economic efficiency of technical choices intervene (Steiner 1987, 1112–14).

28 See Dupont's remarks concerning this which he associates with LeRoy's article "Ferme: économie rurale" (*Ephémérides du citoyen*, 1769, t1, xx–xxi). The extremely detailed questions that Quesnay collects in his *Questions intéressantes sur la population, l'agriculture et le commerce* must also be mentioned (Quesnay 1758) as well as some short papers devoted to œconomy in the *Ephémérides* (1770, t10, 240–62; t12, 260–71).

29 This fact derives from Quesnay's recognition of the importance of using machines that lessen work (Quesnay 1757b, 563; 1766, 901); see also the paper by Baudeau answering Vaucanson's misrepresentation of the physiocratic thesis (*Journal de l'agriculture*, April 1774).

30 "Trade is divided into two parts: it is internal or external; their principles are different and cannot be confused without great disorder" (Forbonnais 1754, i: 54). On the question of the two circuits, we refer to our own study of mercantilist thought (Steiner 1992).

31 Forbonnais is in favor of a positive balance of trade, for the growth of the quantity of money is translated, according to him, into a growth of economic activity (Forbonnais 1754, i: 76–80, 111). He therefore calls the statesman's attention particularly to this aspect: "Such is the effect of trade when it is carried to its perfection in a political body: it is to procure it that the cares of administration aim. It is by a superiority of views, by an assiduous vigilance concerning the methods, the regulations and the motives of the people who are in competition, and finally by the combination of real and relative wealth, that they succeed. The circumstances are infinitely variable but the principles are always the same; their application is the fruit of genius that embraces its various sides" (ibid., 81). Such considerations, especially the insistence on the positive balance of trade, are found frequently in the *Journal du commerce*.

32 "To compare the productions of nature and the arts in different climates; to understand the value of these productions . . . ; varied transportation expenses according to the nature of the commodities and the diversity of the roads, the taxes to which they were subjected, etc., etc.; in a word, to embrace through its entire extent and to follow in its continual revolutions the state of natural productions, industry, population, finances, needs and even caprices" (Turgot 1759, 596).

33 "To discover the hidden causes and effects of this multitude of revolutions and their continual variations; to ascend to the simple motives whose action . . . directs all the operations of trade; to recognize these unique and primitive laws, founded on nature itself, by which all of the values existing in trade balance with each other and are fixed to a determined value . . . ; to grasp these complicated relations by which trade becomes connected with all the branches of political economy; to perceive the reciprocal dependence of commerce and agriculture, the influence of each of them on wealth, on the population and the strength of states, their intimate linkage with laws, customs and all the operations of government, especially with the dispensing of finances . . . ; finally to unravel, in the chances of events and the principles of administration adopted by the different nations of Europe, the

true causes of their progress or decay, is to envision it as the philosopher and as the statesman" (ibid., 596–7).

34 It is not without interest to note that Turgot then brought in an analogy between the formation of value and the physical laws of equilibrium (ibid.).

35 Dupont de Nemours presents the matter in this way: "he [Quesnay] applied all the strength of his mind to the search for physical laws relative to society; he succeeded finally in discovering the unshakable basis of these laws, grasping them as a whole, developing their linkages, extracting and demonstrating these results" (Dupont 1768a, 10). This methodological stance was submitted to many criticisms at the time (cf., for example, Forbonnais 1767; *Journal œconomique*, July 1763).

36 For example: "The opinions pro and contra on different subjects of economic science are the materials of our periodical, but they are not its object; we hope only that light will emerge from the chaos by the very conflict of various opinions, which the learned men will insert in our Journal. We must thus envision opinions pro and contra only as preliminaries that must lead to the truth" (*Journal de l'agriculture*, October 1765, 67n).

37 He assumes this method in a foreword inserted into the *Journal de l'agriculture* in October 1765 (ibid., 172–3; cf. also September 1765, xxxvii, and *Ephémérides* 1769, t4, vii–viii).

38 "The *Gazette* that we present to the public will bring successively to readers the mobile picture of trade in the old and new worlds" (*Gazette de commerce (Province)*, April 1, 1763, 11).

39 The *Gazette*, like other periodicals – the *Journal du commerce* for example – appealed to the public in order to collect information. The public seems to have responded to this request rather quickly; for example, the issue of the *Gazette du commerce (Province)* for November 28, 1763 contains a long letter about the price of grain in Lorraine (299–301); the issue of March 3, 1764 includes seven pages of discussions, letters and analyses and a single page of data (exchange rates and the price of merchandise).

40 The brief editorial of 1765 recognizes that certain readers have complained about the uselessness of the price lists (*Gazette de commerce*, January 1, 1765, 1). Several months later, the *Gazette* published a letter that suggested doing away with the price list and the numerical tables on imports and exports and replacing them by articles and reflections on trade (ibid., April 30, 1765, 281–3).

41 Dupont de Nemours was appointed editor of the *Journal de l'agriculture, du commerce et des finances* in September 1765; he was fired in November 1766 – it was in this period that Quesnay published frequently in this journal – because of his physiocratic bent. In December 1766, the abbé Yvon replaced Dupont and gave a rather anti-physiocratic orientation to the *Journal* until his departure in 1770 (*Journal de l'agriculture*, June 1770, 3ff). His successor, the abbé Roubaud, was a much more moderate physiocrat than Dupont.

42 From 1756, the *Journal* offered a bibliography of recent publications in its January issue. The first of these uses three categories: agriculture, commerce, arts (ibid., January 1756, 8–28); in the following year, the classification becomes more complex by bringing in numerous subdivisions under the general category "arts and œconomic sciences".

43 "Political economy establishes the power of a state, the happiness of a nation on the returns of the land, on agriculture and the export of its products. It is the always renewed wealth of agriculture that extends the population, animates industry, makes all the arts active, and allows trade to flourish" (*Journal œconomique*, February 1759, 76). This appreciation, with its physiocratic tone, is provided in the

review of Patullo's work *Essai sur l'amélioration des terres*, which reproduces important parts of Quesnay's article "Hommes." (This book is mentioned by Dupont in his collection of works that contributed to the making of political economy in France; see *Ephémérides* 1769, t1, xlvii.)

44 A reader who called for advice on how to make Maroille cheese is mentioned (ibid., 11). The *Journal œconomique* sought, moreover, to satisfy this kind of request to some extent, since the issue of April 1764 contained several articles on making cheeses.

45 Let us recall that two major works appeared then: *Théorie de l'impôt* (1760) and *Philosophie rurale* (1763).

46 We mean the theses on price variations that follow from the tables that Quesnay published in the article "Grains" in the *Encyclopédie* and which reappeared in the article "Hommes" (see in this connection the analyses developed by Vaggi 1987 and Steiner 1994). It is very probable that the *Journal* was aiming at the work of Herbert himself as well as at this article by Quesnay; supporting this hypothesis is the fact that the issue of September 1759 contains the entire essay of Piaron de Chamousset ("Observation sur la liberté du commerce des grains"); this essay follows Quesnay's central thesis very closely and even includes the numerical tables from the article "Grains"; this essay is also mentioned by Dupont (*Ephémérides* 1769, t1, xlviii).

REFERENCES

Accarias de Serionne, J. (1766) *Les Intérêts des nations de l'Europe développés relativement au commerce*, Paris: Desain.

Barbier, J.M. (1981) *Le Quotidien et son économie. Essai sur les origines historiques et sociales de l'économie familiale*, Paris: CNRS.

Cantillon, R. (1728–30) *Essai de la nature du commerce en général*, ed. T. Tsuda, Tokyo: Kinokuniya.

Chamousset, P. de (1759) *Observations sur la liberté du commerce des grains*, Amsterdam.

Christensen, P.P. (1989) "Historical roots for ecological economics: biophysical versus allocative approaches," *Ecological Economics*, 1: 17–36.

Cusano, C. (1991) "Fisiocrati e stampa: la strategia giornalistica delle *Ephémérides du citoyen*," *Rivista Storica Italiana*, 3: 557–8.

Delmas, B., Demals, T. and Steiner, P. (1995) "Les physiocrates, la science économique et l'Europe," in B. Delmas, T. Demals and P. Steiner (eds), *La Diffusion internationale de la physiocratie: XVIIIe–XIXe siècles*, Grenoble: Presses Universitaires de Grenoble, 7–29.

Démeunier, M. (ed.) (1784–8) *Encyclopédie méthodique: économie politique et diplomatique*, Paris: Panckouke.

Dupont de Nemours, P.S. (1768a) "Discours de l'éditeur," in P.S. Dupont de Nemours (ed.), *Physiocratie ou constitution du gouvernement le plus avantageux au genre humain*, Paris and Leyde.

Dupont de Nemours, P.S. (1992 [1768b]) *De l'origine et des progrès d'une science nouvelle*, Catania: Cooperativa Universitaria Editrice Catanese di Magisterio.

Forbonnais, F. Véron de (1753) *Le Négotiant anglais ou traduction libre du livre intitulé "The British Merchant"*, Dresde: Estienne.

Forbonnais, F. Véron de (1754) *Eléments de commerce*, 2nd edn, Leyde.

Forbonnais, F. Véron de (1764) "Réflexion sur la nécessité de comprendre l'étude du commerce dans celle de la politique," in *Mémoires et considérations sur le commerce et les finances de l'Espagne*, Amsterdam: F. Changuion.

Forbonnais, F. Véron de (1767) *Principes et observations économiques*, Amsterdam: Rey.

Goutte, P.H. (1994) "Les 'Ephémérides du citoyen': instrument périodique au service de l'ordre naturel," *Dix-huitième siècle* 18: 139–61.

Herbert, C.-J. (1910 [1755]) *Essai sur la police générale des grains*, Paris: P. Guethner.

Herlitz, L. (1961) "Trends in the development of physiocratic doctrine," *Scandinavian Economic History Review* 8: 107–51.

Hoock, J. (1987) "Discours commercial et économie politique en France au XVIIIᵉ siècle: l'échec d'une synthèse," *Revue de synthèse* 1: 57–73.

Kaplan, S.L. (1976) *Bread, Politics and Political Economy in the Reign of Louis XV*, The Hague: Martinus Nijhoff.

Lacombe de Prezel (1760) *Les Progrès du commerce*, Amsterdam.

Le Blanc, abbé J.B. (1754) "Préface du traducteur," in D. Hume, *Discours politique*, vol. 1, Amsterdam.

Linné, C. von (1752) "Principes de l'œconomie, fondés sur la science naturelle et sur la physique," *Journal œconomique* 2: 40–65.

Mercier de la Rivière, P.P. Le (1910 [1767]) *L'Ordre naturel et essentiel des sociétés politiques*, Paris: P. Guethner.

Meysonnier, S. (1989) *La Balance et l'horloge. La genèse de la pensée libérale en France au XVIIIᵉ siècle*, Paris: Editions de la Passion.

Mirabeau, V.R., Marquis de (1760) *La Théorie de l'impôt*, Amsterdam.

Mirabeau, V.R., Marquis de (1763) *Philosophie rurale*, Amsterdam.

Morellet, abbé A. (1769) *Prospectus d'un nouveau dictionnaire de commerce*, Paris: Estienne.

Murphy, A. (1982) "Le développement des idées économiques en France de 1750 à 1756," *Revue d'histoire moderne et contemporaine*, 4: 521–41.

Murphy, A. (1987) *Cantillon: Entrepreneur and Economist*, Oxford: Oxford University Press.

O'Heguerty, Pierre André (1754) "Essai sur les intérêts du commerce maritime," in D. Hume, *Discours politique*, vol. 2, Amsterdam.

Perrot, J.C. (1992) *Une Histoire intellectuelle de l'économie politique XVIIᵉ–XVIIIᵉ*, Paris: Editions de l'EHESS.

Quesnay, F. (1757a) "Grains," in Quesnay (1958, 459–510).

Quesnay, F. (1757b) "Hommes," in Quesnay (1958, 511–73).

Quesnay, F. (1758) "Questions intéressantes sur la population, l'agriculture et le commerce," in Quesnay (1958, 619–66).

Quesnay, F. (1766) "Sur les travaux des artisans," in Quesnay (1958, 885–912).

Quesnay, F. (1958) *François Quesnay et la physiocratie*, vol. 2, presented and annotated by L. Salleron, Paris: INED.

Robinet, M. (1777–83) *Dictionnaire universel des sciences morales, économiques, politiques et diplomatiques; ou Bibliothèque de l'homme d'Etat et du citoyen*, 30 vols, London: Libraires associés.

Sgard, J. (ed.) (1991) *Dictionnaire des journaux: 1660–1789*, Paris and Oxford: Universitas–Voltaire Foundation.

Steiner, P. (1987) "Le projet physiocratique: théorie de la propriété et lien social," *Revue économique* 6: 1111–28.

Steiner, P. (1992) "Marchands et princes: les auteurs dits mercantilistes," in A. Béraud and G. Faccarello (eds), *Nouvelle histoire de la pensée économique*, vol. 1, Paris: La Découverte, 92–140.

Steiner, P. (1994) "Demand, prices and net product in Quesnay's early writings," *European Journal of the History of Economic Thought* 2: 231–51.

Steiner, P. (forthcoming) "François Quesnay et le commerce," *Revue d'Economie Politique*.

Tribe, K. (1978) *Land, Labour and Economic Discourse*, London: Routledge & Kegan Paul.

Turgot, A.R.J. (1751) "Plan d'un ouvrage sur la géographie politique," in Turgot (1913–23, 1: 255–74).

Turgot, A.R.J. (1753) "Plan d'un ouvrage sur le commerce, la circulation et l'intérêt de l'argent, la richesse des états," in Turgot (1913–23, 1: 376–87).
Turgot, A.R.J. (1754) "Sur la géographie politique," in Turgot (1913–23, 1: 436–41).
Turgot, A.R.J. (1759) "Eloge de Vincent de Gournay," in Turgot (1913–23, 1: 595–623).
Turgot, A.R.J. (1913–23) *Oeuvres de Turgot et documents le concernant*, ed. G. Schelle, 5 vols, Paris: Alcan.
Vaggi, G. (1987) *The Economics of François Quesnay*, London: Macmillan.
Weulersse, G. (1910) *Le Mouvement physiocratique en France (1756–1770)*, Paris: Alcan.

INDEX

accumulation: capital 70–2, 73–5, 131; colonialism 157, 160, 161–7
Act for the Attainder of the Rebels in Ireland 1657 159
Act for the Settling of Ireland 1652 159, 162
actor-network theory 6
Adventurers' Act 1642 159, 166
aerodynamics 14
agency, history 6–17
agriculture 70–1, 195–7, 199, 201–5
air warfare 14
d'Alembert, J. 20, 179
alignments 11, 14, 16
American Economics Association 144, 145
anarchists 51
anti-industrialism 51–2
anti-humanism 9
apprenticeship 175
Aristotle 12, 91, 92, 99
Arnold, H. 14
Arrow, K. 130
artificial intelligence (AI) 13, 45
associations 147–52
astronomy 10
atomic warfare 13, 14
Austria 97
Austrian capital theory 133

Babbage, C. 9–14
banishment 159
Bank of England 150
banking system 113
battlefields 7, 14
Baudeau, N. 201
Baumol, W. 22
Bayes' Rule 25–7

Bayes, T. 26–7
Beccaria, C. 95, 96, 97
Becker, G. 48
Bellamy, E. 40
Berle, A. A. 50
Bernal, J. D. 8
Bernoulli, J. 30–3
Bernoulli, N. 22–3
besieging 188
Betz, H. 144, 145, 149
big-business corporatism 105
Blaug, M. 11–12, 70, 146
board rooms 110
Board of Trade 28
Bodin, J. 204
body 9–10, 11
Boisguilbert, P. 189
Boulding, K. 39
bourgeoisie 123, 124
bread 70
Britain 28, 97, 118, 120, 138
Buckle, H. T. 29, 85, 99
business class 108, 109
business psychology 107–8

Cadigan, P. 42
calculators 9, 10–11
calculus 26, 97
cameralism 93
Cantillon, R. 90, 97
capital 8
Capital 157–8, 167
capital: accumulation 70–5, 131; Austrian theory 97; growth 114; marginal efficiency 112, 118, 120
capitalism 11, 12; colonialism 161; crisis 40; development 87–8; foreign trade 73; heterogenous labor 56;

215

Keynesianism 112; literature 49; middle class 50; probability 19, 24; Ricardianism 69; twentieth century 105–27
capitalists 135, 139
cashless society 49
Catholic Church 93, 157, 158, 162
Chamousset, P. de 204
chance 20, 21, 23, 26
chaos theory 16
Cheap Truth 42
Chicago traditions 39–55
Child, J. 173, 187
Choisel, C. 174
Churchill, W. 113
circulation 93–5, 183–4
classes 105–27
classical situations 86–8, 94, 96, 100
classical theories 19–38, 88, 96–8
Clinton, B. 50, 53
cliometricians 144
Cliquot Blervache, S. 174, 180
Cohen, I. B. 25
Colbert, J. B. 174
Cold War 13, 14, 15, 50
Collard, D. A. 130–1
collectivism 50
colonialism 157–71, 197
colonization 72
commercial reasoning 19
communism 92
comparative advantage 70
competition 175–6, 179–82
computers 9, 10, 12, 13
Comte, A. 85, 99
conditionality 27
Condorcet, J. A. 85
consumption 8–9, 15, 71, 75, 122, 177
contextualism 6, 10–11, 14, 16
contracts 20, 21
conventions 110, 111
Corish, P. 160, 162
Corn Laws 70
corporate capitalism 105–7
corporate securities 108
corporations 175–9, 181
Cournot, A.-A. 24, 29, 96–7
Cromwell, O. 157–71
Culpeper, T. C. 173
culture 84, 93, 148, 152
currency circulation 183–4
cybernetics 16

cyberpunk 39–55
Cyberpunk Frequently Asked Questions (FAQ) list 42, 52
cyberspace 47, 52
cyborg science 9, 11–12, 15

Darwin, C. 94
Darwinism 44
Daston, L. 9, 19–22, 24, 27
Davis, J. B. 56–66
Debreu, G. 130
debt 166–7
deductive theory 148
deflation 113
demand for money 107
demand-and-supply theory of exchange values 97
demographic information 29
Denmark 21
destruction 8, 13, 15, 16
determinism 21, 34
Dickens, C. 39, 49
Diderot, D. 179
differential calculus 97
Dilthey, W. 147
diminishing marginal utility 23
diminishing returns 56
distribution dynamics 56
disutility 109
division of labour 9, 10
dogmatics 150
domestic trade 182–4
Dorfman, J. 144
Douglas, M. 21
dual labor market theory 58
dualism 9, 12
Dupont de Nemours, P. S. 200, 201, 205
Dupuit, J. 97
Dutot, C. 189
Dutt, A. K. 56–66, 137
dyadic relations 26, 27
dynamics 86, 96–101, 135–7
dystopias 40, 41, 49

earning class 108, 109
economic journals 194–211
Edwards, R. D. 162–3
efficiency 58, 112, 118, 120
elasticity 130–41
electromagnetism 8–9
elites 109, 122–4
Elizabeth I 159

Elliott, J. E. 105–27
Ellis, L. 24, 29
empiricism 86
employment 178
engineering 10–11, 14, 15, 16
Enlightenment 28
enterprise 107, 108, 115
entrepreneurs 105, 107–8, 110, 112–14;
    Keynesianism 115–20; role 124, 135,
    139; state 115
environmentalists 51
equation systems 97
equilibrium theory 100
evolutionism 85
execution 159
expectations 21–3, 107–8, 130–41
exploitation theory 58
extended state 116, 120
Exxon Valdez 49

factionalism 157, 160, 161–3
factories 7, 9, 10, 12, 14, 175
fair monetary settlements 20
fairness 21, 22, 25
Farquhar, M. 54
Federal Bureau of Investigation (FBI)
    51, 52
Fermat, P. de 19
Feyerabend, P. 12
filiation 88, 89–90, 95, 98, 100
finance capitalists 105, 107
financial markets 110–15, 138
Fine, T. 32, 34, 35
First World War 98, 100, 121–2
Firth, C. H. 167
fiscal policies 118–19
food 70–1, 73, 184–5
Forbonnais, F. V. de 197–8, 199
formal sectors 57
Foucault, M. 8–9
France 28–9, 97, 164, 173–92, 194–211
Francis I 175
free markets 47–8
free trade 69, 71–2, 174; liberalism 189;
    wheat stores 183; workers 76
freedom 174–82
Frege, B. 29
French Revolution 28
frequentist theories 19–38
Friedman, M. 48, 49
full-employment model 60–1
fundamentalism 42, 50

futurology 14, 15

Galbraith, J. K. 39, 49, 50
Galileo 12
Galton, F. 29
gambling 23–4
game theory 12–15
games of chance 20, 23
General Register Office 28
Georgescu-Roegen, N. 34
German Historical School 83, 99, 101,
    143–5, 153–5
Germany 33
Gibson, W. 42–7, 49, 52, 54
gold standard 113
Goldfield, S. 22
Goldsmith, O. 39
Goodwin, C. D. 39–55
Gookin, V. 167
Gossen, H. 97
Gournay, V. de 173–92, 197, 200
Great Depression 39, 112
great gap 92
Greece 91, 100
growth 56, 64–5, 114, 139

Hacking, I. 19, 28
Hafner, K. 52
Hahn, F. 131, 134
Hands, D. W. 130
Haraway, D. 8
Harberger, A. 48
Harrod, R. F. 139
Hegel, G. W. F. 85
Heidegger, M. 145
heliocentrism 12
Helm, G. 29
Henderson, J. P. 1–5
Herbert, C.-J. 204
heterogenous labor 56–66
Hicks, J. R. 130–41
historical narrative 143–55
historiography 6–8, 10–11, 14, 16, 36
history 6–17, 83, 85, 135–7, 148–51
History of Economic Analysis 81–103
History of Economics Society 6
Holland 158
Hoock, J. 195
House, F. 147
Howitt, W. 161
Hughes, H. 43
human agency 7

humanism 9, 12, 39
Hume, D. 27
Huygens, C. 19
hydrogen bombs 13

ideas 6–8, 12, 16
income 108, 109
indifference principle 20–2, 25
individualism 151
industrial capitalists 105, 107, 113
Industrial Revolution 7, 9, 87
industrialization 8–11, 13, 39
inequality 61–6
inflation 113
informal sectors 57
information superhighway 53
information technology 42–54
inside money 130
inspectors 179–80
instability 132–7
institutionalism 39, 48–50, 143–4
institutionalization 12
instrumentalism 87
intelligentsia 109, 116
interest 130–41
Interest and Prices 134
interest rates 107–8, 112–14, 118–19,
    137–84, 183–4
international trade 68–79
Internet 42
interrelations 201–5
investing class 108–9
investment 114–18, 120, 123, 138–9, 183
investors 106
involuntary unemployment 105–27
Ireland 157–71

James I. 159
Jameson, F. 42
Japan 49
Jensen, H. E. 105–27
Jevons, W. S. 12, 98
joint stock institutions 116
journals 194–211

Kant, I. 146, 147
Kaplan, F. 15
Keynes, J. M. 25, 34, 48, 98, 105–27, 130,
    136–7
knowledge 6–7, 176
Kondratieff cycles 87–8
Kugelmann, L. 167

Kuhn, T. 86, 88
Kuznets, S. 88

labor 9, 99, 174–82; atomizing 10;
    discipline 8; heterogenous 56–66;
    remuneration 68–79; social relations
    12; supply 163–5; theory of value 58,
    97
Labour Party 110, 122–3
laissez-faire 78, 123, 124, 173–92
laissez-passer 173–92
Lakatos, I. 86
land ownership 56
landlords 56, 69, 71
language 15, 149, 150
Laplace, P. S. 23, 24, 26
Latour, B. 6, 9
Lauderdale, J. 97
Le Play, F. 28
learning 12
legal reasoning 19
Leonard, R. 8, 13, 15
liberalism 173–92
Liberia 33
Lindahl, E. 130–41
Linné, C. von 196
liquidity 110–15
literature 39–50, 52, 93
Lloyd, W. 97
logarithms 9
logic machine 12
logical positivism 86
long run 33, 34, 40
luxury goods 75
Lyon Chamber of Commerce 174, 175

McCulloch, J. R. 68, 71, 73–4
Mach, E. 91
machinery 8–10, 12, 68–79
McNamara, R. S. 16
macrohistory 7–8
macromodels 130
Malthus, T. R. 57, 97
Man, P. de 145
management 8, 106, 108–10
Mandeville, B. de 39
manufacturing 174–82, 180–2, 197
marginal efficiency 118, 120
marginal productivity theory 97
Marginal Revolution 86, 90, 98
marginal utility theory 97
marginalization 42

INDEX

market creation 163–5
market-clearing models 130, 131
Markoff, J. 52
Marshall, A. 86, 96–7, 109
Martineau, H. 39
Marx, K. 11–12, 40, 85, 95, 99; Cold War 50; colonialism 157–71; constant capital 75; cyberpunk 48; development 100; exploitation theory 58; grand vision 98; revolution 101; socio-economic classes 105; superstructure 84
Marxism 19, 39, 146
mathematics 10, 13–16, 21, 23
Maxwell, J. C. 29
Means, G. C. 50
means of production 157–8, 162–3
medieval theology 91, 92
Melon, J. F. 189
Menger, C. 98
mercantilism 24, 87, 93
merchants 21–2, 24, 95, 163, 181, 185
Mercier de la Rivière, P. P. Le 198
Meysonnier, S. 195
microbiology 8
microstudies 7
Middle Ages 93
middle class 50
migration 61–4, 177
military 14
Mill, J.S. 40, 84–5, 86, 97
mind 9–11, 13, 82–5, 87, 148–9, 153
minimum wages 65
Ministère de l'Instruction Publique 28
Ministère de Justice 28
Mirabeau, V. R. 198
Mirowski, P. 11, 13–14, 16, 19–38
Mises, R. von 29, 32–4
modernism 9, 11
money 107, 113, 130, 132–7
monographs 7
monopolies 56, 176–7, 180
Montmort, P. 22
moral philosophy 91, 92
morality 23, 204
morals 147
Morellet, A. 174, 200
Morgenstern, O. 13, 15
Mote, J. 143–55
multiplier effects 119
Murphy, A. 195

Napoleon, Emperor 26
National Information Infrastructure (NII) 50, 53–4
national interest 180–2
National Investment Board 117
National Telecommunications and Information Administration (NTIA) 54
nationalism 30
natural wage 70, 75, 76
Navigation Act 174, 184–8, 189
Nazism 146
neo-Kantian movement 146–7
neo-Marxism 58
neo-mercantilism 87
neoclassical theory 22–3, 48, 57–8, 143, 148; development 88, 98; probability 24; purge 145; rise 11–12, 96
neoliberalism 47–9
Neuromancer 42, 43–7, 52
New Deal 50
New English 158
Newton, I. 94
non-professional literature 39–50, 52
non-human agency 7
noö-sociology 151–3
Norris, F. 332
nuclear state 116
nuclear warfare 15
numismatics 20

oil spills 49
Old English 158
oligopoly capitalism 105
ontology 9, 15
Orwell, G. 40–1, 49, 54
overviews 7
ownership 108, 109

pamphleteers 93
paradigm development 86
Paris Post Office 29
Parsons, T. 144
Pascal, B. 19
Petty, W. 157–71
philosophy of science 86, 87
physics 15, 203
Physiocrats 93–5, 189, 195, 200–1, 205
Pickering, A. 6–17
pirates 21
Pitavy-Simoni, P. 173–92
place-selection function 32

planned supply 133–7
planning 116–17
plantation 157
Platonism 8
Poincaré, H. 91
Poisson, S.-D. 24, 31–3
political economy 198–201
polymathy 81
Popper, K. 36, 86
population 8, 57, 64–5, 160
Porter, T. 28, 29
positivism 147
posthumanism 9
poverty 120
Prasch, R. E. 68–79
price 23, 70, 73, 76, 130–41
price level reductions 113
Price, R. 26, 27
Principles of Political Economy and Taxation 68–79
prisoners' dilemma 46
probability 19–38
production 8–10, 12, 174–5
productivity 58
professional economists 144
professional managers 106
profits 56, 58–61, 70, 73, 75, 107
Prony, G. R. de 9–10
propensity to consume 107, 108, 115
propertied classes 106
protectionism 173, 185, 188
provisions 71
Prussia 28, 29
psychologism 147
psychology 12

quantification 20
Quesnay, F. 94–5, 97, 101, 195, 198–201
Quetelet, A. 29, 31

racial prejudice 49
radicalism 50
Rae, J. 97
Railroad Trust 49
Rand, A. 40, 41
RAND Corporation 13, 14–15
rationalism 151
Reagan, R. 48
reciprocal alignments 10, 11, 16
regulation, competition 179–82
Reich, R. 50
Reichenbach, H. 29

remuneration 68–79
Renaissance 19
rent theory 56–61
rentiers 106, 108–15, 119–20
rents theory 71
research 7
revolution 88–91
revolutionaries 123
Ricardo, D. 56–66, 68–79, 96–7, 124; Ricardian vice 98
Rickert, H. 147
Robbins, L. 97
Robinson, A. 123–4
Rogers, A. 39–55
Rogin, L. 144
Roman Empire 91
Romantics 40, 149
Royal Prussian Statistical Bureau 28
Rucker, R. 41, 42
Ruskin, J. 40

St Petersburg paradox 22–3, 24
St Thomas Aquinas 92
Samuelson, P. 22, 130
Say, J.-B. 90, 97
Say's Law 60
Schaffer, S. 9, 10
Schelle, G. 182
Schmoller, G. 144
scholasticism 92
Schumpeter, J. 22, 74, 81–103, 105, 145
science 6–10, 14, 86–91, 151–3
science fiction 41–7, 52
Second World War 13, 16, 98
Sécrestat-Escande, G. 173, 174
sectionalism 110
securities 108
servomechanisms 16
Shaw, G. B. 40, 49, 122
Shiner, L. 41, 42
Shionoya, Y. 81–103
shipping 184–5, 187
Shirley, J. 41, 42
Simmel, G. 147–8
Simon, H. 13
Skidelsky, R. 122–3
skills 56–7
slave trade 92, 161
small capitalists 105, 106
Smith, A. 8–9, 86, 88, 93, 97; synthesis 94–7, 101
Snooks, G. D. 143–4

social justice 115
social sciences 8–9, 15–16
socialism 48, 109, 116, 123–4
society 82–5, 87, 147, 149–50, 153
socio-economic classes 105–27
sociology 6, 12–13, 95–101, 144, 146, 151–3
Soisson, E. 199
solidarity 151
Sombart, W. 143–55
specialization 7
speculators 107–8, 110–15
Spengler, J. 90
Sraffa, P. 68, 72
stabilizers 137–9, 139
Stark, W. 87
state 114–16, 119–20, 175–6;
employment 178; entrepreneurs 119;
manufacturing 180–1; socialism
123–4
statics 86, 96–100
statistics 28–30, 83
Steinbeck, J. 39
Steiner, P. 194–211
stereotypes 52
Sterling, B. 41, 42, 52
Stigler, G. 48
Stigler, S. 22
Stock Exchange 107, 109, 138
stock markets 107, 108
structure 135
subjective probability 21, 25
subsistence 57, 71
superentrepreneurs 116–17
Superintendent of Commerce 185
superstructure 84
supply 107, 133–7, 163–5
Sweden 29, 138
syllogisms 12
synthesis 88–91, 99
systems analysis 15–16

taxation 76–7, 113, 157–8, 166–7
technology 7, 13–14, 48, 50, 105–6, 138–9
textbooks 88
Thatcher, M. 48
theology 91–2
theory 148–51
thermodynamics 8–9
thermonuclear warfare 14
Thünen, H. von 96, 97

Thurow, L. 50
Tonnies, F. 147
trade 68–79, 182–4, 201–5
traditionalism 151
transplantation 157, 159
transportation 157
Treasury 166
Tropeano, D. 130–41
Trudaine, C. 174
Tschebyscheff, P. 32
Tsuda, T. 173
Turgot, A. R. 174, 179, 200
Turgot, J. 90, 94–7
Turing, A. 34
twentieth-century capitalism 105–27
two-structure approach 81, 84–7, 100

Unabomer 51–2
underemployment equilibrium 136
unearned income 108, 109
unemployment 58, 63, 66, 105–27
Union of Soviet Socialist Republics
13–14, 50
United States 13, 49–50, 53, 107, 109, 118, 144
universities 12, 51, 95, 96
utilitarianism 92, 99
utility 15, 109
utopias 40, 41, 42

Value and Capital 132–6, 138, 140
value theory 23
values 147
Veblen, T. 47, 48, 50
Venn, J. 29, 30, 33
Verdier 203
Verein fur Sozialpolitik 144
Vico, G. 84
Vietnam War 16
Viner, J. 81, 82
virtual reality 45, 47
Von Karman, T. 14
Von Neumann, J. 12, 13, 15

wage-fund doctrine 69, 73–7
wages 56–61, 65, 70, 113, 121, 137
Wakefield, E. G. 164–5
Wald, A. 29
Walras, L. 90, 95–8, 101, 130
warfare 14–15, 188
wealth 11–12, 121, 174–5

Weber, M. 144
Weintraub, R. 13
Welch, P. J. 157–71
welfare economics 70
Wells, H. G. 115–16
Weulersse, G. 195
wheat stores 183, 187
Whitworth, J. 10
Wicksell, K. 86, 130, 131, 134

Williams, J. 15, 42
Windelband, W. 147
Wohlstetter, A. 15
workers 56, 58–64, 108–9, 135, 139; free
   trade 76; Keynesianism 114, 120–4;
   migration 177
World Bank 48

zero-sum games 13

For Product Safety Concerns and Information please contact our EU
representative GPSR@taylorandfrancis.com
Taylor & Francis Verlag GmbH, Kaufingerstraße 24, 80331 München, Germany

www.ingramcontent.com/pod-product-compliance
Lightning Source LLC
Chambersburg PA
CBHW061158220326
41599CB00025B/4527

*9 781138 880900 *